THE BUSINESSMAN'S GUIDE TO
COMMERCIAL CONDUCT AND THE LAW

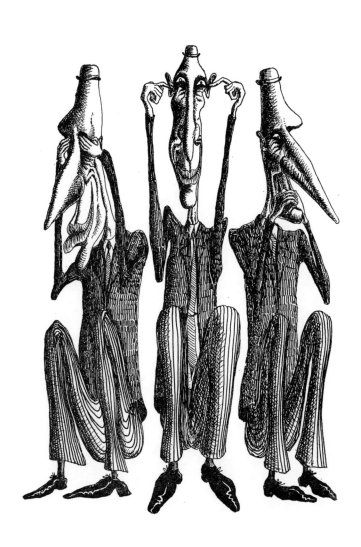

EWAN MITCHELL

The Businessman's Guide to Commercial Conduct and the Law

Illustrations by Nigel Francis

BUSINESS BOOKS LIMITED

London

First published 1972

© EWAN MITCHELL 1972

ISBN 0 220 66808 6

This book has been set in Times (327) 10 on 11pt
and printed in Great Britain by
The Camelot Press Ltd, London and Southampton,
for the publishers, Business Books Limited,
(registered office: 180 Fleet Street, London EC4)
(publishing office: Mercury House, Waterloo Road, London SE1)

MADE AND PRINTED IN GREAT BRITAIN

This book is respectfully dedicated to the following courageous and distinguished Soviet Jewish scientists and to their loyal families; in the hope that they may soon be free to live in the land of their choice, in accordance with the Universal Declaration of Human Rights

SERGEI GUREVITS   PROFESSOR ALEXEI LERNER
ACADEMICIAN BENJAMIN LEVITCH   DAVID MARKISH
VICTOR POLSKI   GABRIEL SHAPIRO
VLADIMIR SLEPAK   VICTOR YACHOT

and to the Ladies of the '35s' (The Women's Campaign for Soviet Jewry)

Contents

CONTENTS

Preface

"The Plaintiffs," said their Counsel, "have perpetrated a desperately dirty trick ..."

"I am very sorry," said the Judge. "I cannot help you. The Dirty Tricks Act is not yet on the statute book." True. But it *is* in operation throughout the field of commerce.

Take employment law, for instance. The wise executive needs to know the legal angles, so as to protect his own position. And remembering that an employee who is 'unfairly dismissed' may now (thanks to the Industrial Relations Act) be awarded as much as £4,160 compensation for his wretched state, the reader will want to study the rules on hiring and firing from two angles. First, how can he ensure that if *he* is dismissed, that *his* dismissal was both 'unfair' and provably so? Second, how can he avoid dismissing anyone else 'unfairly'? After all, he will not have to dismiss too many people at a cost of several thousand pounds to the company before he joins their unemployed ranks. So this book deals with employment law, starting with the Industrial Relations Act itself.

If you do not know your law, you are in for some rude and nasty shocks and a great deal of avoidable trouble. Conversely, it is not enough to know some basic law – you must also understand how best to apply it to your commercial circumstances. The object of this book is to act as a guide to the noble art of keeping within the law—while at the same time, making an honourable living.

Apply the same principles to crime and industrial espionage ... coping with lawyers and with litigation . . . dealing with courts and judges . . . with negotiation, buying and selling, making and breaking contracts ... acquiring or transferring property.... In each case, if you know the law and master the art of its application, you are well away. Bungle and you may be out of business.

Again, how does the law help you to fend off creditors ... to get in the money you are owed, without being prosecuted for 'harassment' ... to deal with those who steal ... to barter with the bank...? This book examines these situations with an eagle, legal eye—pointing out in particular how the deficiencies and defects in the law can be used against you, if you are not well prepared in advance.

Or take disasters. What should you do if you suffer from a fire? How do you handle your insurers? Do you employ loss assessors—and if so, what may you expect of them?

Or how do you cope with contractors . . . estate agents . . . sur-veyors . . . ? We examine them—from the viewpoint of the business-man who wants to make a decent, profitable living . . . to keep out of trouble . . . to behave with legal propriety and to earn success not at the expense of others but with their loyal and happy co-operation, collaboration and consent. Unfortunately, the law is not always his ally in this important pursuit.

Again, I offer the advice of a tax expert, in a splendid appendix devoted to the art of keeping your own tax burden and that of your business to a reasonable minimum. Tax evasion is a crime in the eyes of the law—the payment of unnecessary taxes is an idiocy in any-one's eyes.

At every stage, of course, the paths of commercial law and those of business etiquette keep crossing. There are books on each—but, so far as I know, none on both. Yet how can you keep them apart?

Take an ordinary example. You suspect that you are to be dis-missed. Is the managing director (or other hatchet man) bound to give you notice—and if so, then how much? If you jump the gun and get another job elsewhere, what are your chances of keeping your redundancy pay or obtaining damages for unfair dismissal?

Conversely, if you are faced with the grim necessity of sacking an employee, how can you do so so as to achieve your result with the least possible unhappiness and embarrassment for the employee—and the minimum disruption to your good labour relations? How can the law legitimately help you to cushion the blow?

Or take a takeover. Whether you are in the market for another concern, or others are angling for your business, have you City Code of Practice at your fingertips? I offer it as an appendix.

So here—in as lively and readable form as possible—is a Guide to Commercial Conduct, designed to help the businessman to know the rules of the legal/commercial game. Oscar Wilde once remarked that the beauty of making a mistake is that you can recognise it when you make it again. With good fortune and careful study, this book should save you from making many of the errors which have caused dismay, loss, aggravation, upset—and even catastrophe—to others. And looking at the bright side, it may also help you to increase your profits through sensible application of modern and well-tried laws of conduct, both those of common sense and those of common (and statute) law.

I am very grateful to Mr Brian Clapham and to my wife for their help in preparing this book. Without them, I could not have managed.

The Temple,
London, EC4

EWAN MITCHELL

Part One

Coping with the Industrial Relations Act

Introduction

Whether you like it or not, the Industrial Relations Act is now law. Whatever your branch of commerce or industry, you will have to live with it.

Maybe this will please you—particularly if *you* have the misfortune to be unfairly dismissed, and manage to obtain £4,160—the maximum available under the Act—for your pains. Conversely, dealing with 'agency shops', 'bargaining units'—and the unfair dismissal of others—may drive you into desperation, or out of your job. Either way, it is vital that you know how to deal with the new situations which this legislation presents.

To do that, there are two essentials. First, you must understand what the Act says. As it contains no less than 170 Sections and 9 Schedules, all I can hope to do in this book is to provide you with a digest—and one that is as digestible as possible.

You will also need to know how to find your way about the Act itself (obtainable from HM Stationery Office, or your bookseller at £1.15)—and the explanation in Chapter I will help you if you are forced into contact with any other parliamentary misery.

Finally, having presented and explained the text of the law, I shall offer you the benefit of my own, well-considered bias, on its interpretation.

In the old days, they used to say that if you put two Frenchmen together, you would get three political parties. Certainly if you ask two lawyers or parliamentarians or experts in industrial relations precisely how various parts of the Act will work, during its early years in practice, you may receive more than two answers. So once we come to interpretation, by all means reject my views if you wish—but at least consider them with care. They may be correct. Indeed, I am immodestly convinced that most of them are.

In the House of Commons, it is customary to declare an interest. I voted against most parts of this legislation. But that at least means that I have lived with it, for several legislative months—and discussed it from every angle, with its proponents and opponents alike. I shall therefore give you the benefit of my extremely well-considered bias. It provides a viewpoint which is likely to be somewhat new to readers nurtured on HMSO digests of the Act—but it should be none the worse for that.

The art of commercial conduct, then, is inevitably subjective. But its exercise requires sound information on fact and law, intelligent application to situation and circumstance—and a great deal of good fortune.

I offer you information and interpretation. I wish you—and all others who must put this Act into practical, day-to-day use—the best of good luck.

Chapter 1

The Act—and How to Find Your Way About It

The lawyer faced with an unfamiliar statute often starts at the end. There he finds when the law comes into practical effect—and those parts of the United Kingdom to which it applies.

The Industrial Relations Act (which I shall now refer to as 'the Act') is on the Statute Book. The Secretary of State for Employment has brought the Act into force far quicker than most people expected. As we go to press, problems of docks and railways have produced its early use.

The Act applies in Scotland, as in England and Wales (with only minor variations). But, in the main, it has no application to Northern Ireland, whose Parliament is given the power to bring in similar rules.

Next, interpretation. Section 167 either provides the main definitions necessary to understanding of the Act (from 'action' to 'worker'), or indicates where they are to be found. For instance, 'trade union' has 'the meaning assigned to it by Section 61 (3)'. You turn to that Section and learn that the words mean 'an organisation of workers which is for the time being registered as a trade union under this Act'. Whenever the Act refers to a 'trade union' it means one which is on the register.

If you cannot trace the Section you want via the definitions, move straight to the front. No Act has an index. (The index at the back of this book should guide you to the right pages here, which will take you on to the appropriate Section in the Act, if you then need it.) But the 'Arrangement of Sections' at the front of the statute does at least list the parts of the Act: 'Introductory'; 'rights of workers'; 'collective bargaining'; 'registration of conduct of trade unions and employers' associations'; 'National Industrial Relations Court, etc.'; 'restrictions on legal proceedings'; 'emergency procedures'; and 'miscellaneous and supplementary'. Find the part, look for the Section—and your hunt should be a short one.

If you wish to know the object of the Act, look at Section 1. It is intended to 'promote good industrial relations' in accordance with 'general principles . . . free collective bargaining . . . develop and maintain orderly procedures of industry for the peaceful and expeditious settlement of disputes by negotiation, conciliation and arbitration . . .' and so on. In a word, the Act (in general) is designed to set up a legal framework, within which it is hoped that good industrial relations will flourish.

Sections 2 to 4 deal with the Code of Industrial Relations. This is the Highway Code of the industrial world. You cannot be prosecuted or sued merely because you fail to abide by it, but such failure can be used in evidence against you in any proceedings arising under the Act. It contains basic, elementary and, on the whole, sensible principles upon which good industrial relations should be based. It is set out in Appendix 2.

Chapter 2

Unfair Dismissal—and How to Win or Lose £4,160

Those Sections of the Industrial Relations Act which give an employee the right to compensation for 'unfair dismissal' may be amended, but they will never be repealed. For the first time, employees—and that includes executives up at the very top—are given reasonable protection against capricious or unfair dismissal, whether with or without notice or pay in its stead. Unfortunately, a new premium is placed on keeping the inefficient at their posts, or (at worst) on dismissing summarily. As we shall see.

First, the background. Until now, any employee could be sacked at any time, if he was given his proper notice or pay in lieu. Provided that the notice he originally agreed to was not less than the statutory minimum laid down by the *Contracts of Employment Act, 1963*, he could claim no more than that—even if he was dismissed ignominiously, in humiliating circumstances and without a reference—and then left unemployed as a result.

In the famous case of *Addis* v. *Gramophone Company*, the House of Lords said that you cannot be placed in a better position if you are dismissed summarily than you would have been in, had you received your proper notice or pay in lieu (more on dismissal in Chapter 11). Hence the unfortunate plaintiff got his damages for wrongful dismissal—the money he had lost because he did not receive his proper notice—but nothing for his loss of status or to compensate him because he was unable to obtain another job at the same, high level, ever again.

But Section 22 of the Act gives most people the right not to be 'unfairly dismissed'. Where the business employs four or more people any man under the age of sixty-five or woman under the age of sixty is covered, provided that he has been on the books for at least two years—a minimum period not required where the employee has been fired for exercising his rights to join or not to join a trade union (as the case may be). People ordinarily employed outside Great Britain or as dock workers, shore fishermen or teachers in Scotland are excluded, along with husbands, wives and other 'close relatives', and part-timers who work an average of less than twenty-one hours a week.

Dismiss any other employee and the law presumes that the dismissal was unfair.

How do you prove 'fair dismissal'? First, you may show that its reason 'related to the capability or qualifications of the employee for performing work of the kind which he was employed by the employer to do'. Can you, perhaps, satisfy a Tribunal that the ex-employee's 'capability' assessed by reference to skill, aptitude, health or any other physical or mental qualities was so severely lacking that it was 'reasonable' to sack him? Or maybe you could prove that he did not hold the requisite 'degree, diploma or other academic, technical or professional qualification relevant to the position' in question.

Alternatively, was the 'conduct of the employee' such as to warrant the dismissal? A man properly dismissed for serious misconduct gets neither redundancy pay nor compensation. Conversely, if you can prove 'that the employee was redundant', then if he was dismissed, he will get his redundancy money, and no compensation for unfair dismissal.

If for some reason it becomes illegal to retain an employee on your staff—possibly for security reasons—then you may dismiss him. Alternatively, you may find 'some other substantial reason of a kind such as to justify the dismissal of an employee holding the position which that employee held'.

Once you have proved your reason, the question whether the dismissal was fair or unfair will 'depend on whether in the circumstances the employer acted reasonably or unreasonably in treating it as sufficient reason for dismissing the employee; and the question shall be determined in accordance with equity and the substantial merits of the case'.

What matters, then, is to prepare the case in advance, so that 'its substantial merits' will be obvious to the Tribunal. This should be done in writing.

The more and the better the documentation, the greater your prospects of proving the substance of your reason and the reasonableness of your dismissal.

If in doubt, consult your solicitor or superior and let him carry the responsibility of a dismissal which might (as we shall see) involve a payment of up to two years' pay at £40 per week—£4,160 under the Act alone. After all, your job is unlikely t ɔ remain very secure, if you sack too many people at that sort of cost to the old firm.

Finally, note that these cases now come before Industrial Tribunals, who have the right to recommend re-engagement of the employee. If either employee or employer refuses to accept the recommendation, that is taken into account when assessing the amount of compensation. And (subject to the maximum) the Tribunal may make such award as it considers 'just and equitable in all the circumstances, having regard to the loss sustained by the aggrieved party . . .'. And the extent to which that loss 'was attributable to action taken by or on behalf of the party in default'.

So suppose that you are thinking of sacking an employee who is unqualified to do his job—perhaps because of new techniques or equipment. Give him the chance to acquire the necessary qualifications or your dismissal may be unreasonable.

Finally, remember that, in general, an employee is not allowed to contract out of his rights under the Act. If he agrees to accept a settlement and not to take you to Court, he will only be bound by that agreement if it has the blessing of one of Her Majesty's Conciliation Officers.

7

Chapter 3

Contracting Out of the Industrial Relations Act

In general, 'any provision in an agreement (whether a contract of employment or not) shall be void in so far as it purports' to contract out of the Industrial Relations Act. It must not 'exclude or limit the operation of any enactment contained in the Act, or preclude any person from presenting a complaint to or bringing any proceedings before the Industrial Court or an Industrial Tribunal under the Act. It is the exceptions to this rule that every businessman should understand—and use. The great art of living with the new legislation lies, in my opinion, in keeping as far away from it as possible. Here are a few suggestions.

*   *   *

First, Section 161 removes the restriction on contracting out, in so far as it applies to any agency shop agreement or approved closed shop agreement. An agency shop agreement is an agreement (in general terms) between one or more employers and one or more registered trade unions, under which it is a term of the employee's contract of service that he will join one of these unions. So he is required to contract out of his right not to join a trade union, as provided by Section 5 of the Act.

The only 'approved shop agreements' likely to live on—that is, in ordinary language, pre-entry closed shops—are those of actors and seamen. They, too, may contract out of their freedom to be free of trade union membership.

Next, as we shall see in the next chapter, employees on fixed-term contracts (and that includes apprentices) may contract out of their right to damages for unfair dismissal, if their contracts are not extended when the term expires.

Then, where employer and employee agree to settle a claim for compensation for unfair dismissal and that settlement has the blessing of a conciliation officer, it will be binding on both parties. And this is so even though it precludes the employee from presenting his complaint to the Tribunal.

The most important right to contract out, though, lies in Section 34—the Section which caused so much controversy while the Bill was passing through Parliament. It reads as follows:

'Every collective agreement which is made in writing after the commencement of this Act, and does not contain a provision which (however expressed) states that the agreement or part of it is intended *not* to be legally enforceable, shall be conclusively presumed to be intended by the parties to it to be a legally enforceable agreement.'

Removing the double negative, this means quite simply that *unless* a written agreement made after the commencement of the Act contains a provision—in whatever words the parties wish—which says that the agreement or part of it shall not be legally enforceable, then the parties will be taken to have intended that a party who breaks that agreement may be taken to court. The Industrial Court is given power to deal with breaches of legally enforceable collective agreements. But if you are wise—and even if you are not—the odds are that the Section will be a dead letter. I will explain.

First, a 'collective agreement' is one which applies to the terms and conditions of work of a collection of employees—as opposed to an individual contract of service, which defines the rights and duties of a particular employee. Obviously, it will be made between workers' representatives and employers (or their representatives).

Now, no trade union is going to want the agreements to be 'legally enforceable'. I doubt whether any union (registered or otherwise) will come to an agreement, unless that agreement contains a provision which 'however expressed' states that it is not intended to be legally enforceable.

So even if you would like to be able to chase errant employees to the Court, it is very unlikely that you will be able to do so. If you want agreements, then you will have to allow the flexibility required by the employees.

On the face of it, this is an unhappy situation. In my view, when you consider the realities, it is nothing of the sort—and you should advise your company to avoid legal enforceability, even in those rare cases in which it has the option. Why so?

Suppose that you have a legally enforceable agreement. The union breaks it. What are you going to do? You have the alternative—to sue or not to sue.

If you do not intend to take the matter to the Court, alleging an 'unfair industrial practice', then you would be better off not to have had a legally enforceable agreement in the first place. It is not wise, is it, to have a sabre merely for the joy of rattling it? Your bluff is

9

far too likely to be called—and if you are not prepared to 'put up', then you would have been wiser to 'shut up' in the first place.

If you do decide to take the case to Court, what can happen? You may win or you may lose. If you lose, you would obviously have been better off not to have brought the claim. But if you win, what then?

The Court is given power to fine registered trade unions up to (in rough terms) £1 for each of their members—up to a limit of £100,000 for unions with 100,000 members or more. Unregistered 'organisations of workers' may be fined an unlimited amount.

So the Court may levy a fine—or it may simply order the union to comply with its agreement. What happens then?

If the union submits to the Court's order, all will be well. But surely there must be a very real risk that it will do nothing of the kind. In that case, those who have refused to release the union's funds, or to instruct members to obey the Court's orders—or, worse, who have issued instructions that the Court's orders shall be flouted—will be 'in contempt of court'.

The ordinary penalty for 'contempt', of course, is imprisonment. Until the contempt is 'purged', the 'contemnor' remains inside, cooling his heels.

It is often pointed out that the Act contains no provision for the sentencing of anyone to prison. That is the theory. In practice, the Act enables Courts to make orders—and if those orders are disobeyed, prison is the inevitable, ultimate answer.

Now suppose that having considered my advice, you decide to ignore it. You achieve a legally enforceable agreement—perhaps because no one has remembered on the other side to put in the 'contracting out' clause. You claim—and win. And the leaders of the union concerned refuse to obey the Court's order and are shipped off to jail. What then? Is it not a case of 'everybody out'? And anyway, are you going to find it easier or more difficult to deal with those leaders, when eventually they emerge from behind their bars?

Nor is that all. How long will this process have taken? Wise lawyers invariably advise their clients to keep out of court, if and when possible. This is not only because of the great expense of legal proceedings but also because of the inordinate waste of time and effort, inevitable in legal proceedings—and because of the delays of the law.

No one knows at the moment how long it will be before a case will reach the Industrial Court. But—again in my opinion—the queue is likely to be a long one. Details of the Court's manifold duties are given in Chapter 7.

The essence of first-class industrial personnel management? The speedy resolution of disputes. The sword of justice is often so rusty that it sticks in its sheath. By the time your dispute reaches trial, will your plant still be in operation?

Of course, you may be in one of those industries in which relations are already so bad that nothing could be worse. You may feel that union leaders or shop stewards may not want to be martyred by refusing to obey Court orders. It is possible (although, in my view, unlikely) that you are right. So why not wait and see—and let someone else produce the test case?

If you do decide to contract out of legal enforceability, then remember that this only applies to agreements made after this part of the Act came into operation—28 February 1972. And it only applies to written agreements.

Remember, too, that while the simplest written agreements are documents made at the time and signed by both parties, there are other varieties. For instance, a written agreement may be contained in an exchange of letters. And sometimes there are Minutes, confirming the terms of a previously made oral agreement—and if the Minutes are accepted by the parties as setting out their agreement, then a Court might say that they constitute an agreement 'made in writing'.

So you may want some form of words printed at the foot of letters, Minutes or other documents, saying: 'It is not intended that any agreement contained herein shall be legally enforceable.' The words are a matter for you.

Or you can if you wish, write the words at the foot of each potential agreement—or at the head—or in the centre. The position is irrelevant, but write them.

Chapter 4

Apprentices, Fixed-term Contracts—and the Act

As we have seen, the Act says that a written agreement made after the commencement of the Act shall be conclusively presumed to be intended by the parties to it to be legally enforceable—unless the parties state to the contrary. Contract out, loud and clear.

But now consider another—and potentially equally important—

form of contracting out. It affects apprentices and others who serve under fixed-term contracts for two years or more.

With the new rules on 'unfair dismissal' now in effect, an employee who is 'unfairly dismissed' is entitled to bring his claim before the Industrial Tribunal. Once he proves that he has been dismissed, it will be presumed against the employer that the dismissal was 'unfair'. An employer who wishes to show 'fair dismissal' has to prove, in broad terms, the reason for the dismissal—and that he acted reasonably. If he can prove that the employee was redundant, then no 'compensation for unfair dismissal' is payable. Again, if the employee was 'incapable' of doing the job—or 'unqualified'—for it, or if he was guilty of 'misconduct'—then the first barrier is overcome. But the employer still has to show that he acted reasonably in all the circumstances of the case, in dismissing the employee.

A successful claimant may be awarded as much as £4,160—up to two years' pay, at a maximum of £40 per week. The Tribunal must again look at all the circumstances, including the extent to which the employee has brought about his own loss. It will consider whether to make a recommendation that the employee be re-engaged, and if the recommendation is not complied with, then it will want to know why—and the compensation will be adjusted accordingly. But in any event, the successful employee may acquire a very substantial nest egg—probably tax free.

Now, you will appreciate, of course, that these rules apply to ordinary employees. But very few executives and managers realise that they apply equally to apprentices and to anyone else who is employed on a fixed-term contract for two years or more. Section 30 says that the unfair dismissal provisions do *not* apply:

'(a) to dismissal from employment under a contract for a fixed term of two years or more, where the contract was made before the commencement of this Act and is *not* a contract of apprenticeship, and the dismissal consists only of the expiry of that term without its being renewed.'

So a person who is dismissed from employment under a fixed contract for a fixed term of two years or more which was made before 28 February 1972 will not be able to claim compensation for unfair dismissal if the employer simply refuses to extend the term. But the exclusion applies only where the contract is 'not a contract of apprenticeship'.

The converse obviously applies. Where there is a contract of apprenticeship—whether made before or after this portion of the Act came into effect—the unfair dismissal provisions do apply. If you simply decline to give a contract of employment to an apprentice who has served his term, you may be liable to pay him compensation for 'unfair dismissal'. You will be taken to have dismissed him—and, as usual, the burden of proving that the dismissal was 'fair' will rest upon you, the employer.

Of course, if you can show that the apprentice was unsatisfactory or slovenly—or that he is redundant—all may be well. Equally, the journeyman principal may apply in your industry and you may show that it is not customary to employ an apprentice in the same firm or company in which he served his time. Then you may win your case. But you are certainly at risk. And you may wish to settle many cases for quite a lot of money, rather than risking the wrath of a Tribunal.

Again, in normal times an apprentice may easily find work with some other outfit. But at present, with many hundreds of thousands of people unemployed, the young man may find it very difficult to get other work. If he is left cooling his heels and without work, you may have to pay him wages, as compensation. And if he is out of work for two years, that compensation may equal the pay which he would have received, had you taken him on your books.

What, then, of contracts made after the commencement of the Act? The unfair dismissal provisions do *not* apply:

'(b) to dismissal from employment under a contract for a fixed term of two years or more, where the dismissal consists only of the expiry of that term without its being renewed, if before the term so expires the employee has agreed in writing to exclude any claim in respect of rights under Section 22, in relation to that contract.'

So if an employee who is employed under an apprenticeship contract—or any other which is for a 'fixed term'—agrees in writing that he will not make a claim for compensation for unfair dismissal, he is allowed to 'contract out' of that protection.

Probably the reason for this clause is to enable employees to obtain apprenticeship agreements and fixed-term contracts. Industrialists might prefer to have no more apprentices, if they were absolutely bound to keep them on, when their term expired.

So how do you handle the situation? You are fully entitled to include a clause in the indenture or apprenticeship agreement of any new apprentice whom you employ, stating that he agrees not to invoke the protection of Section 22. This will effectively prevent him from doing so.

Or suppose that you wish to employ an assistant, who would have to set up home in another part of the country in order to take on your job. He says: "Unless you guarantee me two years' employment, I will not risk moving." You may give him his two-year contract—and if you include a term which says that he will not invoke Section 22, if you decide not to renew his contract when the two-year period expires, that agreement will be binding upon him.

"Very well," you say. "In future, we will include such a term in all contracts for our apprentices. But what of those whom we took on in the past and whose agreements contained no such term?"

'If before the two-year term expires and the employee has agreed in writing to exclude any claim in respect of his rights under Section 22', then he has successfully contracted out of those rights. I repeat: 'At any time before the term so expires.' And that means—now.

If you can induce your apprentices to sign an agreement excluding their rights under Section 22, then the company is in clover. But can you?

Remember, first, that any such agreement would require 'consideration'. You would have to provide some 'quid pro quo'. In consideration, perhaps, of your increasing the pay which the apprentice gets, he agrees to give up his rights. Well and good. But simply to get the lad to sign a form just will not do. If he puts his agreement into a deed —duly 'signed, sealed and delivered'—then all is well. But why should he do that?

Any wise apprentice who is offered such an agreement—which gives away a perfectly satisfactory statutory right—will consult his union, his shop steward, his foreman or his parents. And he will decline to sign. In that case, there is nothing you can do about it. You cannot thrust such an agreement upon him. You cannot force him, in effect, to agree to a variation in his contract of apprenticeship, which will work entirely to his detriment. And if he is an 'infant'— aged under eighteen—such a change might be a nullity.

On the other hand, it is perfectly proper to come to some arrangement under which he gives up his right, if you give him something substantial in return. That is a matter which you will have to sort out and, possibly, to negotiate.

In practice, I think that most businessmen will take great care with their fixed-term contracts in future, to include a 'contracting out' term. But they will be equally careful when it comes to the end of the contractual term of their apprentices, either to provide them with jobs or else to make sure that they get work elsewhere.

You will not find it necessarily very easy to satisfy a Tribunal that an employee whom you kept on your books for (perhaps) four or five years was guilty of such serious misconduct that you were justified in dismissing him, when those years came to an end. After all, the odds are that he will have worked for a lower wage than he could have received, had he left you, thrown in his apprenticeship and taken a job (probably) as a labourer. You endured him—and he you. If you do not offer him work when he has completed his term, you will be taken to have 'dismissed' him—and such dismissal will be presumed to have been 'unfair'. If you can show that he was genuinely re-dundant, then you may, of course, be lucky.

All of which (combined with the previous chapter) makes me wonder why this legislation was greeted so warmly by so many employers. Perhaps they did not understand what they were letting themselves in for.

Chapter 5

Contracts of Employment—and Organisations of Masters and Men

Every employee works under a contract of employment. This may be oral or written (see also Chapter 8)—but if made orally, the *Contracts of Employment Act, 1963*, requires particulars of the main terms to be put into writing, within thirteen weeks of the start of the employment.

Under the Industrial Relations Act, those particulars must be expanded. First, holidays. Details must be given of 'entitlement to holidays, including public holidays and holiday pay (the particulars given being sufficient to enable the employee's entitlement, including any entitlement to accrued holiday pay on the termination of employ-ment, to be precisely calculated)'.

In the past, there have been far too many disputes over whether an employee who left between holiday seasons was entitled to holiday pay, on a pro rata basis. Now this must be set out either in the con-tract or in the written particulars.

Every statement given to an employee must also indicate the nature of the employee's rights to join or not to join a trade union, as laid down by Section 5 of the Act, including 'where an agency shop agree-ment or an approved closed shop agreement is in force which applies to him, the effect of that agreement on those rights'.

Briefly, Section 5 says that an employee may be a member of such trade union as he may choose or (subject to agency shop agreements, which we shall consider in the next chapter) to no trade union. Meanwhile, in preparing new written particulars for any employee, you must remind him of his rights—and tell him of any agency shop agreement which may be in force. Pre-entry, closed shop agreements are of course banned by the Act—except for 'approved closed shop agreements', for (it is presumed) only actors and seamen.

Next, the particulars must 'specify by description or otherwise the person to whom the employee can apply for the purpose of seeking redress of any grievance relating to his employment, and the manner in which any such application should be made'. Thus: 'In the event of any grievance, please speak to your supervisor', or: 'If unhappily any grievances should arise, our personnel manager is available during normal working hours in Room 84.'

Finally, the particulars must 'either explain the steps consequent upon any such application'—for redress of a grievance—'or refer to a document which is reasonably accessible to the employee and which explains those steps'.

Note: Whereas the grievance procedure may be given in 'a document reasonably accessible', the same does not appear to apply to the other particulars. To avoid possible doubt, include these in the document actually given to any new employee. And (if you have not already done so) you should give existing employees a note of any new particulars, not already included in their contracts.

Under the 1963 Act, the particulars must include 'the length of notice which the employee is obliged to give and entitled to receive to determine his contract of employment'. And that Act lays down minimum periods—extended by the Industrial Relations Act, as follows:

After thirteen weeks' service (instead of twenty-six), the employee is entitled to seven days' notice; after two years, the minimum goes up to two weeks; after five years, to four weeks—and now, after ten years, to six weeks; after fifteen years, to eight weeks.

These are *minimum* periods only. Although many employers say: 'You shall be entitled to the notice laid down by the Contracts of Employment Act', this is incorrect. And certainly in so far as your own contract is concerned, it is essential to see that you get a good deal more notice than the law requires.

The object of putting particulars on to paper is to enable employees to know their rights. But a new and vast field of paperwork is opened up by the Industrial Relations Act. The newly appointed 'Chief Registrar of Trade Unions' sets up his 'provisional register' upon which all current registered trade unions are automatically registered —in due course, to be transferred to a permanent register. But if the union asks to be taken off the register, the Registrar must comply with its request—provided the union's own rules permit deregistration.

The Registrar is given power to vet unions' rules and procedures— and only those unions whose constitutions are approved will remain registered.

Now, the Trade Disputes Acts are all repealed and equivalent protection is given only to registered trade unions. Again, it is only those on the register who can make agency shop agreements and whose trust funds are (in general) protected, when fines (potentially up to £100,000, in the case of the largest unions) come to be levied.

Will the unions with whom you deal agree to be or to remain on the register? Will they sacrifice their protection and that of their funds in return for either principles or the hope of destroying the effect of the Act? Time will tell—if it has not done so already.

Chapter 6

Agency Shops and Bargaining Units

Just as every employee would be intolerably weak if he had to negotiate on his own behalf, so industrial relations would be in permanent chaos if there were no 'collective' bargaining. The Industrial Relations Act completely alters the basic structures of that bargaining.

Apart from actors and seamen, the pre-entry closed shop is abolished. In its place comes what amounts in most respects to a post-entry closed shop, embedded in a so-called 'agency shop agreement'. This means 'an agreement made between one or more employers and one or more trade unions', registered under the Act—'or between an employers' association and one or more trade unions, whereby it is agreed, in respect of workers of one or more descriptions specified in the agreement, that their terms and conditions of employment' will include a requirement that the employee must (in general) be a member of one or other of the unions concerned.

The word 'shop' is not defined, anywhere in the Act. The agreement may be in respect of 'workers of one or more descriptions specified'. These may work in a 'shop' (either literally, or in the sense in which the word is used, with reference to 'shop stewards'). Or it may mean an office; or plant, or group of workers; or category of workers. . . . What matters is to recognise the vagueness of the term—and to compare it in a moment with the constitution of a 'bargaining unit'.

Under an agency shop agreement, the workers concerned must

either join a trade union or pay an appropriate contribution to it or, in the (probably rare) cases of genuine conscientious objection to joining any union, they must make the same contribution to a charity. As we saw in the previous chapter, details of the agency shop agreement must be included in the written particulars of the employee's contract of service.

If there is no agreement, then the trade unions concerned or the joint negotiating panel (see later) may apply to the Industrial Court, asking for a ballot. The Court will refer the matter to the Commission of Industrial Relations—which will, in general, set up the arrangements for a ballot. If two thirds of those voting on a simple majority of those eligible to vote are in favour of the 'agency shop', what amounts to a post-entry closed shop will be established.

Now for the 'bargaining unit'. This means 'those employees or descriptions of employees of an employer, or of two or more associated employers, in relation to whom collective bargaining . . . is or could appropriately be carried on by an organisation of workers or a joint negotiating panel . . .'. A 'joint negotiating panel' means 'a body consisting of representatives of two or more organisations of workers . . . established for the purposes of collective bargaining and authorised by or on behalf of those organisations to enter into collective agreements on their behalf . . .'.

Now, a 'bargaining unit' may include any 'descriptions' of employees, who can conveniently band together for bargaining purposes. It follows that you may find yourself with one or more—or many—agency shops, within your undertaking—and either more or less 'bargaining units'.

In my view, you should aim at getting your unions (assuming that they are registered) to agree to agency shops, covering the same workers as the 'bargaining units' most convenient to your business.

As with 'agency shop agreements', so with 'sole bargaining agents' —in the absence of voluntary agreement, the Industrial Court, allied to the Commission, may decide the issue. But in those organisations which previously enjoyed good industrial relations, it should (one hopes) be possible to come to an arrangement with the employees' representatives, so that collective bargaining may be carried out in sensible units—preferably being the same as the 'agency shops' in question. But if industrial relations are bad, both parties may (willingly or otherwise) join the queue outside the Industrial Court.

Where labour and management previously got on well, the new rules are a worry and an aggravation. Where there were bad relations previously, the question is: How far will the unions co-operate (or continue to co-operate), so as to enable the new arrangements to work?

If a union is registered, it could use the new 'agency shop' pro-cedure, to strengthen its position. But then there will be competition and dispute between the unions—and employers may find themselves in the same unhappy position as they are in where there is a demarca-tion dispute. Peace in industry and commerce depends not only upon goodwill between employer and employee, but between union and union also.

In the long run, your success in maintaining peace in your unit will probably depend upon your personal relationships with your em-ployees' representatives. But remember: Every written, collective agreement made after the commencement of the Act between employer and employee will have binding, legal effect, unless there is some written statement to the contrary (however expressed). You and your unions will have to contract out of legal enforceability.

If you prefer an informal arrangement, based on trust—rather than the possibility of court battle—then contract out. The odds are that your employees will do so, in any event. This should not worry you, because I doubt whether you will be able to afford to bring proceedings against a union for 'an unfair industrial action', because you could not afford to *win*. And we shall now see why.

Chapter 7

The Legal Framework—and How Not to Use It

The British (we are told) are a law-abiding people. And the Govern-ment hopes that by setting up a legal framework for industrial relations, it will need to be used very little. The existence of law and the workers' respect for the courts should (it is believed) bring more sweet reason into industry and commerce, and less chaos and dis-pute. Certainly the successful implementation of any law depends upon the consent of those afflicted by it. And speed is of the essence in the solution of industrial disputes. Will there be speed—or consent?

So consider the new court set-up; the business with which it must contend; the emergency procedures available—and the powers at the Courts' command.

First, there are the Industrial Tribunals. These are the same bodies that previously dealt (in the main) with redundancy disputes—

dispensing informal, swift and (usually) satisfactory justice. Suitably strengthened, these Tribunals are allocated all disputes in respect of workers' rights to join or not to join trade unions (under Section 5) and those involving unfair dismissal (Section 22). They are unlikely to be unemployed. And their work is reasonably uncontroversial.

Not so the new National Industrial Relations Court. With High Court status and presided over by a judge, with 'other members', the Court is intended to deal (amongst other things) with the following:

1 Disputes over proposed agency shop agreements and 'sole bargaining agencies'.
2 Breaches of collective agreements.
3 Procedural provisions—remedial action where procedure agreement non-existent or defective.
4 Unfair industrial practices in connection with organisations of workers.
5 Appeals from Industrial Tribunals.
6 Other matters affecting contracts of employment and disputes between master and servant.
7 Emergency procedures.

In most cases, the Court will be much too busy to go into details as to the sorting out of the dispute or the conduct of the appropriate ballot. It will refer these matters to the new 'Commission on Industrial Relations' for enquiry, report and recommendation.

The Court is given very wide powers. There is no specific power under the Act to commit people to prison, but consider a typical case:

1 An employer alleges that a trade union has been guilty of (say) breach of an enforceable, written, collective agreement, and lays a complaint before the Court.
2 The Court finds the complaint justified, and orders the union to comply with its agreement, and to pay a modest fine (the £100,000 upper limit—for units with 100,000 members or more —is unlikely to be reached very often).
3 The union declines to do what the Court orders. Its funds can be 'sequestered' to pay the fine. But if it refuses to obey the Court order, what then?
4 The Court, presumably, will not stand by to see its orders flouted and its jurisdiction brought into disrepute. It then has the normal, High Court sanction, for 'contempt of court'— imprisonment for the 'contemnors'.
5 With the union leaders safely in prison, it will be (I would have thought, quite clearly) a case of 'everybody out'.

All this, of course, will have taken a considerable length of time—

the amount of time depending upon the number of Courts and the amount of business they eventually have to do. But the delays of the law are notorious and, in my view, it is a very unwise employer who takes an alleged 'unfair industrial practice' to Court, not so much because of the risks of losing the case, but because of the dangers of winning it. Before you charge into legal battle, at least consider this possibility.

"Courts are for emergencies," you say. "What about a nice, 'cooling-off period'—or a compulsory strike ballot?"

Those are for emergencies also. And you have to go to Court to get either.

In both cases, the Secretary of State makes the application to the Court and before doing so, it must appear to him not only necessary that the cooling-off period be ordered and the strike postponed—or a ballot called—but also that there really is an emergency.* In the case of the 'cooling-off period', the industrial action must have caused or be likely to cause 'an interruption in the supply or in the provision of services of such a nature, or of such a scale, as to be likely to be gravely injurious to the national economy, to imperil national security or to create a serious risk of public disorder, or to endanger the lives of a substantial number of persons or to expose a substantial number of persons to serious risk of disease or personal injury'.

For a strike ballot, there is an alternative. The Minister may be satisfied in the alternative 'that the effects of the industrial action in question on a particular industry are, or are likely to be, such as to be seriously injurious to the livelihood of a substantial number of workers employed in that industry'.

The Minister then applies to the Court, which considers whether there are reasonable grounds for the Minister's belief—and if so, it refers the matter to the Commission, which sets up the agreements; reports back to the Court; and the new rules come into play.

In the case of disputes in the docks, power stations, post offices or sewage plants of Britain, emergencies arise and may be dealt with— effectively or otherwise—by these procedures. But the average executive who thinks that he will be able to force employees to 'cool off' or even to ballot, every Monday and Friday, is in for a great disappointment.

Those, then, are the basic rules—and the legal structure intended to sustain them. Use these chapters with care and they should stand you in good stead. But if dispute arises, either individually or collectively, do consult some lawyer who knows the Act—and pray for peace.

* The Minister must also consider whether or not it is politically expedient to apply for a Court order. During the 1972 miners' strike, the emergency powers were left well alone.

Part Two

Coping with Employment

Chapter 8

Written Particulars

The only contracts which English law requires to be made in or evidenced by writing to be effective are those involving the transfer of an interest in land, contracts of guarantee and some contracts of insurance. A contract of employment does *not* have to be in writing to be effective. However, writing is useful, if only so that the terms of the agreement can if necessary be proved. And the *Contracts of Employment Act, 1963* (as amended by the Industrial Relations Act—see Chapter 5) lays down specific rules in the case of this type of agreement.

In practice, if you break those rules you are highly unlikely to run into any trouble with the law. But you should follow them, not only because to do so will help avoid disputes, but also because if you do get involved in a legal tussle over the contract concerned, your failure to put the terms into writing will not endear you to a Court of Tribunal.

'Not later than thirteen weeks after the beginning of an employee's period of employment with an employer, the employer shall give to the employee a written statement.' If the man was employed, in writing, and the particulars were supplied in the original letter of employment or confirmation of terms of service (by whatever name), then no further particulars need be given under the Act.

What must the statement say?

First, it must identify the parties. In practice, this means that where there are many companies in association, the employee must be told which one is to pay him his remuneration. And if he is liable to be shifted from one company to another in the same group, the written particulars should say so. Naturally, the less the employing company needs its limited liability, the better off the employee.

Next, the particulars must specify the date when the employment began. An employee's right to the statutory minimum period of notice and (more important) to redundancy pay or compensation for unfair dismissal will probably depend upon his period of continuous employment.

Next, the employee must be told 'the scale or rate of remuneration, or the method of calculating remuneration'. Simple enough.

Then come 'the intervals at which remuneration is to be paid (that is, whether weekly or monthly or by some other period)'. So the man can know his pay day.

Fifth: The particulars must include 'any terms and conditions relating to hours of work (including any terms and conditions relating to normal working hours)'. Once the basic hours are known, overtime can be properly assessed.

Sixth, the employee is entitled to know his terms and conditions relating to holidays and holiday pay entitlement (details on page 15).

The particulars must also set out 'any terms and conditions relating to incapacity for work due to sickness or injury, including any provisions for sick pay'. Once again, there is no law that says that the employee must be given sick pay. But if any agreement is come to, it must be consummated in writing, which is given to the employee.

Next, 'Pensions and pension schemes'. These are not yet compulsory by law, but if any is operated for the employee's benefit—then written particulars must be supplied.

Finally, the employee is entitled to written particulars as to 'the length of notice which the employee is obliged to give and entitled to receive to determine his contract of employment'. He should be told of any agreement—or that he is only to be entitled to the minimum periods laid down by the Act (as amended)—or that 'reasonable notice' will apply. A man is entitled, of course, to 'reasonable notice', in the absence of some specific agreement on the point.

If there is a change in the terms to be included or referred to in the statement, the employer is given one month after the change to inform the employee by a written statement. If he does not leave a copy of the statement with the employee, then the employee must be given 'reasonable opportunity of reading it in the course of his employment' or it must be 'made reasonably accessible to him in some other way' (see also Chapter 5).

The employee need not sign his written particulars. But he should, for your protection and for his. He should be encouraged to read the particulars and to raise with you—or with your appointed official —any matters in doubt. He will not then feel that he has been tricked into agreeing terms which are against his interest—and he certainly cannot afterwards successfully allege that he did not receive the document.

Finally, please note that the written particulars do no more than set out what the parties have agreed. They are not to be used as a means of varying the contract without the employee's consent. If you agree certain terms orally, then by all means confirm them in writing. What you must not do is to use the provision of written particulars (in their original or their amended form) as an excuse for introducing entirely new terms—restraint clauses, duties to permit employers to search, limitations on periods of notice or holiday money, or anything else.

The statement is intended to confirm, not to alter. And in practice, Section 4 has helped avoid a considerable number of disputes over the terms under which a period is employed. At least it enables people to know their rights. Enforcing them is, of course, an entirely different matter.

Chapter 9

Tribulations—and Trial Periods

Before you next offer someone a 'trial' or 'probationary' period, pause—and note you may in fact be providing for more protection to your new employee than you ever intended to give him. Conversely, if you are offered a 'trial period', you may be sensible to accept, before your prospective employer changes his mind.

"I'll give you six months' trial," says the manager to the applicant. They agree on salary and duties—and that there shall be a review at the end of the six-month period.

After a few days, the manager realises that he has made a mistake. The man is moderately competent, but not fitting in with other staff. Alternatively, the manager is satisfied that while the applicant may do well today, he will never advance tomorrow.

"I'm afraid you must go," he says. Magnanimously (he thinks) he offers the man four weeks' notice. Unfortunately for the manager, he has succeeded in giving his employee six months' security. In law, the man was employed 'for a period certain'. There being no specific agreement as to any period of notice during the 'six months' trial', a judge would almost certainly read the agreement as conferring a definite period of six months upon the employee.

This is not as unreasonable as it may sound. After all, the man may have had to pull up his roots . . . to move to another part of the country . . . to acquire a new home . . . to change his children's schools. . . . All this is usually only worth doing if he could either get a substantial payment from his proposed employers or a good, long period of notice—or both.

Note, then, that the word 'trial'—or its brother, 'probationary'—does *not* operate in law so as to permit the employer to dispense with the employee's services during that period—without notice or payment in lieu. If you wish to make that sort of arrangement, you should do so specifically and in precise terms:

'At any time during the trial period, your employment may be terminated forthwith.' Alternatively: 'This employment shall be subject to fourteen days' notice on either side, during the probationary period.'

When the trial ends, what then is the basis of the employment?

Originally, both parties agreed that new terms would be arranged. Often this is done. Often—for whatever reason—it is not.

At that stage, the employee remains on the books without there being any agreement as to notice. The law says that the employee is entitled—in the absence of agreement—to 'reasonable notice'. The amount of that notice will depend upon all the circumstances of the case (see Chapter 5).

"We like to specify a trial period, so as to put a man on his mettle," you say.

Then go right ahead. There are employers who think that it is better not to make a new employee feel that you are breathing down his neck, particularly if you wish to see whether his work really will be suitable on a long-term basis. This is a matter of management and not of law.

My advice? Whether during a trial period or any other time, make an express agreement with the employee concerning notice. You will then each know where you stand—which is fair to both. You will avoid disputes—and both haggling and unpleasantness over what period is or is not 'reasonable'. And neither of you will then be taken aback by the firm fact that a man 'on trial' may find himself with either more or less notice than he would have expected.

After all, if the dismissal occurs within the first few weeks of the employment, the man with a fixed, probationary period will do well. But if he is sacked near to the end, he may find himself with less. Those are the dangers of accepting or giving fixed-term contracts. Do so if you wish—but understand the legal implications.

Chapter 10

How to Keep Your Staff Mobile

Some years ago, the manager of the London branch of a Turkish bank was required to pull up his roots and move to Turkey—lock, stock and family. He refused—and was sacked on the spot. He sued for damages for wrongful dismissal—and lost his case. The Court held that there was an implied term in his contract of service that he would take over such branch of the business as his employers might require.

Would the same principle apply to your business? If you want to shift a manager from one branch to another—or, for that matter, to require a representative to operate in a different territory—would he be entitled to decline? Or if he refused to do so, could you sack him?

Everything depends on the precise nature of the case. But there are ways and means to avoid all doubt.

The law will only imply a term into a contract if this is necessary in order to give the contract 'business efficacy'. When it comes to a contract of service, you do not have to say: "Thou shalt not steal . . . thou shalt not purloin our secrets and pass them to competitors. . . ." And, the law will imply a term that the employee will 'obey all lawful orders'. This means that he will carry out all duties which come within the scope of the job for which he is being paid.

Now, whether a particular job is itself stationary will depend upon the nature both of the post and of the business itself. A court would ask: When the man was taken on, must he by necessary implication have agreed to travel from branch to branch, area to area—or even country to country—as the circumstances of the business might require? If so, then the company would be issuing a lawful order, if it required that particular move. If not, then the man would be fully entitled to decline to go.

Employees of a Liverpool electrical outfit were told that there was to be no more work in their particular area. But they were offered alternative and identical employment at the same rates of pay, somewhere in the Cheshire area. They refused the alternative jobs, saying that these were entirely different in that they would have to spend nights away from home, or to move their homes in order to cope with the job.

The Redundancy Tribunal held that the company was not entitled to require its staff to shift to a different area. There was neither an express nor an implied term in the contract which would demand this of the men. Equally, the men were justified in refusing the alternative work on the ground that it would interfere with their normal family and social life and require a great deal more travelling than was anticipated under the original contract of service.

So to discover whether your men would be entitled to decline to move, you have to look at the entire circumstances of the contract. Upon the answer will depend not only the man's potential right to notice or pay in lieu but also any claim to redundancy money.

So how can you cope with this situation in advance? Insert a term in the contract of service of any employee whom you may want to move. Say: "You will transfer to any of our branches, as and when required . . ." or: "In the event of the business so requiring, you will be prepared to transfer to an alternative area, during any forthcoming season . . ."

Once there is something expressed in the contract, then there is no argument. No court has to decide whether or not a term should be implied. Not only is the business protected, but clarity avoids dispute. An express term today keeps the courts far away . . . care in the preparation of this sort of clause avoids trouble. Just as the wise businessman arranges in advance supplies, materials, stock as equipment to be available, so he ought also to give thought and care in advance to the actual or potential movement of his staff and that means taking care when preparing—or, for that matter, varying—contracts of service.

Naturally, these same rules apply in reverse. Your company wishes you to move to a different area or country? To find out whether you risk dismissal by refusing to go, look at your contract of service. If there is an express term, you know precisely where you stand. If the term would require you to obey an order to move, then you refuse it at your own risk. If you do not wish to go, then see if you can induce the men in charge to change their instructions. If they are adamant, then you stand fast at your own risk.

If your contract of service is silent, then you must enquire: Would a court imply a term into the arrangement that I must move, if asked? If in doubt, consult your solicitor. If you decide to take a chance and to sue, you may find yourself—like the unhappy manager of that Ottoman bank, so many years ago—out of both job and money. Naturally, you should have checked to see that your contract stated that you would be stationed in the particular town or area in which you wished to remain. Next time, you will know.

Warning: even if there is a clause in a contract of employment, permitting dismissal for refusal to move, such a dismissal may still (under the Industrial Relations Act) be unfair.

Chapter 11

Tactics for Sacking

Morality apart, an employer may seek to terminate a contract of service at the minimum cost to the business—while the employee hopes to depart to his own best advantage. So consider the legal angles from your privileged viewpoint as the employer or his agent and also (and especially) at the same situation from your angle as an employed executive.

Suppose, then, that you wish to dismiss a senior employee. You may do so either with or without notice. Assuming that you give proper notice or pay in lieu, you are entitled to sack as and when you see fit, and for any reason or none. Subject to the rights of an employee to compensation for 'unfair dismissal' under the Industrial Relations Act (see Chapter 2) the dismissed employee is entitled only to his notice or remuneration in lieu—plus, in appropriate cases, redundancy pay.

Unless you can dismiss summarily, you will have to give notice or pay in lieu. But redundancy pay may amount to an even greater sum. Cut this in half to recognise the reality that the Revenue will meet its share out of the fund into which you have been paying over the years and you may still be left with a sizeable contribution. Where an employer seeks to show that the reason for dismissal was for something other than redundancy, the 'burden of proof' rests squarely upon him to do so.

It follows that if you wish to avoid making a redundancy payment, you must be prepared to prove positively that the employment was terminated out of dissatisfaction with the employee's services, and not because (for whatever reason) his job was no longer available.

Summary dismissal is potentially far cheaper. There is then no notice and no pay in lieu—and as you are only entitled to dismiss summarily if there has been serious misconduct, and as the Redundancy Payments Act specifically says that dismissal for misconduct removes any right to redundancy pay—that money too remains in the company purse.

Summary dismissal may be either rightful or wrongful. To warrant instant firing, the employer must show that the employee has been guilty of such serious misconduct as to amount to a repudiation of the contract of service. The employee must do something which 'strikes at the very root of the contract'. He destroys it and by dismissing him the employer merely accepts the situation that the employee has created.

It is not enough to prove a breach of the contract of service. Minor breaches must be endured—or the employee dismissed with notice or pay in lieu. Only when the breach is mighty has the employee shown himself unwilling to be bound by it.

One really serious act of misconduct may suffice. The employee who steals or gives away even the smallest secret is asking to be sacked. So is the man who lights a cigarette when working with inflammable materials, and so endangering the lives of his colleagues and the property of the company.

On the other hand, while every employee who arrives late, takes too much time during the lunch interval, leaves early in the evening . . . is rude, discourteous, disobedient . . . fails to obey a lawful order . . . or otherwise acts in contravention of some express or implied term in his contract of service, is in breach of that contract— he has not earned himself the summary sack. Minor acts of misconduct will only amount to a repudiation if they are persistent— many small breaches add up to a major repudiation.

If you are satisfied that an employee has repudiated his contract, then you may dismiss summarily. But what of the borderline cases?

Many employers will give notice or pay in lieu, so as to avoid ill will—or through union pressure. But where you are entitled to dismiss summarily and wish to exercise that right, you must do everything possible to ensure that you can if necessary prove that the dismissal was justified. How is this achieved?

First, you do not have to tell a dismissed employee why you are sacking him. It is often wise to keep silent. Apart from your natural reluctance to create ill will, you may find that it is only after the dismissal that the true depths of the man's misbehaviour become apparent. Colleagues who have not liked to speak out against a fellow employee lose their reluctance when the person is a colleague no longer. The truth has a way of appearing late in the day.

Second, you must prepare your documents. Naturally, the letter informing the employee of his dismissal is of vast importance. But it should be backed with a series of memoranda.

If an employee sues for damages for wrongful dismissal, his prospects of success are likely to depend upon the documentation. If the company can produce documents which show that the dismissal was justified, it will probably win its case. So if you start receiving letters of complaint from your boss—mind out! And reply, in writing.

Chapter 12

Take No Notice—Just Go

It could happen, you know. So suppose that you are wrongfully dismissed and you claim damages for wrongful dismissal. Subject to the new rules on 'unfair dismissal' (in Chapter 2), the odds are that you would be in a mess.

The company's first advantage? Time. The longer the litigation drags on, the greater your need for money.

Next, there is money itself. The company can afford the litigation. Can you? Unless you are blessed with legal aid, the chances are that you will not be able to cope with lawyers' fees. The law, alas, is for those with small resources—who get legal aid—or large ones who do not need it. The sacked executive is seldom in either class.

Above all, the law says that an employee wrongfully dismissed must take reasonable steps to mitigate his loss. He is not entitled to put up his deckchair in his own garden and relax, secure in the knowledge that his employers will be liable to pay damages in due course. He must seek to keep his loss to a minimum. In a word, he must seek reasonably suitable alternative employment.

Similar restrictions on the sacked man's freedom to relax apply even in the case of 'unfair dismissal'. In assessing his loss, the Tribunal will take into account the extent to which that loss has been caused or contributed to by his own action or inactivity. In practice, this means that he is still bound to do what he can to mitigate the effect of his employers' wrongful behaviour.

Of course, if you do obtain other work and lose no money, you will have saved yourself the full cost of your wrongful dismissal. But if you get in work which brings in any pay, then the damages (or the compensation) payable by your company will be reduced accordingly.

What if you get no alternative work? Then the company's lawyers will doubtless plead that you failed to take any or any sufficient or any sufficiently energetic steps to find such work.

Finally, the company will argue that it was entitled to dismiss you as it did. True, it is unlikely to succeed in this defence. But (as your lawyers will soon tell you) litigation is a chancy business and you can have no certainty of success.

So you—the sacked employee—will put on one side of the scales your need for cash—soon; your inability to meet your own costs— or (if you lose) those of the company; your need to mitigate your loss—and the probable accusation that you took insufficient steps to that end; and the accusations of wrongful behaviour which they will doubtless level at your head—what will you do? In a word— settle.

The sacked employee, then, will generally accept far less than his true entitlement, simply so as to avoid the risks, expenses and time wastage of litigation. By his meanness today, his employer has saved money tomorrow. So watch out!

Chapter 13

Suing—and Prosecuting—Your Servant

If a salesman or representative is responsible for stock losses, then even if he is acquitted on criminal charges arising out of the deficiencies, he may still be sued by his employers. That is the moral of the recent and extremely important case of *Beeches Working Men's Club and Institute Trustees* v. *Scott*.

Mr Scott was the steward of a club—but, for our purposes, he might have been almost any employee. Under his contract of service, he was liable for deficiencies in cash or stock. A complaint was taken out before the local magistrates, alleging that he had 'withheld certain property in his possession, namely £130'. He was triumphantly acquitted.

The trustees then sued in the local County Court, for the same £130. "You have had one crack of the legal whip," said the manager, in effect. "Your prosecution failed. You cannot now sue in a civil court." The County Court Judge agreed. The club appealed.

Unanimously, the Court of Appeal decided that the issues in the criminal proceedings were different from those before the County Court. In the one case, a conviction could only be obtained if the prosecution could prove that funds had been 'withheld or misapplied'. If he had behaved fraudulently, then he could be convicted and fined. But if there had been no fraud, he must be acquitted.

But what if the deficiency had been caused by the action of a third person? In that case, there was no dishonesty, no fraud, no misbehaviour—and no criminal offence. But he could still be liable to his employers under his contract of service. The case was sent back to the County Court, to decide whether there was a deficiency—and if so, whether there was not a breach of the contract of service.

So these express clauses in contracts of service are valuable to employers—and potentially perilous to those who are employed to sell.

But even without any express agreement, every salesman is bound to take reasonable care to avoid causing loss to his employers. If a deficiency occurs in goods or cash under the control of a salesman and it could be proved that this was caused by the employee's negligence (or, to be precise, as a result of a breach of the implied term in his contract of service that he will take due care of his employer's property), then the employers will have a good claim

against him. What is more, while in criminal proceedings the prosecution must prove its case 'beyond reasonable doubt', in a civil
court all that has to be shown is that the case is proved 'on the
balance of probabilities'. And that is often a good deal easier.

So for once, the law has come down clearly and resoundingly
on the side of the boss. Employees must take good care of their
employer's property or they may be held accountable—even if there
is no provable dishonesty on his part. The legal whip may crack
several times.

Chapter 14

You, too, Can Change Your Job

Most executives have periods of notice built into their contracts.
They are entitled to receive—and must give—the agreed notice.
In the absence of agreement, each side is entitled to 'reasonable
notice', which must not be less than the minimum appropriate
period laid down by the *Contracts of Employment Act, 1963* (as
amended by the Industrial Relations Act). It is generally far more.

Top management may be entitled to anything from (perhaps)
three to twelve months' notice, either by agreement or as 'reasonable
notice'. Top weight under the Contracts of Employment Act,
as amended? As we saw in Chapter 3, eight weeks' notice after
fifteen years' service.

The Act also provides that after three months' service, the employee
must give a magnificent seven days' notice. Once again, this is a
minimum, and subject to agreement (express or implied) to the contrary. Why so short a period? Because Parliamentarians—unlike
businessmen—recognise that any period of notice to be given by
the employee is theoretical only and has no enforceable legal effect.

Suppose, for instance, that you are offered a better post with some
other company. Your presence is required at once. What do you do?

You consult your contract of employment. You find out whether
there is any agreed period of notice. If nothing is agreed, then you
must give reasonable notice. Either way, you will not be able to wait.

Go to the man at the top of your outfit and present your apologies.
Ask him nicely whether the company will waive its rights to notice.
If he agrees, then you part on good terms. If he does not, then con-
sider the consequences if you walk out.

You will be breaking your contract of service. This may cost the company a good deal of money. But how much? "Thousands of pounds," you say. How many thousands, then? No one can tell.

In practice, it is absolutely impossible to quantify the damage caused because an employee leaves in breach of his contract of service. If he is sacked without notice or pay in lieu, then he will lose the remuneration which he should have received during the period of notice, minus anything which he actually manages to earn during that period. This can be totted up very precisely. But the employer cannot assess his damages with precision. And where damages for breach of contract are involved, the law says: "Unless you can prove your loss, you can generally get no damages."

So if you walked out without giving proper notice, your company will not get damages against you. What, then, of 'specific performance'? Can it get an order of the Court, requiring you to serve your notice in accordance with your agreement?

The law will only grant orders for 'specific performance' where damages would not be an adequate remedy. This usually applies only when there is a contract for the transfer of some interest in the land and either the vendor or the purchaser fails or refuses to complete the deal. Orders for 'specific performance' will not be made in cases involving personal obligations. So you need have no worry on that score.

That leaves the possibility of an injunction—an order restraining you from taking the other job. But this would amount to a restraint on your freedom to earn your living. And in the absence of some valid, binding restraint clause in your own contract of service, your company will get no injunction against you.

So at this stage you must check your contract very carefully. No restraint clause will be implied into it. And any clause actually written in will be examined with great care, to see whether it is reasonable in all respects. If it provides the company with more protection than is reasonable, for the necessary sheltering of its business . . . if it imposes an unreasonably wide restraint on your freedom to earn your living . . . or if it is unreasonable from the public viewpoint—then it will be a dead letter.

It follows that you must hope that your contract either contains no restraint clause at all or a very wide one which will be unenforceable. Either way, you may break your contract with legal impunity.

If you do discover a restraint clause in your contract, take it to a solicitor. Let him advise you whether or not the term would be likely to stand up in Court. If it is clearly too wide, then you may move tomorrow to your company's main competitors and you will leave a powerless Board behind you.

Even if the clause would probably be enforced, you may still decide to take a gamble. Precisely because this sort of litigation is so doubtful and every case of its kind is considered on its own facts, it is unlikely that the company can be sure of success, if it does sue. Will it take the gamble? Unless it does so, other executives may realise that the restraint clauses will not be enforced—and act accordingly. Conversely, if it does sue you and fail, then all hopes of future bluff against other members of staff will collapse, along with the company's case.

In this sort of nasty dilemma, most businesses will sigh sadly and wave farewell to their employee. He is entitled to his 'cards'—these do not belong to the business. He must be paid his remuneration up to and including the day he leaves—he has earned it. He may leave on very bad terms, and get no reference at all. But this is unlikely to worry him, if he already has a well-upholstered alternative available.

From the one side, then, the employer may (if he sees fit) dismiss summarily, often to disadvantage of his business. Conversely, the executive who wishes to leave without giving proper notice runs little legal risk. Only if he is bound by a valid restraint clause must he watch his next step with great care.

Morals? Employers should attempt to insert reasonable restraint clauses in all contracts of service of senior executives. But executives should attempt to avoid the acceptance of any restraint clause—except one that is thoroughly unreasonable, in which case it will be unenforceable and the executive can ignore it.

Chapter 15

Never Resign

I once asked a famous politician whether it was true that he had threatened to resign over a particular issue. "Certainly not," he replied. "To resign is to be defeated." In politics, this may be an overstatement. In commerce, it is not. The executive who wishes to retain his legal rights should normally prefer to be dismissed.

Suppose that you get involved in a boardroom dispute and take the losing side. You are invited to resign. "It is much better to part on good terms," says the company secretary, soothingly. "After all, one day you may need a reference. . . ."

True enough. And there is no law which requires an employer to supply a reference—good or bad. But before you take the easy way out, consider the snags.

If you resign, you terminate your own contract of employment. Therefore you are not dismissed.

Naturally, you cannot obtain damages for wrongful or for unfair dismissal, unless you can prove that your employers terminated your contract. Do so yourself and you were not dismissed—and you will therefore lose not only your golden handshake but also your prospect of obtaining damages through action in court or tribunal.

There are two provisos. By all means let your employers describe your departure as 'resignation upon agreed terms', if they have duly feathered your nest. You are, of course, better off (initially at least) to obtain a golden handshake, rather than to earn the money. Unearned income paid as 'severance pay' escapes tax up to £5,000.

Second, an employer owes precise duties to his employee. There are terms implied in your contract of service that *you* will give loyal and faithful service . . . that *you* will not enter into competition with your own company . . . that *you* will obey all lawful orders . . . and so on. Act sufficiently in breach of one or more of those terms and *you* will destroy your contract of service and entitle your employers to dismiss you.

Equally, there is an implied term in your contract of service that *your employer* will not make it impossible for you to do your job. If he makes your life a misery by constant interference in your work . . . by humiliating or belittling you in front of those whom you control . . . by making your life a general misery—then he is effectively making it impossible for you to carry out your work. He is attempting to drive you away from your work. He may put an end to your contract quite as effectively as if he had actually, physically given you notice.

To see the sense of this, consider the situation in reverse. If you resign—with or without notice—you terminate your employment. Equally, if you habitually fail to do your job in a proper manner . . . if you make it impossible for your employers to keep you on . . . then you may 'repudiate' your contract, just at effectively as if you had specifically and deliberately called it to an end.

It follows that it is worth putting up with a good deal of humiliation and wretchedness, rather than to resign. Whether your employer's treatment of you will be sufficiently serious or severe to amount to a 'repudiation of the contract' by him will be a question of degree and will depend on all the circumstances of the case.

Naturally, it will be difficult for you to assess the situation with any impartiality. And even if you can stand back sufficiently from your own troubles to consider matters of degree in reasonably cold blood, you will not be able properly to assess the view likely to be taken by a court. For that, you need an experienced lawyer.

This is one situation in which it is well worth taking your troubles to a solicitor. Write out your problems in advance, if you can . . . provide him with as much information as possible concerning your treatment by the boss . . . and then let him advise you as to whether or not the mistreatment goes sufficiently far to amount to a 'repudiation' by your employer. If it does, then by leaving you are not resigning but accepting the situation he has created—just as he is not destroying the contract if you are guilty of serious misconduct and he asks you to leave.

Now look at the effect of these tactics upon redundancy problems. In order to obtain redundancy pay, an employee must show two things—that he was 'dismissed' and that the dismissal was due to 'redundancy'.

In brief, you are 'redundant' if you lose your job through some change in the employer's business—if he closes down a branch, a department or the company . . . if he moves his business (wholly or in part) to some other area . . . indeed, if you are 'redundant' in the ordinary sense of that word.

What, then, of 'dismissal'? The employer must have put an end to the contract of service.

In one famous case, a highly reputable company informed employees in one department that they should look for other work because redundancies were in the offing. An executive found other work and left his post. He claimed redundancy pay.

The court decided that the man had jumped the gun. He had not been 'dismissed'. He had not received his notice—nor had his employers repudiated the contract. In the circumstances, there was no 'dismissal' and hence no right to any redundancy payment.

Once notice has actually been received, the situation immediately changes. An employee may then find other work and provided that he gives the appropriate written notice to his employers, he may leave before the period expires—provided that they do not serve a counter-notice on him, offering him renewed employment. If that situation arises, once again you should consult the experts before you act.

Indeed, it is often worth obtaining the help of a lawyer in the drafting of what you would (wrongly, I hope) describe as a 'letter of resignation'. That letter should put your case into clear, precise words. You are not leaving voluntarily but because you have been thrust out of your job. It is not a question of resignation by some other name. When your employer destroys your contract of service you acquire new legal rights. But put an end to it yourself and those rights are likely to disappear.

Naturally, when acting for the company, you apply the same rules in reverse. If you can induce unwanted employees to resign you are likely to save the old firm a good deal of money.

Chapter 16

Poaching Staff

There is no close season for the poaching of people. Provided that your competitors do not induce your staff to break their contracts of service, they are fully entitled to invite your employees to leave your service and to join theirs.

Morality apart, you would only be able to prevent your competitors from enticing your employees away from you if you could show two things. First, you would have to prove that the employees left without giving the notice required under their contracts of service. In that case, they would have broken those contracts. Second, the court would have to be satisfied not merely that the employee had acted in breach of contract, but that the new employer had 'procured' that breach.

There is nothing to prevent your competitor from saying: "Join my staff. I will give you higher wages . . . better conditions . . . improved prospects. . . ." What he must not do is to say: "Leave now . . . do not bother to give proper notice . . . I need you at once. . . ."

If you can show that a number of employees have left in breach of their contracts of service, then you might get an injunction—an order of the court, restraining any future breach. And you could also claim damages. But no breach of contract means, in general, no rights.

Naturally, if you could prove that your employee had moved to your competitor in breach of an enforceable restraint (or radius) clause, then you could claim an injunction against the employee—and also against the new employer, restraining him from employing the person, in breach of his restraint clause.

Finally, if you could show that your competitor was sending talent scouts on to your premises, then you might be able to prove a trespass. And while trespassers cannot be prosecuted, they may be ejected—and sued for injunctions.

In practice, though, your chances of taking your competitors to court and emerging with a successful result are not great. If you want to keep your customers, you have to provide goods at the most competitive rates. If you wish to retain your staff then, in the long run at least, you will have to make it worth their while to stay.

Naturally, the converse applies. The freedom which the law gives to your competitors to poach your employees applies equally to you. By all means enter the labour market and steal them back again. Provided that you do not trespass or induce them to act in breach of restraint clauses or contrary to their contracts of service, all will be well.

Chapter 17

Bottoms up—and Spare-time Misconduct

The temptation to lay hands on other people's property is only equalled by the urge to lay hands on other people. There are, of course, those who do so legally as part of their healing arts. But even they have their troubles. Every so often the patient of a doctor or dentist alleges that she has been raped—and the unfortunate healer finds himself dragged before his Disciplinary Committee. For a professional man, it is 'conduct unbecoming' to allow one's physical pleasures to become involved with one's professional studies, even in one's spare time.

Businessmen suffer under no such off-duty restraint. Even those who manufacture beds are fully entitled when at home both to make and to lie upon them. But there are limits. The laying on of hands should not be done without the consent of the other party.

To touch another without his consent amounts to an assault. Even if no 'bodily harm' is caused, the offender may be prosecuted. And in the case of 'actual' or 'grievous' bodily harm, a conviction might prove serious.

More important (and more likely) in the world of industry is the smacking or pinching of the female bottom, out of fun or frustration. The man who lays hands on his female colleague in this way is probably breaking his contract of service and if he does it often enough the breach may be sufficient to amount to a repudiation and

41

to warrant summary dismissal. This, in effect, was the defence which failed in one recent case in which an executive sued for damages for wrongful dismissal. Even though a couple of technical assaults were proved against him, the judge was satisfied that these left the contract of service intact. Like the ladies.

Of course, you are not bound to keep a rapist on your staff or even a man who assaults indecently. What he does in his own time may be his own business—but serious misconduct in your time affects your business.

There was once an unmarried governness who became pregnant and was sacked on the spot. Even though her loose living was carried on outside her employer's premises, they were entitled to demand that she set a good example to her charges.

But the executive who saw fit to commit adultery and to ruin his own matrimonial life gave no cause whatsoever for his company summarily to sack him. If his amours (or, for that matter, his matrimonial unhappiness) had preyed on his mind so as to leave insufficient thought for the business . . . if as a result he was not doing his job properly . . . if he was guilty of persistent negligence, in and about his employment . . . then he would have shattered his contract of service. It was then his behaviour at work and not his promiscuity or infidelity outside it that gave his employers the right to show him to the door.

There are, of course, borderline cases. The executive who seduces his secretary when they are both working late at night is asking for trouble, commercial as well as matrimonial. Whether he had behaved in such a way as to make it impossible for him to carry on in his job is a question of fact. The odds are against it. But seduce enough secretaries sufficiently often and your position becomes untenable.

The chairman of a family company once called the managing director into his office. After five minutes, the next senior director received a summons . . . then the next . . . and the next . . . until only the most junior director was left in the boardroom. Eventually, he too was called in.

"Well, Brown," said the chairman. "Do sit down. Now tell me. Have you slept with Miss Jones?"

"Certainly not," Brown replied.

"Never?"

"Never. In fact, I've never laid a finger on her."

"Do you swear it?"

"Certainly."

"Then," said the Chairman, "you sack her. . . ."

It is not always easy to separate business and pleasure. What a man does in his own free time is generally his own business, provided only that it does not affect his work. He must not compete with the company. He must now show himself to be a thief, and hence unfitted to be trusted in the company's affairs. But otherwise, his conduct is usually up to him. Similarly, if he is a drunk on duty, he may show himself unwilling to be tied by his contract of service—he may destroy it by 'striking at its very roots'. But if he sees fit to drink too much in his own time, that is a matter for him—at least until his delerium tremens or cirrhosis of the liver render him incapable of carrying his commercial burdens.

Or suppose that you get convicted of a traffic offence. If it takes you off the road, so as to ruin your social life or to make it impossible for you to cart your children to school in the mornings, so much the worse for you. Only if your disqualification makes it impossible for you to carry out your duties at work will you have driven yourself out of work.

An operative came crying into the office of the personnel director. "I've been raped," she said.

"By whom," enquired the executive, with grammatical calm.

"I'm not sure," she said. "But I think it was the foreman."

"Why?"

"Because he wore a white coat and brown shoes and I had to do all the work."

In that case, the odds are that the gentleman concerned had not earned himself the sack. Anyway, who wants to upset the unions? And it's a free country, isn't it? And all work and no play makes Jack a dull boy. "I have no concern for your predicament, Jack," says the law. "I'm all right. . . ." In other words, so long as the employee does not repudiate his contract of service, his employers acquire no right to throw him out.

Chapter 18

Making the Best of a Bad Reference

You cannot force a reference out of your former employers. If they wish to keep silent, they may do so—however unfairly.

Suppose, then, that you leave your employment in a state of dispute. Maybe there was a split on the board and you backed the wrong side . . . perhaps you were wrongly accused of misconduct. Whatever the cause, you cannot get other work today because you fell out with your former employers yesterday. What should you do?

First, forget about suing. As you have no right to a reference, you have no legal remedy if your employers refuse to give one.

"What about defamation, then?" you say. "By saying nothing, they are indirectly defaming my character."

True enough. But there being no duty to speak out, your employers are fully entitled to remain silent. You will not get damages for defamation because words of praise remain unspoken. Anyway, how do you know that your employers are not supplying (orally or in writing) bad references for you?

"It's one or the other, isn't it? Either they are damning with their silence or with their words. Either ruins my prospects."

Too bad.

"How about asking prospective employers to show you any references?"

Do not waste your time. They will almost certainly refuse. And even if they were to provide evidence of bad references, the occasion would be 'privileged'. Unless you could prove 'malice'—that your employers gave a false reference with the deliberate intention of harming you, not out of any wish to assist your prospective employers —they would have a water-tight defence. They could successfully plead 'qualified privilege'.

Of course, if the reference were both untrue and negligently supplied, you might theoretically have some remedy. But in practice, I do not know of even one decided case in which an employee obtained damages on that sort of basis.

So the outlook for the employee left without a reference—or (which is equally bad) supplied with an unfavourable one—is bleak. On this occasion, what matters is to know and appreciate your own weakness, and to cope accordingly. Knowledge of the law is necessary not merely in order to make use of the weapons it provides, but (as here) to know when you are in a hopeless, legal plight, so that you may look for other ways around your problem.

"What can the unfortunate employee, bereft of both job and reference, do then?"

Use intelligent tactics. It is hopeless to apply for a job on the basis that the prospective employer will appoint you 'subject to references'. Put your cards straight on the table. Like this:

"The best reference I can offer you is ten years' service with the company, starting as a junior and working up to executive. The reason I left? No fault of mine. Disputes within the company— a situation in which I became involved, against my will." Or: "Reference? Hopeless. Mr X is in charge and I am afraid that we did not get on. That, in fact, is an understatement. Had he not arrived on the scene, I would still be there. As it is, I am at your service, if you want me."

Naturally, the prospective employer may still check up. He may want to know what Mr X has to say about it. And he may prefer the word and the opinion of Mr X to your explanations. On the other hand, he may not. That, at least, must be your earnest (and only) hope. You must build yourself a career, and as you have no references upon which to lay its foundation, then it is up to you to exercise your wit, craft and personality and to overcome a situation which certainly creates difficulties but which has not prevented many excellent men from clambering back into well-paid posts, after unhappy disputes with the old firm.

The only alternative? Sink your pride. After all, you may have a wife and children to provide for. Phone up the man who has spurned you . . . invite him to meet you . . . splash your last few pounds on lunch, drinks and potential goodwill—and see if you cannot induce the man to bury the hatchet—and (at no cost to himself) provide you with a reference. Hopeless? Sorry.

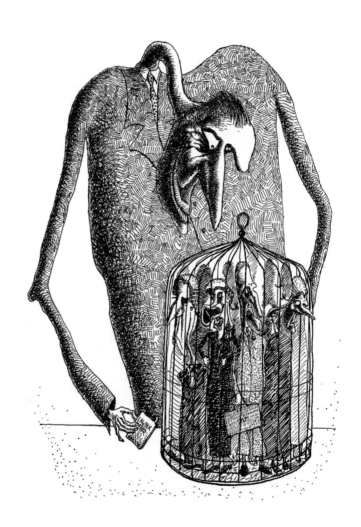

Part Three

Coping with Lawyers, with Litigation and with
Members of Parliament

Chapter 19

Calling on Counsel

When do you need a barrister on your side? Precisely what do 'Counsel' do for their living? Should you choose your 'Counsel' or leave that problem to your solicitor? And anyway, would it not be better to let the solicitor cope with your litigation on his own? Important questions, these, to every businessman, caught up in the mesh of the law.

* * *

Barristers are the consultants and (usually) the professional advocates of the legal world. You feel ill? Then you go to your general practitioner. He requires specialist advice on your condition? Then he will pass you on to the appropriate consultant, almost always of *his* choice. An operation may be needed? Then (apart from minor miseries, such as the lancing of boils) you will be despatched to the appropriate hospital or (in the case of a private patient) to a surgeon (once again, of the doctor's choosing).

Solicitors are the general practitioners of the legal world. Barristers (or 'Counsel') are the consultants. The client, like the patient, may not consult direct. You go to your solicitor. He 'takes Counsel's opinion' on your behalf, if necessary.

Litigation is the surgical procedure of the law. Your solicitor *may* appear in any County Court (which, in general, deals with cases involving £750 or less), before any Tribunal or (in criminal matters) in a Magistrates' Court or (in some cases) a higher court. Still, unless he specialises in advocacy, or unless the case is very minor, he will probably 'brief' Counsel. Barristers have a right of audience before any Court in the country.

"When do *I* need Counsel, then?" you ask.

If you have confidence in your solicitor, you can leave that decision to him. But if you are doubtful about the advice you are getting, you are fully entitled to demand that Counsel be instructed. You may

49

insist upon a conference with your barrister. Alternatively, you may require your solicitor to obtain Counsel's written advice.

If you are involved in minor litigation, your solicitor may prefer to get on with the job—and if he knows what he is about, you may save a good deal of money if no barrister is needed. But if there are complicated points of fact or law, you will probably need the application of a barrister's mind and tongue. He may know less than your solicitor . . . he may be young and inexperienced, while your solicitor is mature and learned. . . . But the chances are that your solicitor will be so involved in the everyday administration of his practice and in dealing with his flood of routine work that he will not have time to do the necessary research.

"No barrister, however learned, can know all the law of the land," a wise old practitioner once remarked. "But he *can* know where to find it . . . and he *must* find the time to dig it out."

If there is to be litigation in the High Court, then you have no option. A solicitor may draft (or 'settle') the writ. But at that stage (if not before) Counsel will have to be instructed. He will settle the necessary 'pleadings', i.e. the documents that set out your case. He will advise at the various stages. He will sharpen the legal knives, on your side of the table.

"What will a barrister charge?" That entirely depends upon the seniority and skill of the barrister and the nature of the case. The younger and the less experienced your man of law, the lower (in general) his fee. The more substantial and involved the case, the higher the cost.

Sometimes, there are scales laid down in Rules of the Court. Usually there are none. The barrister may charge what the market will bear—and if he is not prepared to work for you at the fee suggested by your solicitor, then your work will go elsewhere unless, of course, you tell your solicitor to pay the fee that Counsel wants. The fee will normally be negotiated between your solicitor and the barrister's clerk (who acts as a strange combination of business manager and secretarial factotum, receiving a commission on all fees which come into his 'Chambers').

If Counsel is to be instructed, ask your solicitor to estimate the cost in advance. He should be able to give you a rough guide. And remember that payment for conferences, opinions and 'interlocutory work' tends to be moderate—only commercial, tax, patent and other specialist or absolutely top grade Counsel receiving mighty fees. But when cases come to court, Counsel may do very well. So next time your barrister advises you to settle a case, do not take umbrage. He is the one who is certain to lose financially if the case is compromised.

"What precisely is a Queen's Counsel? And when should I employ one?"

A QC is sometimes called a 'Silk', because he may wear a silken gown—or a 'Leader', because he usually has 'junior' Counsel, instructed with him. A barrister may 'apply for Silk' when he has been in practice for at least ten years. He is unlikely to 'get Silk' unless he has a very substantial practice, is a man of personal distinction and irreproachable integrity and unless he is 'learned in the law'.

You will only need a 'Leader' for your most difficult or lengthy cases. He will be called in either at the advice of your solicitor or of your 'junior Counsel'—or both. He may advise on some particularly intricate point of law or procedure, or appear in court on a major matter. In certain cases (such as town and country planning applications) he may appear on his own. Usually, a 'junior' will have to be instructed with him. But the old, restrictive practice requiring that the junior be paid two-thirds of his Leader's fee has now been abolished.

The lawyer, then, must know his law and his judges. What matters to you is to know—and to trust—your lawyers.

Chapter 20

A Solicitor's Services

There are occasions when you can save money by *not* employing a solicitor. But *not* when you buy or sell property. There is no law that says that the seller or buyer of premises must employ a man of law. But not to do so is asking for trouble.

As a seller, what matters is to get hold of the purchaser's money. You want to tie up the deal as swiftly and securely as possible. You will be paid a deposit 'subject to contract', and it is up to you to make sure that the contract which is eventually drawn up—or, to be precise, the contracts that are exchanged—are to your benefit.

Next time some completed contracts come your way, have a look at them. You will probably find that they are covered in amendments in red, green, mauve, brown or other coloured inks—each one indicating that the bargaining has been going on. The solicitors have done this, each in their own client's interest. You do not *need* to have someone acting for you. But there is much truth in the old saying: "A man who is his own lawyer has a fool for a client."

The situation is even more serious for the buyer, on his own. How will he know what he is getting for his money? Worse, how can he find out where the pitfalls lie?

Smith Limited bought an office building on a down-town street. Unfortunately, no one had bothered to check with the town hall to find out whether any development scheme was in prospect. In fact, the place was scheduled to be pulled down within five years. And the compensation payable under the *Land Compensation Act, 1961,* is seldom enough to satisfy the uprooted occupier.

Jones Limited did their own conveyancing. To their horror, a road widening scheme lost them their forecourt, and neighbours' rights of way across their yard at the back prevented them from using the place as they wanted.

Now, solicitors might have made the same mistakes. In that case, the chances are that they would have been negligent and the purchasers could have claimed damages from the solicitors, to compensate them for any loss which they could prove that they suffered because the lawyers had not done their job and found out the facts. If you go it alone, then you take your own risks. Your ship may be sunk because you begrudge the necessary quantity of legal tar—and however expensive that may seem at the time, it is quite small, when compared to the loss you could suffer if you do not know how to handle your legal affairs.

* * *

"If we employ a solicitor when we buy our new business, can he charge us whatever he thinks that the market will bear?"

Solicitors' conveyancing fees (at present, at least) are generally laid down on fixed scales, the amount chargeable depending upon the value of the property to be conveyed and whether or not the land is 'registered'. When you know the value of the property, tell your solicitor—and he will tell you the amount of the standard charge for the job. The scale fees will certainly apply, if there is no agreement to the contrary.

Of course, there will be extra fees if you need to take on a mortgage. And you must not forget stamp duty—which, once again, will vary according to the price. Anyway, when you give your requirements to the solicitor, he can look up the fees with no difficulty at all and then you will know exactly where you stand.

*   *   *

"We are desperate. We have sold our old premises and cannot get our solicitors to complete the purchase of our new ones. We have a bridging loan from the bank, but interest charges are heavy. And we are working in a temporary place with only half our equipment. Can we sue the solicitor?"

Your solicitor may be negligent. If so, then you may claim damages from him. But the odds are that the delay is not his fault. What usually happens is that the vendor cannot get into his proposed premises, so he sits tight—and then the man who is buying his property just has to wait—and so on down the line.

You should go to your solicitor's office and see him. Ask him whether he could not serve a 'notice to complete', requiring the vendor to let you into possession of the property within the stated time. If notice to complete is not complied with, then the purchaser can go to court and ask for an 'order for specific performance', requiring the vendor to carry out his part of the contract. But this is a last resort; it does involve expense; and the mere fact that completion has not taken place on the due date is certainly no guarantee that your solicitor has failed in his duties.

At present, solicitors' fees for conveyancing are in the political melting pot. You may soon be able to get the job done at cut rates. But whatever the necessary price—pay it.

Chapter 21

The Delays of the Law

A magistrate recently berated a company whose witness was not available at the hearing of a summons under the *Trade Descriptions Act, 1968*, which then had to be adjourned. Adjournments, alas, are a hazard of the law. And if this time the fault lay with the business-man, usually it is caused through the defects in the legal set-up itself. So consider for a moment how you can use the law's delay to your own best advantage. If you cannot beat them, join them.

In criminal matters, where (for instance) you are at the receiving end of a summons, you are fully entitled to ask that the proceedings be delayed so that you may bring up your cohorts of witnesses. Equally, the prosecution may make the same request. But adjourn-ments are within the discretion of the Court. Do not take it for granted that you will be granted the indulgence you seek. Let the prosecution know in advance that you will be asking for delay and if they consent, your chances of obtaining the Court's agreement are greatly improved. But there can be no guarantee. The Court's time is valuable and justice must be reasonably swift.

It is the desperate efforts of the Court to keep itself busy that cause the most upset to litigants (civil and criminal). The enormous pressure on Court time . . . the queue of cases waiting to be heard . . . the anxiety of the Lord Chancellor's office to ensure that the courts provide the speediest possible trials—all these contribute to the unwillingness of the judiciary, at every level, to allow the Court to be left without work for a few minutes—even if re-organisation of the list would result in vastly improved convenience for lawyers and litigants alike,

Suppose, for instance, that you are faced with a civil action. You turn up at Court, only to find that your case is well down the list. It may not be reached until late in the day. Or maybe it is adjourned, without any hearing at all. Or perhaps the Court was counting on earlier cases being settled. Perhaps an action which the parties thought would last an hour stretched into a morning.

Unfortunately, patience is an essential virtue for the businessman in Court. Still, there are occasions when delay is very useful indeed. Maybe you are being sued for money which you fear that you will eventually have to pay, but you want to put off the evil day for as long as possible. Or maybe your lawyers insist that you produce accounts or documents or other evidence, and you are too busy earning a livelihood to devote yourself to litigious research. Whatever the reason, explain your difficulties to your lawyers and with any luck they will be able to turn the tardiness of the law to good account.

In general, rules of Court prescribe specific time limits for the carrying out of various steps in civil litigation. Alternatively, the Court will 'give directions', requiring litigants to take the stated steps within prescribed times.

If your lawyer knows that you need extra time, then he can ask the other side to extend courtesy to you . . . he can sit back and do nothing in the hope that the other party will be equally glad of the delay or, perhaps, that their solicitors will not notice the passage of time and will allow the action 'to go to sleep'. . . . Or he may apply to the Court to grant extra time, to allow you to prepare your case.

Courts recognise, of course, that businessmen with interests and staff out of town or abroad will often require more time than usual in order to obtain statements or documents from far-flung places. But just as your bank manager is far more likely to meet your requirements for cash if you keep him well informed, so your lawyer will do much better in his efforts to obtain time for you, if you keep him well informed of your need for time.

By judicious planning, then, it is often possible to use the delays of the law for your own purposes. But (I repeat) do not take delay for granted. Every Court—civil or criminal—gets infuriated when a litigant tries to get an adjournment at the last moment. Both courtesy and commonsense require you to plan for delay, well in advance—and to leave last minute applications for real emergencies. If the executive spared as much forethought for delay as he does for speed, he would have a lot more success in using the law to his own best advantage.

Chapter 22

The Science of Paying Money into Court

For the businessman who wishes to use his time and energy in the noble pursuit of profit, the art of keeping out of court is worth careful study. And a great deal often depends upon an understanding of the science of paying money into court—both at the right time and in sufficient quantity.

Suppose that (alas) you have a dissatisfied customer. Efforts to buy him off for some sensible payment all fail. You receive a High Court writ (where the client hopes to recover over £750) or a County Court summons. What should you do? Consider a payment into Court.

The rules are these. If you pay in a sum and the Plaintiff gets judgment for that sum or less, then (once costs have been dealt with) he will be allowed to take out of Court the amount of the judgment; any balance will be paid out to you—but, much more important, you will be entitled to an order that the Plaintiff pay the legal costs incurred from the date of the payment in. Not only will *you* not have to pay *his* costs from that date—even though he has won his case—but *he* will actually have to pay *yours*. And it may well be that the costs he has to pay will exceed the amount of damages recoverable from you.

On the other hand, if the Plaintiff decides to accept the money paid into Court, he does so in full settlement of his claim. He will keep the sum paid in and you will have to pay his costs to date. But that is the end of the case.

Suppose, for instance, that you are sued. You decide to pay (say) £100 into Court. If the Plaintiff accepts that sum, you have got rid of the case—and of all the possible bad publicity, worry, aggravation and expense attached to it—not for £100, but for £100 plus the Plaintiff's costs and your own, incurred up to the date of the payment in.

Conversely, if the Plaintiff accepts your £100, you will have laid out money which you might not have had to pay, had you fought the case to the bitter end—but then the end might have been more bitter than the loss of £100 plus costs.

Naturally, the sooner money is paid into Court, the smaller the amount of costs already incurred. Equally, the larger the sum paid in, the greater will be the temptation to the Plaintiff to accept that sum—and the greater the risk for him in carrying on with the legal battle.

On the one hand, the more you pay in the less likely it is that the Judge will award less than that sum—and hence the better your chances of keeping the cost of the litigation to a minimum. On the other hand, the money paid in may be accepted by the Plaintiff— and if you pay in too much, you may lose a good deal more than the Court would have awarded to the Plaintiff, even had he won his case.

Payments into Court are normally made with a denial of liability. The Judge is not told that there is money in Court—so he cannot know what (or whether) you thought it was worth paying to get rid of the litigation. Only if and when you lose your case will the Judge consider the 'payment in'. If you have judged the amount of that payment in correctly, then even if you have lost your case, you may save yourself a good deal of money. If you have paid in too little, then you will have tied up some of your cash between the date of the payment in and the date of the trial—but otherwise, the tactical move will have cost you nothing but the interest on that money.

The timing of the payment in is important and should be discussed with your solicitor. Pay in too early and your litigious opponent may regard this as a sign of weakness and hope that you will either pay in more or else put up your bid, at the door of the Court. He will be told by his lawyers that there is no finality about a payment into Court. It may be increased at any time.

Conversely, you may decide to put up the risks of the litigation, right from the start and to pay in a modest sum, in the hope that the Plaintiff will accept it. You may know that you will in fact, if necessary, pay more in due course—but the Plaintiff will have to guess your intentions. Like business, the law is often a matter of bluff and counter-bluff.

Naturally the same rules apply in reverse. Suppose that you are injured in a car crash. The other driver involved denies liability and you have to sue. He makes a payment into Court. You think that the payment is very mean. But bearing in mind that you may fail to establish liability . . . that you may be found guilty of contributory negligence . . . that you may face a mean judge, who takes a dim view of your alleged injuries or damage . . . and that if you recover no more than the sum paid in, you will have to bear the defendant's costs from the date of the payment in—can you afford to leave the money in court and to hope for the best?

Once there is money in Court, the problems of a Plaintiff multiply. But if you know these rules, you can at least transfer many of the worries to the other side of the legal fence.

Chapter 23

When Your Lawyer Does Not Turn Up

If your case does reach court, then you will undoubtedly be upset if the barrister of your choice fails to arrive. So what can you do about it?

*   *   *

Unfortunately, courts generally take the view that a case cannot be adjourned or fixed 'for Counsel's convenience'. Judges forget that when they oblige a barrister by adjusting the court lists, they are not only helping him to make a living but enabling the client to have the advocate of his choice. Usually, that is not a consideration which outweighs 'the convenience of the court'. A judge's time and that of the officials who surround him—is regarded as invaluable.

Why should a lawyer not turn up at the hearing? After all, he keeps a diary, doesn't he? A businessman books his appointments, doesn't he? Yes—but what about emergencies? Things go wrong, even in the best regulated business.

With lawyers, the situation is far more complicated and aggravating, for one good reason—that cases get settled. The vast majority of them, in fact, never reach trial.

Take a typical example. You get involved in a battle with your builder. In due course, the case is set down for trial. A hearing date is fixed. At this stage, the haggling process begins in earnest. The day before the hearing, the case is settled and the barrister's services are not required.

Multiply this instance by several hundred and you have the barrister's typical year. He cannot afford to keep dates free for one particular case because, on the balance of probabilities, it will settle. I repeat: The majority of cases (to the client's eternal benefit) do not reach trial.

Hence any barrister who wishes to make a living must keep his options open for as long as possible. If he puts two cases down for one day, the chances are that both will disappear from the list. Conversely, if he reserves a week for a case, it may easily take longer than expected—and the people for whom he should be appearing during the second week will complain bitterly that their barrister does not arrive.

The answer may lie in a brief adjournment. But that would involve waste of the court's time. "I would like to help you, Mr Jones," says the Judge, when the Barrister applies for an adjournment, "but I'm afraid that Counsel's convenience cannot be the overriding factor. I appreciate the excellent way in which you would carry out your duties—but there are other members of the Bar. . . ." Yes, there are—and some at least may be better at the job than Mr Jones. But the client has confidence in his Counsel and is very unhappy at the unwanted change.

So there can be no guarantee that you will get the Counsel of your choice, even if he has dealt with the preliminary stages of your case. The more eminent the barrister, indeed, the busier he will be—and the less likely you are to have him at the hearing. And as the court's lists become increasingly crowded, so the pressure on the court's time increases—and the less likely it becomes that an adjournment will be granted, for the convenience of Counsel or that of his client.

Naturally, barristers depend for their livelihood upon doing cases —and upon keeping the goodwill of their solicitor clients. If the barrister cannot attend at the hearing, the lay client is upset—and so is the solicitor—and he will take out his wrath upon the barrister, who may lose him as a client.

Unfortunately, the only barrister you can be sure of getting is the one that no one wants—he will definitely be free to look after your business. Otherwise, you must hope for the best—and trust that your solicitor will apply such pressure as he can on the Counsel's clerk, to ensure that he is there to represent your interests when the day of trial arrives.

Chapter 24

Handling the Court

Judges are human. They invariably do their best to do justice and— making all due allowances for human error—they usually succeed. If they fail, this may well be the result of the behaviour of the parties or the witnesses. After all, if someone 'puts your back up', you are hardly likely to incline subconsciously in his direction.

So for the businessman who enters the world of the law—however unwillingly—here are some hints on how to emerge victorious.

*   *   *

First, remember that the judge is watching you. Perched on high on his dais, he observes the participants—and not only when they are giving evidence.

A short time ago, a young man was convicted of murder at the Old Bailey. When passing sentence, Mr Justice Thesiger specifically referred to signals made in the dock. "People think that I don't see this sort of behaviour," he said. "They are wrong."

Few judges actually mention their observations—but all observe. So when you sit in the back of the Court, your demeanour matters.

Control yourself then. Still, it is demeanour in the witness box that matters most.

First, unless your evidence is heard, it cannot possibly be believed. Modest mumbling into the beard is a fruitless occupation. Speak up. Imagine that the Judge is deaf. He probably is.

Then remember that the Judge must write down all important evidence. He keeps a careful note, so that he can deliver a reasoned judgment—or, in criminal cases, a careful and proper summary of the evidence for the benefit of the jury. Some judges write quicker than others. Watch the man's pen and do not irritate him by leaping ahead too quickly.

Next, stand up straight—or, if you are invited to sit, be still. Do not rattle coins in your pocket, scratch your nervous knuckles on the witness box, click the wooden panels or otherwise display signs of the anxiety which no doubt you feel. Calmness pays.

Above all, do not slouch with your hands in your pockets. Do the Court the courtesy of behaving as if you regarded it as important.

Obviously it is worth coming to Court suitably attired. Businessmen who arrive in sports jackets—or worse, sweaters—make a bad impact. If you happen to wear your hair long or dishevelled, this is hardly likely to do you any good. Most judges are middle-class gentlemen, of moderately old-fashioned views. If you wish to win your case, pander to their tastes.

Any barrister will tell you that a judge has to be flattered. Even if you disagree with him . . . think him foolish or stupid . . . it is decidedly unwise to say so. After all, he is the Judge. If he sits alone, he will decide your case—whether you like it or not. You cannot choose your Judge, nor he (in general) his case. You are in his hands —so be nice to him.

Equally, jurymen are usually middle-class citizens—rate-payers and householders. If by any mischance your son or daughter has to appear in court—whether as witness or (heaven forbid) a defendant or accused—insist that he (or she) put aside permissive or progressive tastes in garb, if only for the course of the trial. An appearance of conformity today means a better chance of non-conformity tomorrow.

Finally—and above all—answer the questions you are asked. However great the temptation to think four questions ahead—or two behind—restrain yourself. If you are asked an improper question, the Judge will almost certainly intervene. If not, Counsel for your side will do so. If there is no interruption, answer the question. If possible, say "yes" or "no"—then qualify your answer, if necessary. Witnesses who dodge, fence and prevaricate do their case no good.

Nor should you answer one question with another. "What is

your name?" "What is my name?" "Yes, what is your name?"
"My name's Jones. What's yours?"

It is not for you to question but to answer. Fail to do so and you
will damage the case you seek to serve.

Remember, of course, that Counsel on your own side cannot
suggest the answer he wants to the question you ask. In legal terms,
he is not allowed to 'lead'. "What happened next?" he will enquire.

Counsel on the other side may cross-examine and 'lead' to his
heart's content. "You were doing this, I suggest," he says. "I put it
to you that what happened next was . . ." "Don't you agree that . . . ?"

Do not get cross with the other side. The barrister is doing his
job. Whether he likes it or not, he must carry out his duties. Take
heart—not umbrage.

Know your case and put it across honestly and faithfully . . .
answer the questions you are asked, clearly, loudly and coherently—
and you should have nothing to fear from the witness box. But the
prevaricator, the liar and the teller of the half-truth is liable to be
in trouble. That is the object of the exercise, is it not?

Chapter 25

The 'Hearsay Rule'

"Every time I opened my mouth in the witness box," said the unhappy businessman, emerging from court, "the Judge jumped down
my throat."

Knowing the great courtesy with which judges generally treat
businessmen, the likely solution probably lies in one word: Hearsay.
So in case you have to give evidence spare a thought for the rule which
says that you must only say what you saw or discovered and not
what you were told in the absence of the other party to the proceedings.

*   *   *

It is a basic, time-honoured rule of evidence that your witness
may say what he heard, unless those against whom his evidence is

directed has the opportunity to hear the same. In general, then, the expression, "he told me . . ." must be exorcised from the witness's vocabulary, except where 'he' happens to be the other party.

Worse, witnesses sometimes say: "He told me that he had heard that . . ." This is known as 'double hearsay'.

In practice, it is hard enough to give accurate evidence of what you saw with your own eyes. If you made a note at the time, you are entitled to refresh your memory from that note. Otherwise, you rely upon that inner eye which is the bane of truth. Recollection is faulty and even the most honest of witnesses can be wrong—and often is. 'Memory plays tricks. . . .'

The moment you cease to testify about what you saw and can only say what someone else told you what he saw, two doubtful memories come into play, yours and that of your informant. So the prospects of inaccuracy are doubled.

Worse, if you tell the Court what your informant told you what he was told by someone else, the prospects of the description of the event concerned reaching the ears of the Judge or jury in an accurate form are remote in the extreme—so remote, in fact, that the evidence itself is normally excluded with even greater vehemence than 'single hearsay'.

If the other party is present at the conversation, the situation changes. Then he had the opportunity at the time of contradicting the second-hand account. If he failed to do so, then that is at least an indication that the account was correct. If he fought back then so much the better.

There are a number of exceptions to the rule excluding hearsay evidence. First, if the other side raises no objection, the evidence is often accepted by the Court. If the other man's advocate thinks that the hearsay evidence will rebound to his client's benefit, he will stifle his urge to leap up, crying: "I object".

Next, while the prosecution in a criminal case is expected to prove its case strictly, beyond reasonable doubt and in accordance with all rules of evidence, a good deal of leeway is often given to the defence. If the accused wishes to say what he was told by his daughter or doctor, then he will usually get away with a technical breach of the hearsay rule.

Finally, the *Civil Evidence Act, 1968*, Section 2: 'In any civil proceedings a statement made, whether orally or in a document or otherwise, by any person, whether called as a witness in those proceedings or not, shall . . . be admissible as evidence of any fact stated therein . . .'

Nevertheless, the 'leave of the court' has to be obtained and notice must normally be given to the other side. These rules are rarely invoked.

So the witness who really tries to tell 'the *whole* truth' (as well as 'the truth and nothing but the truth') finds himself frustrated.

Suppose, for instance, that you are giving evidence about an ordinary car smash. You say what you saw and then add: "The driver of the other vehicle said to me . . ."

"Stop!" exclaims the Judge. "Was the Defendant present?"

"No."

"Then I'm afraid that you cannot tell me what the other driver said."

If you did not know before, then at least you do now. And if you wish to keep your foot out of your mouth, then you should remember to remove the hearsay from your lips.

Chapter 26

How to Get the Last Laugh—at Law

In law as in war, it is the final battle that really counts. If you can make the first the last, then you are lucky. But if you are going to lose, then you are far better off to do so from the start.

Jones Limited owed £10,000 for materials supplied by Smith Limited. Credit was short; Messrs Jones could not meet their account; so they scraped the bottom of the legal barrel and came up with some queries on the invoicing, doubts about deliveries and complaints on quality.

Smith Limited sued, and sought summary judgment under that famous, High Court procedure laid down by Order 14 of the Rules of the Supreme Court. The managing director swore an affidavit, saying that he knew of no genuine defence to the claim. He attached (or 'exhibited') to his affidavit a bundle of correspondence which included letters from Jones Limited, asking for indulgence for late payment.

Jones Limited 'filed' an affidavit in opposition, saying that they had a 'triable issue'—that there were disputes between the parties which were at least arguable, and that they should be given permission to take their case forward to trial. But their arguments were so tenuous and unlikely to succeed that the Court made 'leave to defend' conditional upon their paying into court the full amount of the contract debt. Jones Limited considered appealing to the Judge and from the Judge to the Court of Appeal but decided, on their lawyer's advice, that they would merely be throwing away some more legal costs. The evil hour for payment had arrived. Instead of paying the money into court, they did a deal with Smith Limited. In return for dropping their appeal and their allegations of delays and defects, they knocked 10 per cent off the bill and Messrs Smith agreed to accept the balance by reasonable instalments.

So Jones Limited had snatched a limited victory from the jaws of swift, legal defeat. Quite properly, they had used the law as a commercial lever.

Now for another imaginary (but entirely typical) case. Brown Limited owed £10,000 to Black Limited. Black Limited sued, and tried their luck under Order 14. They failed. Brown Limited were given unconditional leave to defend.

In due course, the case was tried by a High Court Judge, who decided in favour of the defendants, Brown Limited, on a point of law. The plaintiffs appealed.

Unanimously, the three Judges of the Court of Appeal decided that the trial Judge was in error. Messrs Black were entitled to their money. The appeal succeeded.

The winner of a law suit is normally awarded his costs. (In legal terms 'costs follow the event'). So Brown Limited had to pay not only the costs which resulted from the hearing in the Court of Appeal, where they had been unsuccessful, but also those of their successful battles before the Master and the trial Judge.

The Court of Appeal awarded the plaintiffs their costs 'here and below'. So in return for delaying the payment of their debt by a year or two, they were saddled with extremely heavy legal costs, even in respect of the skirmishes which they had won. And as the Court also awarded the winners interest on the debt, Brown Limited were heavily out of legal pocket. They would have been a great deal better off to have lost the initial, short, sharp pre-emptive strike under Order 14.

Note that the eventual losers had to pay all the costs of the original trial and of the Court of Appeal hearing, even though the appeal was really made necessary as a result of an error in law, made by the trial Judge. Judges make mistakes. You cannot avoid an order for costs on the basis that a man who tried your case (or some preliminary issue) should not have found in your favour. If you (or your lawyers) were guilty of unwarranted success, eventual failure may prove highly costly.

So apart from improving your bargaining position or delaying dread dates for payments due, if you are going to lose at law, the general rule is: The sooner you lose, the cheaper. The greatest misery is to win all the way up the line—and then to lose in the House of

Lords. And do remember that when it comes to appeals, it is the losers who are the choosers. If you win, then assuming that the loser has the right of appeal, he is entitled to exercise it.

Chapter 27

Sacking the Solicitors

Are you entitled to dispense with your solicitor? If so, then when and how should you do it? Suppose, for instance, that your solicitors, or those of the company, are taking an intolerable time to complete a conveyance. . . .

*   *   *

The first question is: Have your solicitors in fact done anything which warrants the sack? There are, of course, slack lawyers. But very often when there are delays in 'conveyancing' matters (as land transfer arrangements are called, in law) these are not the fault of the purchaser's lawyers at all.

For instance, you may have agreed on a date for completion. The seller may have promised to give you vacant possession by a specified day. But when the time comes, he finds that he cannot move into his new premises. Or, if you are buying from a builder, perhaps the job is just not finished.

If the solicitors are doing their job, they will press the other side to get on with it. But they cannot force them to do so. They can only do their best.

So go to your solicitors and discuss the whole matter with them and see if you can ascertain whether they have been inefficient. Ask to see the correspondence. Read your file—and check on the dates of the various letters. If there has been a break of a month or two without your solicitors chasing up the other side, then you can certainly give your man a rocket. But if, on the other hand, there are frequent letters from him and constant excuses from the vendor's solicitors, the fault will not be that of your solicitors. Then you should discuss with them the question of proceedings for specific performance.

If you do decide to get rid of your solicitors, then you are fully entitled to do so. You may take your custom elsewhere. Of course, the lawyers will be entitled to keep your documents until they get the money you owe them. So try to prevent them from 'exercising their lien'. Forewarned is forearmed. . . .

Chapter 28

Letters Before Action—and When Should You Sue?

Is it worth chasing the company's debtors to court? Or is it simply throwing good money after bad? Should I get a solicitor to chase up my accounts? Or am I better off to have another go myself? How far can the law help the businessman to get in his money—before his own cheques begin to bounce?

* * *

If your demands for payment are ignored . . . your invoices torn up . . . your statements added to the waste pile . . . then the sooner you put the case into the hands of your lawyer, the better. It is remarkable how many poor payers leap into action when they receive solicitors' 'letters before action'. They don't mind ignoring colleagues in the trade, but they don't like to tangle with the law.

"How much would it cost to have a lawyer write?" enquires the careful client.

Less than a pound. And worth every new penny.

"And if that doesn't work?"

Then every case must be considered on its own facts. First, can the debtor be easily found? If he can't and if you have to pay professional process servers to deliver your writ, then, if the amount involved isn't large, you'd best forget it. Then again, is he a man of straw? It's no use getting a judgment against a penniless defendant. You can't eat moral satisfaction.

"I thought that the courts could make judgment debtors pay by instalments. . . ."

So they can. You get an order for £1 a month . . . it's not complied with . . . you send a lawyer to question the debtor in court . . . the debtor gets the order reduced . . . and so on. It costs you more to chase your debt than it would have done to write it off. Of course, petitions, threats of liquidation proceedings, garnishee orders and such-like legal thumbscrews, often force the unwilling debtor to liquidate those hidden securities, and convince him that the rainy day has arrived. Or you might get an 'attachment order', so that instalments are deducted from his pay, at source.

"Suppose that you know where the debtor is and he has got money. What then?"

Then you must ask, has he a defence to your claim? Would he convince the Court that the goods were substandard or not up to sample, the work delivered too late, the machinery defective . . . ? After all, it's not much good prosecuting a claim that you're going to lose, is it?

"Not unless you can get a good settlement."

I agree. Well, anyway, there is not much to lose by issuing a writ or a summons. If the claim is under £750, you bring your action in the County Court. If it is for a higher amount, then the High Court is for you. In either case, you will probably find that the little piece of paper from the Court will shake your debtor into activity. The vast majority of cases that are started never reach trial—unhappily for the legal profession! Where a solicitor's letter fails, writs and summonses often succeed.

"How much will this little lot be costing?"

A few pounds, not more. And if this doesn't bring results, you can always quit, even at that stage.

"How much will a case cost if it does get to trial?"

£50—£100—£1,000 . . . impossible to tell. Everything depends upon its complication, how long it will last, how high-powered the counsel briefed on your behalf. But one thing I warn you: even if you win, you will not get *all* the legal costs back from the other side. The costs will be 'taxed' (that is, assessed) by an officer of the Court, and he will divide them, generally speaking, into three groups.

First, there will be 'party and party' costs, necessarily incurred for the doing of justice and usually paid by the losing litigant. Then come the 'solicitor and client' or 'common fund'—costs, properly incurred, but not absolutely essential and therefore not to be laid at the loser's door. Finally, there are those which the Court feels were really unnecessary and the lawyer can forget them altogether. They will be struck off his bill.

"And do 'solicitor and client' costs usually amount to much?"

Again, it all depends. So write your letters . . . consult your solicitor . . . get him to write . . . and even issue your writ or your summons. But before you sue, make quite sure that you really want to. Litigation is a luxury, and a very expensive one at that. It should be kept as a very last resort. Meanwhile, negotiate . . . and see Part Four.

Chapter 29

Making Use of Your Member of Parliament

Having a dispute with your local authority? Worried about noise or nuisance from your neighbours, disturbing your trade? Having planning problems or troubles with the Local Authority? What can you do?

First, you could consult your lawyer. This might prove expensive—and there are many cases in which the law can be of no help. So that leaves your Member of Parliament. What could he do to help you? When is it worth the businessman's while to write to his MP.

* * *

A Member of Parliament has very little actual power. He cannot, for instance, initiate or prosecute planning appeals for his constituents, develop property or make orders preventing such development—nor take any of the steps which are open to the Government, local or national. He is only a 'member' of the House of Commons—one of hundreds. And even if he happens to be a member of the Government party—or, even, a powerful Minister—in his capacity as a local MP, he has no executive authority.

On the other hand, because of his position, an MP is endowed (metaphorically, if not literally) with a very loud voice. He can make representations on behalf of his constituents to all sorts of authorities and individuals, and largely because of the adverse publicity which he can give to official bungling or private injustice, his actual power to assist his constituents is very considerable.

Suppose, for instance, that you are badly treated by your Local Authority. Maybe they are 'messing you around' over some proposed 'development' for which you need planning permission. Or they fail to keep up the roads or pavements outside your premises. Your complaints produce no results? Then splash the price of one stamp and write to your MP.

Or maybe a Government department is behaving unreasonably—or not at all. Write to your MP, and let him chase up the Civil Servants on your behalf.

In practice, what will your Member do if he gets your letter? Assuming that you have elected the right man and that he does his job, he will give you a prompt answer, telling you whether it is a matter upon which he is able to help. In most cases, letters from constituents are sent on to the appropriate local or government department or agency, with a covering note from the MP, requesting advice or action. When a reply is received, it will be sent to the constituent, again with a covering letter containing the Member's comments.

The very fact that an MP is on the trail will often needle the Authority into action. They will know (even if the constituent does not) that an MP's remedies are not limited to writing letters.

First, between 2.30 and 3.30 each day, Ministers answer Members' oral questions. 'Question Time' in the House of Commons is one of the best guarantees of a citizen's rights. Grievances and complaints of all sorts, private as well as public, are given an airing—and often find their way into the press. What is more, there is 'absolute privilege' for statements or observations made on the floor of the House.

If a Member thinks a subject sufficiently important, he can seek leave to raise it 'on the adjournment of the House'. You may find yourself with a special debate on your own problem.

Whether or not a Member of Parliament would be prepared to pursue your worries is another matter.

Disputes between neighbours are generally matters for the law, not for the legislators. But it is still worth buying a stamp, to see whether your Member can help you out of your dilemma. Maybe a prod from him will galvanise your Local Authority into action which it was otherwise unwilling to take. You never know your luck until you try it.

Of course, the service you get from your Member depends to some extent on his efficiency and interest.

If he does his job properly and knows what he is about, then he can often get quite splendid results, speedily and helpfully. If he is inefficient or disinterested, then you might as well have saved your stamp.

In practice, many MPs find businessmen among their most frequent correspondents. There are problems with Government departments, local authorities, manufacturers, wholesalers, importers, exporters, excise men . . . all of whom are hesitant to ignore an MP's letter. After all, would you like to have your name attacked in the House of Commons?

The MP's powers provide a vital stimulus to the freedom of the British individual. And that at least should be a source of satisfaction to businessmen and public alike.

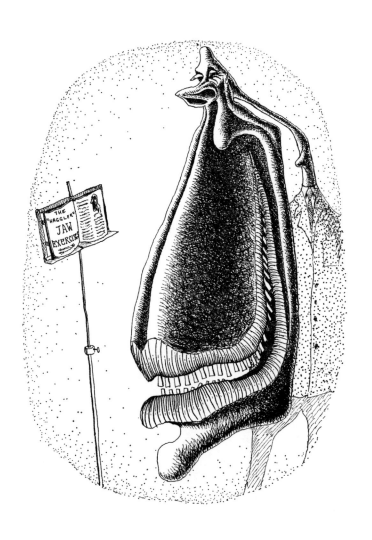

Part Four

The Arts of Negotiation

Introduction

Whether you are negotiating a sale or a settlement, the purchase of a business or a property . . . whether you are dealing with debtors or creditors, bankers or builders . . . whatever the commercial occasion . . . nothing so becomes a successful executive as the ability to negotiate.

To some extent, the arts of haggling are inborn. With a combination of flair and experience, the businessmen may work wonders. But whilst some are born negotiators, the majority of mankind has negotiation thrust upon it. So the conduct of a successful negotiation is well worth some thought.

Recognising that the negotiation—like each negotiator—will differ, there are nevertheless some sound rules, evolved by experience and hardened through use. Adapt them to your own purposes and you increase your prospects of success. So consider the arts of a negotiator, from a multitude of commercial angles.

Chapter 30

When it Pays to Negotiate

Lawyers spend a vast proportion of their working lives haggling on behalf of clients. This activity is commonly called 'negotiation', but it has its origin in the market place.

Litigation is extremely expensive, and if a case can be won through bargaining, then the victory is real as well as apparent. The lawyer who can keep his client out of court saves him time and anxiety, as well as cash. The only people guaranteed to emerge from a legal action, well in pocket, are the men of law themselves. And that is fair enough. That is how they make their living. But the 'costs' have to come from someone's pocket.

The two partners in a firm of builders fell out. Their lawyers failed to settle the case, which eventually reached the door of the court. There everything was agreed, with one sole exception—who was to pay the costs?

Eventually, one of the partners said to his lawyer: "You have failed. Why don't I have a chat with Joe? After all, we once got on well?"

Once a case is in the hands of lawyers, it is usually unwise for the lay clients to engage in their own haggling. But sometimes the process is worth while, with the lawyer's full knowledge and agreement. Why keep a dog and do your own barking? Because, on occasion, the sound coming from a new direction may produce the desired results.

Anyway, Joe was willing to negotiate and the two men went off into a corner to chat.

Ten minutes later, they were back, arm in arm.

"We've agreed on everything," said Joe.

"That's good," says the lawyer. "Have you agreed on costs?"

"Certainly—we are in complete agreement on that, too. He's not going to pay his lawyers and I'm not going to pay mine!"

That's what they thought. In fact, one of the main advantages of a settlement, even outside the door of a court, lies in the sad fact that even the winner seldom emerges from court with his winnings intact. He will normally obtain an Order for costs to be paid 'on a party and party basis'. This means that the loser will be ordered to pay all those costs regarded by the appropriate official (known as a 'taxing officer', in general) as having been necessarily expended for the doing of justice. There is generally a balance of costs properly incurred, but payable by the winner to his own solicitor. These are called 'solicitor and client' costs—and the heavier the case and the longer the trial, the more these will be (see also Chapter 28).

When your case reaches court, the bulk of the costs may have been incurred. Heaviest items? Generally, 'discovery' and 'preparation for trial'. 'Discovery' is the legal term for the inspection and copying of all relevant documents. The mightier the pile and the more abundant the file, the larger the charge will be.

Second, there is preparation for trial, instruction of counsel and counsel's initial 'brief fee'. This is the fee actually, physically marked on his brief and payable to him once his brief has been delivered. He will have to prepare the case and be ready to argue it, even if it does settle at the door of the court. He will obtain his brief fee, no matter what happens—but, of course, if the case is settled, he loses his 'refreshers'—that is, the fees payable for additional days in court. The longer the case is likely to last, the more the parties will save if they can settle it, even within sight of the judge.

In practice, even where cases do not settle before trial, vast numbers are never in fact decided by a judge. Within sight of the witness box, parties suddenly become remarkably reasonable. Anyway, they are brought face to face, albeit at opposite ends of a corridor. Aggression tends to disappear in the face of what is now obvious—the prospect of cross-examination—and possibly of days or weeks of boredom—and the knowledge that the expense will be great.

If the negotiations break down, then, of course, the judge must do his job. Then the thoroughness of your preparations for trial will become obvious. The best man does not always win.

Not long ago, a businessman had to leave court before judgment was delivered. When the case was over, his solicitor sent him a tele-gram: "Justice has been done," it read. The client immediately cabled back: "Appeal at once."

Judges do their best, in the exercise of their judgment. But they make mistakes. Even if you are satisfied that you are completely in the right, the Judge may not agree with you. Negotiate a settle-ment and at least it provides you with the certainty that you will avoid complete disaster. Whether you will look back on the nego-tiated result with eventual satisfaction depends upon your skill and that of your lawyer, in the light of the haggle.

Chapter 31

The Art of Negotiation

Lawyer and client should always consider together the financial strength of the opposition, combined with the legal costs at risk if the case reaches trial. Take, first, the legally aided opponent—and run for your life!

In order to obtain legal aid, a litigant must satisfy the Law Society that he has a reasonable prospect of success in the proceedings and that his income and capital come below the current maximum levels. A man who has a good case but no money with which to fight it will normally get free legal aid. If his case is good but his pocket only moderate, then he may well have to make a contribution towards his costs—usually payable by instalments, and recoverable if the costs are eventually paid by the other side. If he has too much money. then he will get no legal aid at all. And at present no middle-income executive can hope to get legal aid, free or otherwise.

In law, then, it is as well to be very rich or very poor. Those with no money pay nothing for the legal aid and advice they need. Those with stacks of money can afford to pay. Middle-income men are in trouble. They get no legal aid and they could be ruined by the costs of litigation.

One of the great delights of the legally aided litigant comes if he loses his case. The chances are that his contribution towards the winner's costs will be limited to the sum which he has to pay in return for getting his legal aid certificate—probably something under £150, payable by monthly instalments. Only in incredibly rare cases will a court decree that the legally assisted person must pay all the winner's costs—and then only when it can be shown that the winner would suffer grave hardship if he were left to bear his own costs.

I pause with relief, to note that legal aid is not available for the luxurious pursuit of defamation proceedings. I shed a tear at the sad fact that however hard up the limited liability company may be, it can never obtain the help of the welfare state in promoting its litigation—so yet again, the individual trader or the partner in a hard-up firm may be lucky. And I emphasise that if you are faced by a legally aided litigant, you cannot win.

Suppose that you are sued by a company and can satisfy a court that if the company loses its case, it would not be able to pay your costs. Then you may apply for 'security for costs'—for an order, that is, that the corporate plaintiff pay a reasonable sum into court to cover at least part of your costs, if you win. You may also get 'security' from many overseas litigants, without assets within the court's jurisdiction. But there is no security for costs available, when your opponent is legally aided.

Suppose, then, that you are owed money by a client or customer who succeeds in obtaining legal aid. Unless the sum is very large or you know that he has a house upon which you could 'levy equitable execution', or goods which could be clawed in by the bailiff, it is probably not worth your while to waste legal powder and shot upon him. Conversely, if you are sued by a legally assisted plaintiff, then unless he wishes to extract an extortionate price, you had better pay. If the costs that you will have to lay out even if you win would exceed the sum which you would have to spend on a compromise, then even if you consider that you are in no way liable, the chances are that good business would recommend even a bad settlement.

"Blackmail!" Extortion!" you exclaim. "I will fight him on principle!"

Lawyers eat off other people's principles. If you have enough money to spend on resisting extortion or blackmail, then well and good. Before you decide to do so, take out your pencil and pad and work out the figures with your lawyer.

In any event, you must rely upon your solicitor to give you some sort of idea of the likely costs involved in the proceedings. Unless he happens to be a prophet, he will be able to provide no more than an inspired estimate. Still, without some idea of the stakes, you cannot decide whether the particular legal is worth playing.

Then you must assess the strength of your opponent's case. Is he simply putting up a smoke screen? Is there any real likelihood that a court would accept his allegations? Is he a plaintiff who hopes that you will cave in the moment that a writ is issued—or would his lawyers be likely to advise him that his case is worth taking to trial? Is he a defendant, engaged in delaying tactics—perhaps because he has not got the money to pay?

If you are negotiating a business deal, then you will do your best to put yourself into the shoes of the other man. "What is he thinking?" you ask yourself. "What would I do in his position?" Apply exactly the same tactic to your legal problem.

Presume in your opponent's favour that he will take the best legal advice available. Do not underestimate the opposition. Then put the questions that I have posed, into the minds of your opponent's advisers. Your financial standing is satisfactory? Then that is one of their worries out of the way. The other man cannot get legal aid? Then could he afford to risk losing? Looking at the correspondence and at the documentary evidence—is it likely that his lawyers would advise him to do more than to fly a legal kite?

You may be able to assess the moral fibre of your opponent, from past experience. Is he a fighter? Is he a settler? How far will he call your bluff—or should you call his? You may have never seen him and have to judge him through the poker face of his letters. Reading between the lines of correspondence is a great deal more difficult than judging a man whom you can see across the table. So maybe you should invite him to lunch or to meet on neutral ground, so as to judge him the better.

Your lawyer will apply the same principles to his opponents. Before an important bout, the manager of a boxer will not only assess the known strength and tactics of the fighter in the other corner, but also the man's manager. What advice will he be given? The same consideration applies in the ring of the law. It may be that the solicitor will have been selected by the client for the particular battle—'horses for courses' is not a bad principle when it comes to litigation.

More likely, though, your opponent will use his lawyers for all his litigation, if not for the bulk of his affairs. With luck, your own solicitors will have a shrewd idea as to the strength of the legal opposition.

At this stage, you must decide whether negotiations are appropriate. Usually, they are. It is rare that a case is not worth settling (see Chapter 32). So the next question is: Should we wait for an approach from them or should we seek a peaceful solution?

No litigant can afford to show weakness, if he can possibly avoid it. Hence the letters that begin: "It must not be taken that this offer arises from anything other than a desire to deal with the situation amicably. . . . We are quite content to take this case to court or to arbitration, if necessary, but . . ." You may take it, though, that the man who makes an offer is not generally spoiling for a fight.

Often, the best opportunities for settlement come through the contact which the opposing lawyers are forced to have, for the sake of their clients. For instance, documents have to be inspected at a stage called 'discovery'. One lawyer will come to the office of the other and go through the documents which may be important, selecting those which should be placed before the judge. Characteristically, he will sigh to his opponent: "How sick I am of this wretched case."

"Yes, isn't it boring," says the other man. "What a pity we can't settle it."

Maybe they can. As we saw in Chapter 30, once the ball is set rolling, the chances are that it will come to rest somewhere between the hopes of each party. As a result, both will save the costs of trial.

Once you have instructed solicitors, you are generally better off to allow them to deal with the negotiation. They may on occasion ask you to go direct. If you remain on reasonably good terms with your opponent, then you may be able to break the deadlock. If you cannot stand the sight of the other man but the solicitors get on well together, then they should achieve a settlement.

Still, in some cases, the solicitors are as human as their clients and make the mistake of getting emotionally involved in the proceedings. Then the best results are usually achieved by the Counsel on each side haggling towards a compromise. One of the justifications for the separation of functions between solicitor and counsel is that barristers rarely get so deeply into the legal woods that they cannot see the individual trees.

So before you dodge the column and try to negotiate direct, discuss the proposition and the tactics with your solicitor. And never forget the vast number of compromises which collapse because the parties cannot decide who shall pay the costs. The nearer the case comes to court, the larger the 'costs item' looms in the negotiations.

Chapter 32

Make Me an Offer

A famous carpet buyer used to approach the pile in the showroom and throw back the corners, one by one. "Very nice . . . lovely . . . beautiful colours . . ." he would exclaim. Then he would come to the one he wanted. "How much do you want for that rubbish?" he would ask.

They laughed at him, of course. He was an eccentric. "Rubbish Robinson," they used to call him. Never mind. His business was to buy carpets as cheaply as possible. He knew that business, inside out. And his first rule was: "You make *me* the offer."

If the other side speak first, what can you lose? You know that they are prepared to negotiate. You have an idea of the price they may eventually accept. And whether your hand is strong or weak, you can judge your response because they have made the opening bid. The contract is yours, if you want it. In business, silence often presages a slam.

What if each side declines to make the first move? Then you get a situation like this.

Brown: "We are open to offers."

Jones: "You name your price and we will consider it."

"Sorry, but we're not anxious to sell at the moment. If a sufficiently attractive offer is made, I will consider it. But we're not prepared to make the running."

"Sorry."

Maybe nothing will happen at all. At worst, you might lose the deal. But the chances are that you could come back tomorrow. Anyway, if you speak first, you at once weaken your position by revealing that you are more anxious to do business than is your adversary. So he starts from a position of strength, which you have given to him.

If you find that you must make the offer, then give yourself as much leeway as you dare, consistent with not appearing ridiculous.

"All right. You insisted I name a price. How about £X00, then?"

"No. Out of the question."

"Well, I set the ball rolling. Now you tell me what you *would* take. . . ."

You are attacking. And attack is generally the finest form of defence. You have not come out into the open; so you retain your room for manœuvre.

Take a leaf out of the lawyer's book. He spends far more time than you might think, haggling in the corridors of legal power. He knows that if he can produce results for his clients, without all the worry, aggravation and potential cost of litigation, then he will have one success. In general, a sensible compromise is even better than a court victory. A good lawyer is an experienced negotiator.

Curious, isn't it, that no one has ever thought of teaching the arts of negotiation as a commercial subject? The professional military strategist will spend months of his life poring over the tactics of his successful predecessors. The master of moves on the chess board will memorise entire series of gambits, evolved by masters, past and present. Commercial negotiation is an art as intricate as military planning or chess manœuvre. So let us at least spare it some thought. And who better to teach us than the lawyer at his best—a man whose professional etiquette requires integrity, uprightness and honesty and whose clients demand accuracy. Triumph will often evade him. Never mind. "Ah, but man's reach should exceed his grasp, or what's a heaven for?"

The initial 'letter before action' is of vital importance.

Chapter 33

Brinkmanship at Law

No one—least of all a reader of this book—relishes a legal battle. Still, there are times when writs must be issued, because otherwise you simply have to say farewell to your money. Equally, there are occasions when unjustified and warranted legal actions have been started against you. You must then either defend or pay up. If you do not wish to give in, then you must at least file a defence. And attack often being the best means of defence, in law as well as in business, you may also decide to throw in a counter-claim for good measure.

So it is that many a businessman wends his way towards the Law Courts, with the same lack of enthusiasm a child displays on his way to school on examination day. The youngster may not know the contents of his papers, but he understands that examinations are inevitable. The businessman knows that if his case reaches trial, he cannot be certain of success. His lawyers may call the odds, but legal horses have a hair-raising propensity for collapsing at the final fence. So business litigants always ask themselves—and usually their lawyers—the same question: "Will the other side fight?"

So now let us consider the everyday, tactical rules on legal brinkmanship. How do you judge the other man's willingness to do battle? How far can you rely upon a claim or a defence collapsing? What are the chances of a settlement before trial? How can you improve the prospects of a satisfactory compromise—and what are the best tactics for negotiation?

*   *   *

"Don't worry," says the client to his solicitor. "They'll never go to court." Famous last words, these—regularly eaten as the other man marches into the witness box.

"He'll never dare risk his reputation by letting his inefficiency . . . their shoddy goods . . . the company's dishonesty . . . be paraded before the world, in a court of law. . . ." Contrary to all form and expectations, the opponent does just that.

So while the vast majority of legal actions do in fact bring results long before the day of trial, and while still more actually settle at the very door of the court, when you start a legal action or defend one, you must always reckon on the possibility of having to put your own words or actions or your lawyer's advice to the test of trial.

If you prepare your case from the start on that basis, then there are three beneficial results. First, you will not underestimate your opponent's courage or foolhardiness (as the case may be). So you will not be disappointed if the case does not collapse before trial. Second, if battle there must be, you will be fit and ready for it—and hence far more likely to win. Third, you actually increase the chances that trial will be averted by your opponent deciding to call your bluff, because he is actually welcome to do so. Deterrence has its place in law, quite as much as in business or politics.

Suppose, for instance, that you represent a powerful company, well able to sustain the costs of lengthy, expensive proceedings. Realising that there is a large sum at stake, you decide from the start that you will need to engage prominent leading Counsel (see Chapter 19) if the case gets to court. Then you are probably well advised to do so at once. If you are faced with an opponent of limited means, he will realise that if he loses his case, it may cost him his business, his home, his fortune. Then even if his solicitors advise him that his prospects of success are excellent, he may not wish to chance his hand.

Alternatively, you may be faced with an opponent of equal wealth and strength to yourself. In that case, he will see the prospects of a long-drawn-out, expensive battle, with highly paid QCs on each side, backed by 'junior Counsel' and solicitors—and may well see reason at an earlier date.

A negligent driver once knocked down a man who had a very thin skull. He died. His widow sued for damages. It was agreed on all sides that had the man's skull been of normal thickness and strength, he would still be alive. "I should not be penalised because I had the misfortune to strike a thin-headed man," argued the driver.

"You take your victim as you find him," answered the Judges of the Court of Appeal. So if you must be negligent and hurt someone, you should do your best to choose a victim with a thick skull, sound constitution and excellent recuperative powers.

A businessman knocked down an old lady and killed her. It cost his insurers only a few hundred pounds because the unfortunate deceased had no earnings, actual or potential, and a very low expectation of life.

Another driver was involved in an accident in which his passenger was killed. The driver was only partially responsible for the mishap, but could be made wholly liable for the damages—which were enormous. The deceased was a young company executive with excellent earnings, splendid prospects and a wife and three children.

You may have your 'victim' thrust upon you, and you 'take him as you find him'. But you should do your best to choose your legal enemies with care. You take them as you find them and you must judge each one as best you can. The answer to the questions: "Will he fight? Will he compromise?" will depend on the identity, strength, will-power, finances, personality and advisers of the opponent in question.

When legal battle is in prospect, then, you must do your best at the very start to sum up both your opponent and his case. You may need to obtain a status report on the man, the company or the business; to check up on references; or to make discreet enquiries as to the outcome of previous litigation. There are those who delight in court battles, or who at least believe that these provide the lesser of the various ills inevitable in commercial disputes. There are others who have never allowed a case to reach trial. If you can categorise your opponent, then you are well on your way to judging him.

Assume, then, that you decide to sue or to defend, as the case may be. You must then put yourself on to the attack, as swiftly, firmly and decisively as possible.

If you are the plaintiff, then it is essential to get your claim into proper order. The more accurate your 'Statement of Claim', the more likely it is that your claim is properly prepared—and that your opponents will know it. Conversely, if you have to amend, re-amend, then re-reamend, your opponents will realise that your case is in a mess, and will treat your prospects accordingly.

If you are on the defensive, then it is extremely important that you serve your defence—that is the document in which you set out your contentions—as quickly and fully as you can. The weaker your case, the more important it is that you get it on to paper and into the hands of the court as speedily as possible. The chances are that you will not only show your opponents that you mean business, but also head off a summons for 'summary judgment'. The 'plaintiffs' will only be entitled to a swift judgment without a trial if they can satisfy the court that there is no 'triable issue'—no arguable case against them which has any real substance. If you have served a defence which sets out an argument on fact or in law, you are well away (see also Chapter 26).

You should also counter-attack if you can. The larger and more apparently substantial your riposte to the Plaintiff's initial thrust, the more real the prospects of a settlement become.

In some cases, there is no defence. But you can find a counter-claim. So you ask that your 'counterclaim' against the plaintiff be 'set-off' against his claim against you. In commercial terms, you have a 'contra' claim—which comes to exactly the same result, in almost the identical words.

Take some typical examples. A manufacturer sues for the price of goods supplied. His customer admits first that the goods were supplied and second that the sums claimed were the prices agreed. But he contends that goods were defective . . . instalments delivered late . . . and that he suffered loss as a result.

What does the defendant then do? He puts in a 'Defence and Counterclaim'. He pleads express or implied terms that the goods will be 'of merchantable quality' and/or 'reasonably suitable for the purpose supplied'. He maintains that time of delivery was 'of the essence' of the contract. He then sets out the breaches of contract and while on the one hand he admits the sums claimed, on the other he seeks to 'set-off' the money which he has lost as a result of those breaches. Alternatively, he may be willing for the court to grant judgment on the claim, provided that there is a 'stay of execution' pending trial of the counterclaim.

Or consider the case of the professional man who sues for his fees. His client maintains that he is being overcharged . . . that the work has not been properly done . . . that as a result of negligent attention to that work, he (the client) has suffered loss. He will both defend and counterclaim, warding off the blow with one hand while lashing out with the other.

Naturally, the smaller the finances of the plaintiff, the better the prospects of the defendant, if only he can fend off 'summary judgment'. Provided that the plaintiff cannot get a swift order that the sum claimed be paid, delay immediately becomes one of the defendant's finest assets.

In some cases, delay may be on your side. Perhaps you owe money to your suppliers. Liquid capital is short. Your bank manager declines to oblige. If you are sued by your creditor, it becomes extremely important for you to postpone the evil hour of payment. So you employ delaying tactics.

First, you put in a defence and, if necessary, an affidavit in answer to any application for summary judgment. Then your solicitors drag their feet. They take each step in the proceedings at the last possible moment or even apply for extra time. One way or another, they fight to delay. The lawyers on the other side do their best to drive the case forward towards trial.

At each stage, negotiations are liable to take place. The question of delay and who can afford it is another of the elements involved in the haggles. Each side pretends, of course, that it is quite prepared to take the case to trial. It plays down the elements of time, as much as it sensibly can. It puts on a bold front, even if cold financial winds are blowing from the rear. The art of legal brinkmanship is well worth careful study.

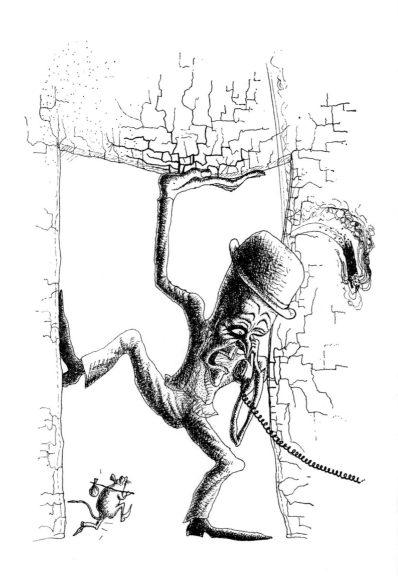

Part Five

Coping with Property—including Insurance
and Fires

Chapter 34

How to Pay the Minimum Rent

Is your lease approaching its end? Then the odds are that you will receive a letter from your landlords, inviting you to agree a rent which is at least double that which you are at present paying. To add insult to financial injury, the chances are that your landlords will assure you that the only reason why they are offering you such a moderate increase is because of their high regard for you as a sitting tenant.

Do not be fooled. This is merely the opening shot in a campaign which you can never win but which need not be as disastrous as the letter suggests. But to obtain any satisfaction, you must know the rights conferred upon you by the *Landlord and Tenant Act, 1954*, as amended by the *Law of Property Act, 1969*.

*　　*　　*

Rule 1: Unless and until you receive a written notice, in the form prescribed by law, you cannot be evicted. The notice must extend for at least six months, to end not before your current tenancy would normally expire. If your landlord forgets to send a notice, sit tight. The law will automatically extend your tenancy. And at the same rent as before.

If you want absolute certainty as to the terms of your extended letting, then you are entitled to serve your own notice on the landlord. But why bother? Let him sleep or haggle, just so long as he does not serve the prescribed notice on you. Negotiate . . . delay . . . haggle. . . . At this stage, time is still on your side.

The situation alters dramatically the moment a written notice to quit in the prescribed form is served upon you. Then action is imperative.

If the landlord wishes to oppose the grant of a new tenancy, he can only do so on specified grounds. In brief, he generally has to show that the tenant has been persistently late in paying his rent or has failed to comply with other terms of his letting—or that he (the land-lord) wishes to demolish or reconstruct the place. If he has held his interest for at least five years, then he may get possession in order to use the premises wholly or partly for the purposes of his own business or as his residence.

More on these terms, in Chapter 35. Meanwhile, remember that unless your landlord has some good reason for evicting you, you will be entitled as of right to a new tenancy.

If the landlord says that he would not agree to your staying on, then he must give his reasons. Do not panic. Many landlords bluff. Take the notice to a solicitor and let him investigate the position and ascertain whether the grounds are solid, stated in good faith and sufficiently well documented to stand up in Court. Once you know the strength of your landlord's case, you can decide whether or not to fight it. Meanwhile, I repeat: You have in any event six months from the date of the notice. And even where a landlord could obtain possession, he may be prepared not to do so, if you can negotiate what are from his point of view reasonable terms for a renewed letting.

Most notices state that the landlord would be willing to grant a new tenancy. Then the negotiations begin. Then, too, the tide of time turns against the tenant. If you receive such a notice, take it at once to a solicitor. You must serve the appropriate 'counter-notice' saying that you are unwilling to leave . . . you must then attempt to agree new terms . . . and if agreement is not reached, you have the right to apply to the court to fix such terms as are reasonable in the circumstances.

If you do not serve your counter-notice within the appropriate time and if you do not make any necessary application to the Court within the period prescribed, the Court will be unable to help you. It has no power to extend your time. You will have lost your rights.

Once your case is in the hands of solicitors, it is up to them to note the limits and to make the applications on your behalf, within the times limited by law. Occasionally, a solicitor fails or forgets to do so. If it can be shown that you missed the legal boat because your solicitor was negligent, then you may well recover damages for negligence against him. The basis of your claim? The difference between the rent which you have to pay in order to keep the premises and that which a Court would be likely to have decided was appropriate. There are, of course, problems in proving the amount of such damages—but if you decide to do your own negotiations, and if you cannot keep to the time limits, then you will certainly have no rights against anyone.

Equally, if your landlord knows that you have a lawyer on the trail, he is more likely to be reasonable than otherwise. He appreciates that you will be properly, professionally advised—and that if he is not reasonable, he may have to contend with court proceedings—which (he will know) are always uncertain in their outcome. You are putting up the odds in his gamble. And the chances are that your solicitor will earn his fee, many times over.

Anyway, when the first letter arrives from your landlord, do not panic. The future is not nearly as gloomy as the 'suggested future rental' might indicate.

Chapter 35

How the Court Fixes Rent

Under the *Landlord and Tenant Act, 1954*, a Court has the power to decide on the terms of a new letting. If the landlord of business premises is willing to grant a new lease—or unable successfully to oppose an extension of the current tenancy—then it is up to him to haggle with the tenant, to see whether they can agree on terms. If so, then the Court does not interfere. But if negotiations reach deadlock, the tenant may apply to the Court to decide on what terms would be appropriate.

The Judge must follow rules laid down by law—and if you wish to win your case (either outside the door of the Court or as a result of legal battle itself) then it is up to you to know the legal rules and at least to be prepared to present your case in the most favourable light.

*   *   *

Section 32(2) of the 1954 Act provides that where the Court has to fix the rent, this shall be that 'at which, having regard to the terms of the tenancy (other than those relating to rent), the holding might reasonably be expected to be let in the open market, by a willing lessor'. In other words, if the landlord were willingly to put the property on to the market, how much rent would it fetch?

93

As this Section points out, this will partly be determined by other terms. For instance, who is to pay the rates? And who is to keep the property in good repair?

In practice, the Court generally spends its time considering evidence of the prices fetched by similar properties, in the same area. The more comparable the property and the letting, the greater its evidential value.

Each party will produce experts. And the only real certainty about the evidence of one expert is that you will find another who will contradict it.

Generally, each side will find at least one local valuer and estate agent who will arm himself with a 'schedule of comparables'. This list will set out lettings in the district, as recent in date and as close in area as possible. The landlord's list will show the very high prices fetched by similar business properties. The tenant's list will indicate the modest extent to which properties of the particular kind in question have appreciated in the market.

The unfortunate Judge listens (generally with great patience) to the evidence of each side. He is not bound to find completely in favour of one party or the other—and in practice, he seldom does. Generally, he comes down somewhere in the middle.

The odds are, then, that the landlord will get less than he claims and the tenant have to pay more than he offers. But of this, there can be no guarantee. I have known cases where the landlord has got very near to his asking price—and others where the tenant's surveyor or estate agent has been accepted as the reliable, accurate witness, whose valuation is 100 per cent correct.

What matters, then, is to find yourself a surveyor who is notably reliable and highly regarded in your district. If you are the landlord, then ask him to tell you the maximum which he thinks that a Court would award—and ask your tenant for that sum. Conversely, if you are worried about an increase in rent, leave it to your valuer to assess the minimum which he thinks that a Court might reasonably take to be the 'open market letting value' of your property. Then offer that sum to your landlord.

Section 34 of the Act requires certain matters to be *ignored* in the Judge's assessment of rent. These include the following:

(a) Any effect on rent of the fact that the tenant has or his predecessors in title have been in occupation of the holding.

So the premises are to be looked at as if they were empty in the market. And no account is to be taken of the extra value of the holding to the 'sitting tenant'. Obviously, this is to the tenant's advantage. He is not to be charged more because of the miseries of moving.

(b) The Court must ignore 'any goodwill attached to the holding by reason of the carrying on thereat of the business of the tenant (whether by him or by a predecessor of his in that business)'.

So the Court must disregard the effect of the goodwill attached to the premises by the tenant or his predecessors in title. Once again, one up to the tenant/applicant.

(c) No account must be taken of 'any effect on rent of any improvement carried out by the tenant or a predecessor in title of his, otherwise than in pursuance of an obligation to his immediate landlords'.

So if you improve your business premises, you are not to be charged higher rent as a result. Exception? If you carried out the improvement because your lease or your tenancy agreement required you to do so. Voluntary acts of improvement are not to lead to penalties when the new rent comes to be fixed.

So much for rent. What of other terms? The new tenancy will be on such other terms as may be agreed between the parties—or, once more, if the parties cannot come to terms then the Court may decide between them.

How will such decision be taken? In the light of 'all relevant circumstances'.

Usually, the Court will be inclined to follow the terms of the current tenancy, other than those regarding duration and rent. But sometimes changes are made.

So how long will the new term be? In default of agreement, 'such tenancy as may be determined by the Court to be reasonable in all the circumstances'—but in any event not more than 14 years, commencing from the end of the current tenancy.

So the Court will look at all the circumstances, in the light of all the evidence which the parties see fit to put before it. You should prepare your evidence well in advance and bring it to the Court. If the other side sees that you are strong . . . if it admires your 'list of comparables' . . . if it sees that you mean business and are likely to win your case, then you may find yourself getting a very good settlement, right at the door of the Court. Impressing the Judge is only half the battle. Impressing the other side may be equally effective—and a good deal less expensive.

Chapter 36

How to Keep Possession

Like all good things, leases come to their end. And as most business-men occupy their premises as tenants, consider the owner's rights—and how to retain possession of your premises.

First, remember that residential occupiers are protected by the Rent Acts and business occupiers by the *Landlord and Tenant Act, 1954*, as amended by the *Law of Property Act, 1969*.

It is a criminal offence to evict the occupier of a dwelling, without an order of the court. Even a 'service occupier' (or 'mere licencee') is protected to that extent. If a landlord wants possession, then he must go to the court. If a residential tenant declines to leave when asked, his landlord may try to buy him off. But under no circum-stances must he use 'self help' and thrust him out into the street.

So if your employee lives 'above the shop', you must not throw him out—even if the 'dominant use' of the premises is as a business.

Business tenants have (in theory) no such rights. But (as we have seen) their tenancies continue at least until they have been served with written notice under the 1954 Act, in the prescribed form—and that notice has expired.

It follows that in order to obtain possession of business premises at the earliest possible date, the landlord must serve his notice, not more than twelve months nor less than six from the date when the tenancy would normally expire. If he can arrange for the notice to terminate on the date when the tenancy would otherwise come to an end, round one of the fight is his. Conversely, if he forgets to serve his notice, the tenant may stay on until six months after memory leaps to life—at the same rent as before.

Of course, if you happen to be the landlord, the best way to avoid forgetfulness is to instruct your solicitor, well in advance. Let him prepare and serve the notice on the appropriate date. If he fails or forgets to do so, the odds are that he is negligent—and you get damages from him.

What are the landlord's chances of obtaining possession? If the tenant has been persistently late in paying his rent; if he has not carried out proper repairs; if he has flouted the terms of his tenancy agreement—then the landlord may be fortunate.

Alternatively, has the landlord held his interest in the property for five years and could he show that he wishes to use the place wholly or partly for the purposes of his own business? Or does he wish to demolish or reconstruct the premises, and need physical possession in order to carry out the work?

These are the most likely grounds for getting possession—and if the landlord can prove any one of them, then the court will not be able to grant an extension of his term, to the tenant.

As always, in law, it is wise to prepare a potential case in advance. To judge your landlord's intentions, watch out for the following:

1 A landlord who is likely to rely upon breaches of the lease or tenancy agreement will usually complain to his tenant—in writing. Pass written complaints to your solicitor for his attention—and comply with the terms of your lease.

2 The landlord who intends to occupy premises himself makes clear, preliminary plans—both genuine and provably so. Has your landlord taken any steps in this direction?

3 The landlord who wishes to demolish or reconstruct will normally consult solicitors and architects regarding planning permission; set plans in motion to obtain all necessary consents; and (without, if possible, spending too much money) he will take sensible steps in order to prepare for the day of possession. If no one has come to look over your premises, to measure up or to make plans, the chances are that your landlord is not going to seek possession for this reason.

Now, if you do receive a notice in the prescribed form, pass it to your solicitor for his attention. Leave it to him to prepare and send a counter-notice.

If the notice says that the landlord will not oppose the grant of a new tenancy, the time for haggling has arrived.

It is a well-known dirty trick in the property world to keep negotiations going, in the hope that the tenant will forget to apply to the court and will lose his rights. If a landlord and tenant cannot agree on the terms of a new tenancy, then the court can decide between them. But if the tenant does not apply in due time, he will lose his rights.

There is no need to rush into a premature settlement. But it is vital to ensure that you apply to the court in due time. The law gives the judge no power to extend time, in this case. If you have left the matter to your solicitors and they forget to apply on your behalf, then they will be liable to pay damages to you.

Naturally, you will have to pay what is (roughly speaking) a fair market rental for your premises. To find out how much that is likely to be, you will probably need the help of a local estate agent or valuer. The odds are that your landlord will start the bidding high, and will be prepared to come down quite considerably, in order to obtain an agreement and to avoid the necessity of court battle.

As always, though, when it comes to bargaining you must judge the business prospects. The law's only interest is to step into the breach if the parties reach deadlock—and this (I repeat) it can only do if the tenant makes prompt application. If he fails to do so, then the landlord is home and dry and the tenant will have to pay whatever the market will bear, if he wishes to stay on.

It follows that if you wish to make use of the very considerable protection which the law has given to you, in your occupation of your premises, it is vital that you act promptly. And on this occasion, it is most unwise to go it alone, without the help of your lawyer.

Chapter 37

Service Occupiers—and Penalty Clauses

Just as a woman's beauty may be skin deep, so the mere fact that a building looks good from the outside will not of itself make it habitable, sound or long-lasting. As with buildings, so with the law.

Legal terminology bristles with pithy sayings and wise epigrams. One of the most famous? "The law looks at the reality and not at the form." To find out the truth of a transaction, the law considers not the form in which appears, but the reality of the situation. Just as a builder may disguise a crumbling, poor quality building with a magnificent, plaster façade, so the legal truth may be hidden behind false verbiage. Consider some important examples.

First, there is the so called 'service occupancy'. Suppose that you convert premises for the use of your staff. The intention? That the moment the employment ends, so will the right to occupy the premises. A document is prepared, intended to make employment and occupation 'coterminous'.

Unless the document is carefully drafted, it may in fact confer a tenancy instead of a service occupancy (or 'licence'). If, for instance, the agreement contains the words 'rent', 'landlord' or 'tenant'—or other terms which are only consistent with a 'tenancy', the occupier may find himself blessed with the protection of the Rent Acts. The owner may manage to get him out when his employment comes to an end, but only by showing that it is reasonable that he be granted possession, and that he has some other employee either on his books or waiting to join the business, who requires the accommodation concerned.

Now, had the appearances of the document been different, the employee would have had trouble in staying on. As he occupied a dwelling, he could not have been thrown out, if he were unwilling to depart. The employer would have to go to court and to claim an order for possession. But the judge would have no power to refuse one. No tenancy, no protection.

The appearance of these documents is vital. But the mere absence of words denoting a tenancy will not of itself mean that the employee is a 'mere occupier'. Looking at the reality, the court will (if necessary) consider whether the person concerned was 'required to occupy the premises for the better performance of his duties'.

Suppose that you wish to attract employees to your staff. Finding the accommodation an employee wants, you make it available for him—but in order to induce him to stay on the staff and so as to have the accommodation readily available for others, you grant him what you please to call a 'service occupancy'. He pays 'money for use and occupation', and no rent. You keep away from the word 'landlord'. But 'looking at the reality', the employee's occupation of the premises does not enable him to do a better job. After all, his home may be miles away from your office . . . he is not available at all times of the day and night, like a caretaker or like the family that lives above the shop.

If ever a court had to decide whether the employee had a tenancy, it would look at all the circumstances—the form of the transaction, agreement or document—and the reality of the relationship between the parties.

Or take 'penalty clauses'. Suppose that you agree to complete a job or a delivery by a specified date. Your contract may contain a term that you are to pay a certain amount for every week during which the job (or delivery) is delayed. If this is a 'genuine pre-estimate of damage', then you delay at your peril and the sum specified will be payable to the unfortunate client. But if it is a penalty, designed to punish rather than to compensate, then it is a dead letter.

A startling example? Suppose that a day for practical completion of a building is given and the contract says that the builder will be liable in the sum of £100,000 for every month during which the building work is incomplete, after the due date is passed. "The said sum of £100,000 is a genuine pre-estimate of damage, and not a penalty," said the contract.

If the law finds that it is in fact a penalty, the builder's clients will not get the money, even though they have seen fit to call it compensation. 'The law looks at the reality and not at the form.' The more fanciful the figure, the less likely it is that the form will satisfy the law.

The moral, then? Just as advocates try to tear down the façade of lies, put up by a perjured witness, so the law seeks the truth beneath the surface of words, thrown out by lawyers and their clients alike.

Chapter 38

Purchase and Sale

Whether you are buying or selling a factory, office, shop or ware-house—or, for that matter, a house or a flat—a little knowledge of basic law may save you a lot of money. Here, then, are some of the most important rules that every vendor and purchaser should know—for his own profit and protection and for that of the public.

Own the 'freehold' and you hold your property free from any interest other than that of the Crown or public. Subject to local by-laws and regulations and Town and Country Planning Rules, and provided that you do not cause a 'nuisance' to your neighbours or to the public, you may use the property as you see fit.

A 'leaseholder', on the other hand, holds his property thanks to a lease (or some other form of tenancy agreement). The nature of his holding will depend upon the terms of his tenancy. But Parliament has intervened to provide considerable security to business tenants (thanks to the *Landlord and Tenant Act, 1954,* and the *Law of Property Act, 1969*)—and to residential tenants of lower priced dwellings, by virtue of the Rent Acts.

Most contracts are just as valid and binding if made orally as they would be if every term were set out in writing. Even contracts of employment do not have to be made or confirmed in writing to be effective—the Contracts of Employment Act simply makes it (technically at least) an offence if you do not at least provide written particulars of the main terms of the contract, within thirteen weeks of its commencement.

Contracts for the transfer of an interest in land and contracts of guarantee are the two exceptions to the general rule. Unless sufficiently evidenced by writing, they may be unenforceable.

Anyway, important deals should be confirmed in writing, if only to make them easier to prove. And when it comes to dealing with land (or 'conveyancing', as it tends to be known), you should not only have the job done in writing, but let your solicitors get on with it.

Solicitors' costs in conveyancing matters are laid down on pre-scribed scales (but note that changes are in the legal offing). The amount will depend upon the value of the land . . . whether or not the property is 'registered' . . . whether mortgages are to be obtained. . . . Ask your solicitor to quote in advance. He should be able to tell you the likely cost with some precision. Naturally, if you purchase a freehold and then sell it and lease back the property, various transactions are involved and the legal costs will go up. But the more complicated the deal, the more vital it is that your interests are protected by having your own solicitors acting on your behalf—and not simply the solicitors for the other side. In general, my advice is: Do not agree to the same solicitors acting for both vendor and purchaser, landlord and tenant.

Here are some questions which the solicitor is trained to answer:

1 Are there any proposed road widening, slum clearance or other development schemes likely to affect the property within the foreseeable future?

2 Will the purchaser have all necessary rights of way—and how will he be affected by rights of others, over the property he wishes to occupy?

3 Has the seller a good title to the property?

There is still no law against selling a tumbledown house—or any other decrepit premises. In general, only if you are buying property in the course of construction are you entitled to a building which is habitable.

It follows that there is no substitute for a first-class surveyor. Where the law will not protect you, you must call in professionals to do so.

The law does not require vendor or purchaser to employ an estate agent. If you can find a purchaser and know the true value of your property, then if you sell you can save yourself a good deal of money by making the deal direct. And as a purchaser, you are not forced to pay your deposit to an agent—you are fully entitled to pay it to the seller direct (or, in practice, preferably to his solicitors).

However, estate agents (and business transfer specialists) perform a valuable function. They introduce purchasers to vendors. And they can often assess the value of a property far better than the vendor.

It follows that an estate agent should be entitled to his commission if—and only if—he introduces a person who eventually buys. Check the estate agent's documents to make certain that you will only be liable to pay, if and when a deal is done, through the agent's intervention.

Estate agents' charges are normally laid down on a scale. But there is no compulsion to adhere to any particular scale. To find out what a proposed agent intends to charge, ask him. If you sign a document agreeing to pay above the market rates, that is a matter for you.

Equally, estate agents are normally paid by vendors. If you, the purchaser, agree to pay an agent a retainer, for finding you the property you require—or for acting on your behalf in dealing with the vendor's agent—that is entirely a matter for you. Do so if you wish—but with your legal eyes well open.

Agents will usually request payment of 'the standard deposit of 10 per cent'. There is no such 'standard deposit'. Because every deposit should be paid 'subject to contract'—to ensure that it will be repaid, if and when the deal goes off prior to exchange of contracts —the initial deposit can be no more than an 'earnest of good faith'. Once received by the estate agent, it ceases to earn for the purchaser. He gets no interest on it. He should keep it to the minimum. Try paying an initial deposit of (say) £100—often this will suffice. By all means agree to pay 10 per cent on exchange of contracts, if you will. Meanwhile, do your best to keep your money for yourself.

Normally, a vendor is entitled to employ as many agents as he wishes. He will only have to pay the one who eventually introduces the purchaser. And if he finds a purchaser without an agent's help, he will avoid payment of any commission.

If, though, the vendor gives an agent 'sole agency', then he will have to pay commission to that agent, even if another agent eventually introduces the purchaser. The first agent will get his money, even though he has not achieved success.

There are cases in which it is reasonable to give a 'sole agency'. Perhaps the agent is prepared to spend a good deal of money on advertising the property. But a 'sole agency' should be given for a limited time and only in special circumstances.

If the vendor gives an agent 'sole selling rights', he is agreeing that the agent will have his commission on the sale of the property, even if the vendor (his principal) finds a purchaser.

Do not give 'sole selling rights' in any circumstances.

When employing estate agents—or doing any other act in relation to the transfer of property—there is one final and basic rule: Mind what you sign (see also Chapter 44). Provided that the document comes within the same class as that which you think you are signing, you cannot avoid the legal effects of your signature. So read before you sign. If in doubt, ask your solicitor to explain any document that concerns you. Take care of your own interests . . . employ skilled professionals to assist you . . . and there is still money to be made in the world of property. But there is no surer way to lose your fortune than to act in property matters without due care and skilled advice.

Chapter 39

Problems of Insurance

Before you can conduct negotiations with insurers, you should under-stand the basis of an insurance contract. Even if you decide to pass off the bulk of the burden of negotiation on to loss assessors (see Chapter 40), solicitors (Chapter 20) . . . or anyone else . . . they are working for you and you should ensure that they do their job properly.

You start with the policy. This is the contractual document. It sets out the deal made between the insurers and yourself (or your firm or your company). In consideration of your undertaking to pay the premium, set out in that policy, the insurers agree to provide you with the stated cover.

The terms of the contract are contained in the policy. If you want to know what you are to get for your money, read the policy. If you do not understand it, get it explained.

If you run into trouble over your insurance, then it is useless to ask for legal guidance without showing your policy to your lawyer. He can only advise you on your rights if he knows the terms of the contract—which, I repeat, are in the policy document.

The wise businessman shops around before choosing his supplies to make sure that he is obtaining the best value available. It is for him to get what he wants at a fair price. If he pays too much or buys goods which do not suit his purpose, then—assuming that he was not misled by any misrepresentation, and that the goods were not defective—he is out of luck.

Precisely the same principles apply when you purchase insurance. When you buy insurance cover, it is up to you to make the best bargain you can. The insurance world is highly competitive. The

103

range of policies and cover available is considerable. If you do not get what you bargained for, the fault will probably be your own.

You can ask individual insurers to quote for the cover you require. You may rely on one company, which you have learned to trust, to supply the insurance you need. Or you may put your affairs in the hands of an insurance broker.

At present, the services of a broker usually cost little or nothing. They generally get their commission from the company with which they place your business. It may be that the situation will change. Meanwhile, good brokers are worth their weight in gold—and their services normally come both free and freely to the insured.

Usually, before an insurance is made, the proposed assured will fill in a proposal form. It is absolutely essential that every fact contained in that form should be stated, fully, and accurately. Any concealment or misrepresentation of any material fact known to the proposed assured destroys the contract of insurance 'whether of life, fire, or sea or other risk'.

Examples:

1 If other insurers have declined the proposal, that is a highly material fact.
2 If previous claims are not mentioned, the insurers will be able to avoid payment, in the event of a claim.
3 Even if the assured is not specifically asked to reveal a fact, he will lose the benefit of the policy if he does not state any fact which would be likely to affect the mind of a prudent insurer, considering providing the cover concerned.

"Insurance is a contract of speculation," said Lord Mansfield in a famous judgment. "The special facts upon which the contingent chance is to be computed lie most commonly in the knowledge of the assured only: the underwriter trusts his representation, and proceeds upon confidence that he does not keep back any circumstance, in his knowledge, to mislead the underwriter into a belief that the circumstance does not exist. The keeping back of such circumstance is a fraud, and therefore the policy is void.

"Although the suppression should happen through mistake, without any fraudulent intention, yet still the underwriter is deceived and the policy is void. . . . The policy would be equally as void against the underwriter if he concealed . . . Good faith forbids either party, by concealing what he privately knows, to draw the other into a bargain from his ignorance of the fact, and his believing the contrary."

So (as another Judge put it) "insurance is a contract of the utmost good faith and it is of the greatest importance to commerce that the position should be observed".

Fail to observe the position . . . fail to reveal all relevant, material facts within your own knowledge, even if you are not asked to give them . . . conceal, mislead or (worse) defraud—and do not be surprised if the insurers refuse to pay, when you make a claim.

One fact that is far too often misstated is the value of the goods in the premises covered. 'Under insure' and you may get nothing. Insurers may pay out a proportion, but they may well be entitled to decline so to do. Check to make certain that your insurance is adequate.

Conversely, 'excessive over-valuation of the subject matter of an insurance for the purpose of a value policy is a material fact which if not disclosed will render the policy voidable'. Even if you over-value by mistake, and even if the over-valuation 'does not affect the actual risk', the insurers may be entitled to avoid payment (see also Chapter 43).

If you suffer loss, then make haste and inform your insurers. Policies often contain conditions requiring notice of loss and details of damage to be given within a stated time and making the policy void if steps are not taken as specified. This is not unreasonable—insurers must be given prompt opportunity to inspect the circumstances of the loss, for their own protection.

Fraud on insurers is far too common. Those who deliberately and dishonestly deceive insurers or who attempt to do so may be convicted under the *Theft Act, 1968*. Those who set light to their own buildings in order to obtain insurance monies are guilty of arson. Many who have been caught are now in prison.

Fraudulent exaggeration of a claim (as where a vehicle owner 'piles on the agony', adding previous damage to that caused in an accident) is not only criminal but fully entitles insurers to repudiate liability.

Where the assured had acted fraudulently in relation to insurance policies and failed to disclose this when applying for further policies, a Court has held that he had concealed a material circumstance. Once the assured has a bad name, he keeps it—and others are entitled to know. Good faith, a good name and complete honesty generally leads to prompt payment of claims and a satisfactory relationship with the insurers.

The converse applies. It is worth choosing reputable, well-established insurers, who pay promptly—even if their premiums are higher (which is far from inevitable). Often, the best insurers will meet claims even though they could, if they wished, avoid them on some technical ground—such as late notification or accidental non-disclosure. There are laws curbing 'fly by night' insurers. But there is still a good deal to choose between the companies—as well as between the policies they offer. And if in doubt, you can, of course, see what Lloyd's underwriters can do for you.

Choose well, then . . . make your choice with care . . . tell the truth, the whole truth and nothing but the truth to your insurers . . . and your insurance policies should enable you to sleep well at night. But ignore the legal snags and you will have paid your money for nothing.

Chapter 40

After the Fire is Over

What do you do if you are faced by a fire? Many a businessman has stood in dismay, watching helplessly as his business went up in flames, not knowing where to look for help. At this crucial moment, who will happen to arrive? A loss assessor, no doubt. So how do you deal with him—and with the dread after-effects of a flaming disaster?

*   *   *

In the old days, solicitors were reputed to keep fit by chasing ambulances. Nowadays, the tout is out. Dignified, the solicitor sits behind his desk and waits for the work to come in. Alternatively, he plays golf or bridge, hoping that his talents will be noticed. Not so the loss assessor. His job is to scent the first smell of smoke and to offer his services, as urgently as possible, to the businessman bereaved of his stock or premises.

There is nothing wrong in this. The man of commerce who is quick off the mark improves his prospects of making a living. And however much the professional may pretend to squint down his spectacles at the man who assesses losses, he may more than earn his percentage.

Loss assessors work on a percentage basis. Some charge 5 per cent, others as little as 1 per cent. Much depends upon the nature and size of the claim and the amount of work likely to be involved . . . and upon the strength of the assessor's desire for the job. The higher the flames and the claims, the lower the commission *should* be. But the amount of work involved should also be reflected in the commission charged.

X Limited keep poor stock records. They do a cash business and are either inefficient or dishonest in their book-keeping. When the fire is extinguished, they have a terrible time in piecing together the fragments of their trade and the remains of their records. A tough assessor may be their sole potential saviour.

Y Limited, on the other hand, keep excellent records—and these are preserved, either because they are in one of the fireproof safes in the basement or because they are at Head Office. Their entire premises and stock are destroyed by fire. They can prove their loss without difficulty. An independent loss assessor is not normally needed. Alternatively, he should charge a low rate of commission.

Z Limited are on the friendliest of terms with their insurers. The insurers appoint a chartered loss adjuster. He gently hints that he would prefer to deal directly with the company and without the intervention of some other assessor. He is a professional man, who considers that he has a duty both to the insurers and to the assured. Expressly or by implication he indicates that certain named assessors, who arrived on the scene before the fire had even taken proper hold, would feel very at home in a tropical, shark-infested ocean.

Z Limited's directors are in a dilemma. They are (happily) inexpert in dealing with fire claims. They cannot interpret their policies. They want someone on their side. "For every 1 per cent you pay us," say the assessors, seeking the company's custom, "we reckon to earn at least 2 per cent for you. We are experts in our business. . . . And anyway, we'll take the burdens of negotiation and preparation off your shoulders. Haven't you got enough to do, trying to get back into business . . . ?"

Wisely, the company calls in its solicitor and its accountant. The solicitor peruses the policy; the accountant assesses the ease (or otherwise) with which a detailed schedule of loss can be drawn up. They work out how much the assessors would be paid, on the basis of their claim succeeding in full. As a commercial proposition, is it worth paying that price?

Factors in favour of employing their own assessors:

1 Someone else will take the responsibility, and be available for advice and questioning.
2 That 'someone' will be an expert, skilled and experienced in dealing with fire claims.
3 The assessor should be able to ensure that his client's interests are fully protected . . . and all proper claims are made . . . and

107

that the insurers 'do not pull a fast one', costing the company money.

Factors against:

1 The assessor has to be paid—often, a good deal of money.
2 If the assessor falls out with the adjuster, appointed by the insurers, the prospects of a swift and satisfactory settlement are diminished.
3 The company's executives will, in any event, have to assist in preparing the accounts and schedules; and unless the employee of the assessors happens to know the particular trade, a good deal of time and effort may have to be spent in teaching the assessor the company's business.

In the Z Limited Boardroom, the discussion raged furiously. To appoint or not to appoint, that was the question. In the event, it was decided to 'go it alone', on the following basis:

1 The company's accountant would in any event have to do much of the preparatory work, connected with the claim.
2 The company's solicitor was perfectly capable of interpreting the difficult clauses—and in case of dispute, it would be much cheaper to spend a few pounds on obtaining Counsel's Opinion, rather than a few thousand pounds on assessors.
3 In so far as the claim was complicated, there was no point in appointing outside experts; the staff would have to ferret out the information in any event.
4 That in so far as the claim was uncomplicated, why pay strangers when no work was involved?
5 Above all, the relationship with the insurers concerned was a very happy one; the company was well known for its integrity and square dealing; the assessor was a man of experience, brightness and goodwill, in whom the directors could place great trust— and whom they did not feel was acting solely on behalf of the insurers—and he made it quite plain that even if assessors were appointed by the company, he would still wish the directors to be well in the picture.

On the other hand, before the decision was made, the following points were decided:

1 The directors were prepared to give such time as was necessary in order to salvage what they could from their past business— and they accepted that (assessor or no assessor) their time would in any event be involved.
2 The company's solicitor and accountant really knew their busi-

ness, so that even if they had no previous experience of fires, they could cope with the situation. And

3 They were dealing with a loss adjuster who was prepared to spend a good deal of time, going over details in the policy with them; advising them as to the steps which they should take, in the company's interests—and with whom they felt happier to deal direct.

They had already decided that if an assessor was to be appointed by them, it would be upon the following basis:

1 That they were assured (in writing) that their claim would be dealt with by a senior employee of the firm of assessors, who was prepared to spend time in their part of the country, in order to cope with the work. They were not prepared to accept 'just any old clerk'—their claim was a major one, so they were entitled to get if not the boss, then a very senior person.
2 They would negotiate terms—probably with several assessors, to see who would do the job at the most reasonable rate.
3 They would ask for recommendations from other firms in the trade, upon whom they could rely. They recognised that the better the name of the assessor, the better the results he would be likely to get.
4 All arrangements with the assessors would be confirmed most carefully in writing—the letter of appointment being checked beforehand by the company solicitor.

*　　*　　*

If you are faced with the horror of a fire, then it is vital that you choose your salvage team with care and perspicacity. You should assess the situation with patience, before you appoint any particular assessor—or any assessor at all—to act for you. Fire creates panic. The less you are insured, the greater your panic is likely to be. However fully you are covered for losses of stock, the chances are that you will not have enough cover to provide you with an indemnity against loss of profits, during the period when your business remains closed . . . or operating at half-steam . . . or being carried on in temporary premises. Never mind. While you retain your health and sanity, you can rebuild. The spur of the panic-stricken moment is not the time to decide on the manner in which your claim is to be presented nor the people who should make the presentation. To-morrow is also a day.

Finally, do take advice. You have a solicitor . . . an accountant . . . an insurance broker . . . a brother who suffered a fire loss some years ago . . . an uncle who is an architect? Then let your advisers (voluntary or professional) rally round. Now is the time when your good deeds will come home to roost. Kindnesses will flow in as fast as the hose-water squelches out of your sodden premises. Be not ashamed to accept the goodwill offerings of those whom you trust. Above all, seek the best advice . . . consider it . . . and then make your decisions and stick to them.

* * *

Just in case this book is consumed in *your* fire, here are some suggested rules on self-conduct, if you are afflicted by fire—to be read now:

1 Do not despair. You have your life and your health? Then you will rebuild your business—like many thousands before you. You wish you had increased your insurance cover? Too late now. This set-back may yet provide you with the means to leap forward. What matters now is to preserve your 'cool' despite the heat.

2 Do not panic. Gather your senior staff around you and then take stock—literally and metaphorically. Until you have analysed your losses, you cannot decide how your profits may be rebuilt.

3 Call in your trusted advisers—professional and commercial, voluntary as well as employed. Take your problems; explain them; 'kick them around'—and by sharing them, they will cease to appear insoluble.

4 Inform your insurers, forthwith. They will doubtless appoint their own 'loss adjuster' or 'assessor'. Deal with him frankly and openly. Discuss your problems; take his counsel; benefit from his experience and knowledge—and do not start off by regarding him as an enemy. If you have behaved with honesty, and if your insurers are (as one would expect) solid and reputable people, it will be their appointed assessor's duty to see that you get a fair deal. Note: He is *not* the

servant of the insurers, appointed to ensure that they pay as little as possible.

5 Having considered the various angles discussed in this chapter, decide on whether or not to appoint your own independent loss assessor. Choose your man with care; negotiate your terms; remember that moths and assessors alike are attracted by flames and smoke. Do not necessarily choose the first people to arrive. You have something substantial to sell, even if this is only the product of your own mishap. So let the buyers gather round . . . keep them at arms' length, if you will . . . find who will do the best and quickest job . . . then make your appointment.

6 Naturally, the firemen, perhaps helped by your staff, will have saved what they could from the wreckage. But now leave everything alone. For instance, it may be extremely unwise to remove goods, dummies or anything else from the shop window, the office floor or the building roof.

Maybe your neighbours are uninsured? Did they suffer loss as a result of the fire which started from your premises? Then they may wish to prove that it started due to your negligence. If you tamper with the evidence, you may destroy the means by which your own experts could show that the fire (on the balance of probabilities) started spontaneously or at any event without any lack of due care on your part.

The police and fire authorities have first call on the forensic experts. But if there are any doubts, you may be sure that the insurers will call in the experts. If they do, be not offended. They may, of course, be looking for evidence of arson—unfortunately, there are still commercial crooks whose ambitions are fired by the prospects of dishonest profits, paid for by their insurance premiums. But these gentlemen are rare. And the forensic men are generally sent in by insurers in the hope that liability to third parties under public liability clauses may later be avoided.

7 Assuming that you are covered (even for a short period) against loss of profits, it will be to the insurers' advantage that you should suffer as little as possible. They will want you to get back into business, within the shortest conceivable time. You will need to preserve your good name and your goodwill and to ensure that when the period of cover is passed, you will be back in the money.

So as it suits both of you to 'mitigate the loss', you may (once again) expect to work with the insurers, as a team. You may therefore expect them to authorise reasonable expenditure, designed to reopen your business. This will include renting and preparation of new premises, the buying in of stock, supplies or equipment and the increase of layout on advertising. But before you spend, ask your insurers' advice. If you are spending £1,000 in order to earn £1,500, approval will be forthcoming. Conversely, to spend £1,000 to earn £500 would be a business stupidity—not to be perpetrated at the insurers' expense.

8 Get out your policies and read them. If in doubt as to their meaning, have them explained by your solicitor and/or insurance broker and/or by the company's loss adjuster. If the document has gone up in smoke, then ask your insurers for a copy. Without the policy, the extent (or lack) or your cover cannot be known. Without an understanding of the precise meaning of its terms, you cannot plan your next step with sufficient understanding.

9 When drawing up schedules of loss, rely on your experts. Remember, for instance, that smoke often causes a great deal more damage than fire or flame. And the smell of smoke is insidious. Garments, for instance, may have no smell at all when hanging on the rack or in the wardrobe. The moment the wearer puts them on and hence heats them up, the smell appears. Even furniture or fittings may (literally) stink of smoke. But modern methods can kill the most pungent smells. Once again, call in the experts. If you need to destroy the smell of smoke in order to preserve your business, then your insurers may well pay the cost of the smell-killers.

10 Watch out for the public relations angles. Example? Fire destroyed a famous furniture shop. But its warehouse was two miles away. Customers who then received goods asked (quite reasonably) for an assurance that those goods were not fire-damaged. When the company set up in business in new premises, the public needed reassurance that the goods sold were not salvaged stock.

The answer, then? Call in the local press—and ask for their help. The more friendly and helpful you were to them in good times, the more likely they are to assist you, now that you need them. Particularly if you happened to be an advertiser in their columns, they will wish to oblige. So provide them with a story, to be included amongst the editorial content. When it appears, put it in your window . . . 'blow it up' in size . . . and let the world know the happy headline: 'Jones Limited Back in Business. . . .' "Stock saved, thanks to new warehouse," says managing director. . . . Feed the headlines to your friends on the press. With any luck, they will help you.

11 Offers of help will come flooding in. Grasp them, wherever required. Now is no time for being bashful. Whether you are offered the loan of office equipment . . . extra credit from your suppliers . . . or good advice from trusted friends—help yourself. Others will get pleasure from helping you—just as you would have helped them, had the misfortune been theirs.

12 Consult your bank manager. However tight the credit squeeze, banks do use their resources to rescue the businesses of their trusted customers, in times of disaster. Treat your bank manager as a friend in need, and with any luck he will act like one.

13 Before you borrow, discuss payments on account with the representatives of your insurers. They will know that even if the bank manager will oblige, interest charges are heavy. If you have the right relationship with your insurers, you may reasonably hope for substantial payments on account. It may take years before you can estimate accurately your loss of profits? But you can assess your stock losses within weeks? Then you may reasonably hope that your insurers will pay you an advance today, on the losses which you can now prove—if only to keep down their payments for your loss of profits tomorrow . . . and tomorrow . . . and tomorrow. . . .

Chapter 41

The Cost of Free Advice

A Mr Evatt was a policy holder in the Mutual Life & Citizens Assurance Company Limited. He asked it for information and advice concerning the financial stability of another company, which was itself a subsidiary. He alleged that 'by virtue of that association the company had better facilities than himself for obtaining full and up-to-date information'.

The company, we are told, employed officers who were 'capable of forming a reliable judgment of financial information obtained'. In reply to his request for information, the company advised him that the other company 'was and would continue to be financially stable and it was safe to invest therein'.

Mr Evatt alleged that as a result of the information and advice given, he had invested in the other company and suffered financial

113

loss. He maintained that the advice was supplied negligently. The company denied negligence and in any event maintained that in the circumstances, they should not be held liable in law. The question to be decided by the Privy Council was whether—assuming that Mr Evatt could prove the facts alleged—these were 'in themselves sufficient to give rise to the duty owed by a company to Mr Evatt to take care in giving him the information and advice which he sought'.

Now, in the famous case of *Hedley Byrne & Company* v. *Heller & Partners Limited*, the House of Lords decided, in effect, that where someone gives advice or information in the knowledge that this would be acted upon, he is under a duty to the recipient. He 'owes a duty of care'. If the advice is both negligently given and incorrect and the recipient can prove that he had suffered loss as a result then (in the absence of a suitable disclaimer) the adviser will be liable in damages. And this applies whether or not he was paid.

In Hedley Byrne's case, the merchant bankers who had given the wrong information had added a disclaimer, saying that they accepted no legal responsibility for the accuracy of the information. The House of Lords unanimously decided that this freed them from responsibility.

But in Mr Evatt's case, there was no disclaimer. But by a majority of three to two, the Privy Council decided in favour of the insurance company.

First, all five Law Lords agreed that the giver of the information had no duty (beyond the duty to give an honest answer) when advice was given casually. For that, all businessmen should be grateful. If you deliberately advise a man to take poison, then you must take the legal consequences. Otherwise the casual nature of your kindly answer will free you from legal responsibility.

The majority of the Privy Council also held that unless the adviser 'carried on the business or profession of giving advice, he could not be reasonably expected to know whether any or one degree of skill was called for, and he could not be reasonably held to have accepted the responsibility of conforming to a standard of skill of which he was unaware, simply because he answered the enquiry with knowledge that the advisee intended to rely on his answer'. Only if you 'carry on the business or profession of giving advice of the kind sought' may you be held responsible for negligence in the giving of that advice.

So take care—and provide a disclaimer with any reference—e.g. 'No legal responsibility can be accepted in respect of this reference, howsoever arising,' or: 'This reference is given on the strict understanding that no legal responsibility is accepted therefore by the company, its servants or agents.' Also, say to your customer, where possible: "In our view, this product will be excellent. But you will appreciate that we cannot accept legal responsibility." A counsel of perfection? Perhaps. So ignore it if you must. But then at least ensure that you are properly insured against risks of this kind. The fact that Mr Evatt lost his case will not mean that you are bound to win yours.

Part Six

Coping with Contracts, Creditors and Companies

In Contracts it's the Last Word that Counts— or: How to Cope with 'Standard Terms'

No doubt your company's terms and conditions are carefully drafted by its lawyers, for its own protection. But when the executive buys or sells goods or services on the company's behalf, it is up to him to make sure that he has the last word, or—in time of contractual strife —those terms may not be worth the paper upon which they are so neatly printed. To understand this legal truth, you must appreciate the essentials of a binding contract.

To be effective, an agreement must result from an unconditional offer, unconditionally accepted. An offer is conditional if it is made (for instance) 'subject to the consent of the Board'. Until that consent is both obtained and communicated, the offer may be withdrawn.

Equally, an offer must itself be distinguished from a 'mere invitation to treat'—such as goods on display at a trade exhibition or in a shop window. They are not 'offered for sale'. Customers are invited to make offers to purchase.

Now suppose that you order goods. The odds are that you are unconditionally offering to buy them, upon your terms as to delivery and otherwise. If you receive an unconditional acceptance—oral or written—the deal is done. But what if you get back a so-called acceptance, which reads something like this:

'We are pleased to accept your order numbered —. For the Company's terms of trading, see back hereof.'

Inevitably and invariably, the supplier's terms will differ from your own. In law, then, they are not unconditionally accepting your offer but making a 'counter-offer' of their own. They are saying, in effect: "We offer to accept your order, but upon our own terms and conditions. In so far as those terms differ from your own, ours— which came later—will prevail."

The executive who does not know his law will probably arrange for the 'acceptance' to be filed, and he will await the supply of the goods or services. These will then be accepted—and by their acceptance, the Company will be accepting unconditionally the supplier's counter-offer. In the process, the Company's original terms and conditions will have disappeared. They will form no part of the deal.

If, then, the supplier has agreed to deliver upon a specified date but 'no responsibility is accepted for delay, howsoever caused', you will have no legal remedy if a delay occurs—no matter how firmly your own order will have stated that a time of delivery was essential to the deal.

Or maybe the supplier's terms say: 'No complaints or returns accepted unless made within — weeks of delivery.' If you wish to make some complaint thereafter—perhaps because you had no prior opportunity of examining the goods or inspecting the results of the services—that will be your own downfall. You should have taken more care in the making of your contract.

How, then, can you avoid this sort of misery? Quite simply, by ensuring that your terms and conditions arrive last. Thus:

'We have noted your terms and conditions of trading set out in your letter of the —. We regret that we cannot place orders other than upon the terms set out in our original order. Please indicate that our terms are acceptable to you.' Or:

'Your condition No. 7 concerning delivery is not acceptable to us. Unless you can ensure and guarantee delivery by the date specified in our order, we shall not be prepared to accept the offer set out in your letter.'

The wording is not important. What matters is to get yours in last. He who writes last contracts best. Conversely, he who allows the other side to get in the final terms, will find himself bound by them.

Naturally, these rules apply equally where you are the supplier. By all means attempt to secure your position by the imposition of terms prepared to protect you. But if your customer decides to cry off before the goods have been delivered by you and accepted by him, the chances are that you will have no legal answer. Yours was a mere counter-offer? Then until it becomes accepted either through some express words or through acceptance of the goods—but either event unconditionally—there is no agreement. You did not unconditionally accept your customer's conditions of trading but instead attempted to substitute your own. Unless and until he unconditionally accepts those, the contract is not binding upon either of you.

Naturally, just as your customer may, in those circumstances, take his order elsewhere, so you may feel free to cancel if you wish. You have provided a loophole available for either side. The one certainty about contracts is that (with rare exceptions) they are binding on both sides or neither.

Chapter 43

Beware of the Small Type

Beware of 'usual terms', 'standard conditions' and our 'normal terms of trading'. There is no such thing. You should bargain your way into the right position—otherwise you may find yourself at a great legal disadvantage, if things go wrong.

Take a contract of hire, for instance. Not long ago, an accountant wanted a complete installation of office communication equipment. He signed on the dotted line, undertaking obligations for fourteen years. Before the equipment was even delivered, he changed his mind and cancelled the deal.

"We shall be pleased to accept the return of the equipment," said his suppliers, "upon the terms specified in the agreement." They demanded the rent for the full period of hire, less the presumed cost of maintaining it over that period.

The accountant refused to pay, and his case eventually reached the Court of Appeal. He lost. The judges held that the owners of the equipment were fully entitled to claim as a genuine pre-estimate of damage such money as would be necessary to put them into the same financial position as they would have been in, had the hirer honoured his obligations. The contract was upheld.

With that unhappy case in mind, I once carried out a small experiment. Having been informed by various firms, renting out equipment, that their deals were made upon their 'usual terms' regarding period of rental, I set about beating them down. I found to my delight that all were prepared to be reasonable, in return for the business they wanted. Sometimes it was necessary to agree to pay a slightly increased rental in order to have a substantially decreased period of hire. But I discovered that it was possible to have that period reduced to as little as twelve months.

Each company that wanted my custom offered different terms— but each was prepared to allow these terms to be varied. Their basic, printed conditions were regarded by most of their customers as immoveable. But once you realised that these conditions were the beginning and not the end, of negotiations, you were well away.

Now, in order to make your living, you will obviously realise that these rules apply to your own particular business contracts. But, in practice, it is remarkable how few businessmen apply the identical principles to the deals they make with their suppliers. There are the 'standard' terms on the front of the contractual document which are swiftly seen and readily accepted—too readily. There are also the printed conditions on the back, which are equally important and seldom read.

Even if you do not know of the existence of these terms—or if you do not understand their factual or legal importance—the odds are that you will still be bound by them, once the deal is done. There is, of course, a good deal to be said for energetic negotiation to solve disputes. But it is far more sensible to avoid those disputes through clear appreciation of contractual rights and obligations, before the bargain is struck. As we shall now see.

Chapter 44

The Effect of a Signature

Every businessman signs order forms. But what is the effect of a signature? Suppose, for instance, that you are under some false impression about the goods or supplies you order. When they arrive, they are not what you had in mind. Are you entitled to return them?

Or suppose that you do not notice the terms and conditions on the back of the form. Maybe you did not read them or, if you did they were incomprehensible because of their legal jargon. Do they affect your contract?

In general, unless there is a genuine agreement between the parties, there can be no binding contract. But what is the effect of a signature? That was the question considered by the House of Lords in an extremely important recent case.

*   *   *

In the case of *Saunders (formerly Gallie)* v. *Anglia Building Society*, the House of Lords gave a grim warning to businessmen of the danger of signing documents without knowing their contents. Even if that signature was procured by fraud, you may still remain bound by it unless you can show that the document is of an 'entirely', 'totally' and 'fundamentally' different class from that which you had intended to sign.

Mrs Gallie intended to make a deed of gift of her house. One day, when her glasses were broken and she could not read the document, a fraudulent third party induced her to sign a mortgage deed, in the mistaken belief that this was in fact a deed of gift. When she found out the truth, Mrs Gallie attempted to have the document set aside. Eventually, the case reached the highest tribunal in the land.

First, the Court re-affirmed the old rule that you cannot rely on your own negligence, if you want to have a deal set aside on the ground of mistake. If you are careless and decide not to read or understand a document you are signing, then that will be your misfortune. It is certainly not a misery which should be passed on to innocent third parties (such as the Anglia Building Society, in Mrs Gallie's case). It follows that you will be bound by terms and conditions contained in a contractual document, provided that these are sufficiently brought to your attention. And if there is a note on the front referring you to conditions on the back, this will normally suffice.

If you have signed a document, it will normally contain contractual terms. Sometimes suppliers attempt to slip in new terms in delivery notes, receipts, invoices or the like. These are 'post contractual documents' and rarely affect the terms of the agreement. But when you sign any order form—beware.

What, then, of fraud? Mrs Gallie, it appears, was not negligent. But she was induced to enter into the arrangement by a false statement made to her concerning the nature of the deed she was executing.

The general rule is that 'a party of full age and understanding is normally bound by his signature to a document, whether he reads or understands it or not'. So as Mrs Gallie was 'of full age' and of eminently 'sound mind', her lack of physical or mental disability created a legal obligation upon her.

"Suppose that the very busy managing director of a large company has a pile of documents to be signed in a few minutes before his next meeting," said Lord Pearson. "His secretary has arranged them for maximum speed with only the spaces for signature exposed and he only 'signs them blind'. He might be exercising a wise economy of his time and energy. But if some extraneous document involving him in unexpected personal liability has been fraudulently inserted in the pile, the person who signs documents in that way should be held bound by them and not entitled to shift the burden of loss on to an innocent third party."

So even if you are induced to sign as a result of fraud, your signature will generally bind you.

The exception? There are cases where you can plead 'non est factum'—that your agreement was not a fact. "The plea ought to be available in a proper case for the relief of a person who for permanent or temporary reasons 'not limited to blindness or illiteracy' is not capable of both reading and sufficiently understanding the document to be signed—at least to the point of detecting a fundamental difference between the actual document and the document as the signer has believed it to be."

Provided that the signer is not negligent and that 'the actual document is . . . fundamentally different from that the signer believed it to be', this plea may succeed.

So it is a 'fundamental difference' that matters. Other Law Lords refer to 'radical' or 'total' difference. But if the document is of a similar class to that which you think you are signing, you are in trouble.

In Mrs Gallie's case, she knew that she was disposing of her property. That was enough to make the disposition effective, even though its nature was quite different from that which she had intended. She lost her case.

It follows that you cannot reject goods and supplies merely because they are different from those which you had in mind. You signed an agreement to acquire goods? Then you will not be able to avoid your legal responsibilities by showing that the goods were not as intended.

So what should you do? See your solicitor. Maybe you were induced to buy some by false statement of fact, so that you could rely upon the *Misrepresentation Act, 1967*? Perhaps you could induce the supplier to exchange the goods for more expensive ones, which are to your taste and satisfaction? So you will have to do your best to negotiate your way out of your present troubles. In future, please mind what you sign!

Chapter 45

The Dangers of 'Holding Out'

If your employee places an order without your consent, the chances are that you will be bound to honour it, like it or not. If you have 'held out' your employee as having your authority to make the contract on your behalf, then you have 'clothed him with your apparent authority'. In so far as third parties are concerned, 'apparent' or 'ostensible' authority is quite as good as 'actual authority', when it comes to pinning liability on to the boss.

Suppose that a company secretary orders you to prepare accounts or an audit. After you have put in a good deal of work, the Chairman discovers that the job has been given to you, although he would have preferred some other firm. If he wishes to dispense with your services, he must pay you for the work you have done, and, quite possibly, damages to compensate you for the profits you will lose as a result of the company's breach of contract. Even if the Secretary was not actually authorised to make the arrangement with you, he had the company's 'ostensible authority' to give you your instructions. And in law, that is quite sufficient.

Clearly, a company can only make contracts through its 'servants or agents'—its officers, employees and other human beings, entitled to act on its behalf. A company as such has no human identity. Equally, those who deal with companies will be entitled to rely upon the authority of those placed in apparent positions of trust.

As with companies, so with firms and with individuals. You must be careful to limit the apparent, as well as the real, authority of those who act on your behalf, or you will be bound by their deals.

Suppose, for instance, that you send your assistant to look over some new computer, at a trade exhibition. In an excess of zeal—and probably encouraged by the assurance that unless he acts at once, he will lose his chance to get to the head of the queue for the chosen model—he places a firm order. You will be bound by it. After all, you have placed him in a position in which the supplier is entitled to presume that he was empowered to make the particular transaction on your behalf.

Naturally, this 'doctrine of holding out' places considerable power in the hands of apparently authorised agents and employees. If they exceed their actual authority, they may have given their employers the right to dismiss them. But the only way to protect yourself against unwanted contracts, entered into by your agents in excess of their authority, is to put the contracting parties on notice. "We are pleased to introduce our Office Manager, Mr X. Kindly show him your latest lines. We would remind you that this firm will only be bound by orders signed by one of the partners. . . ."

Once the suppliers know the limits placed by you on the authority of your agents, you have destroyed any appearance of excess authority and have successfully protected your position. Conversely, if you fail to put the suppliers on notice, you must rely upon the good sense, intelligence, accuracy, obedience—and honesty—of those whom you employ. Good luck!

Incidentally, a candidate in a Bar examination is reputed recently to have defined 'holding out' as 'a form of indecent exposure'. From the contractual point of view, he was probably right.

*   *   *

Chapter 46

The Perils of Buying and Selling

Every businessman is both a buyer of goods and a seller of services. As a buyer, the law does its best to protect him against fraud, misrepresentation and false trade descriptions. As a seller, he must mind what he says.

*   *   *

The seller who tells lies may run into trouble from two directions—the civil law and the criminal law. The former gets its strength from the *Misrepresentation Act, 1967*—and gives a remedy to a buyer deceived. The latter is mainly the product of the *Trade Descriptions Act, 1968*.

The seller is not bound to tell the whole truth, and provided that he sticks to opinions, he has few problems. But the moment that he strays into the realm of fact, he must watch his words.

Every seller is expected to engage in 'commercial puffing'—exaggerated praise of his products or services is inevitable.

So you may say: "Our goods or services are the best . . . the finest value . . . the most marvellous in town. . . ."

Those who sell to you may maintain that they provide 'the buy of the week . . . superb value . . . tremendous opportunities . . . unrepeatable bargains. . . .' Every time a puff.

Once you turn to facts, though, you must beware of fiction. So if you offer (say) a '24-hour service . . . delivery within a day . . .' or that you will supply goods of a specific size, quality or finish—then these are facts.

Equally, those who supply to you may puff but not lie. They are not permitted by law to mistake facts.

126

Suppose, now, that you are deceived. What are your rights?

If you have 'entered into a contract after a misrepresentation has been made to you' then you may 'rescind the contract'. You may return the goods or refuse to accept any further services—and you may demand the return of any money which you may have paid. Alternatively, the Misrepresentation Act says that if you would be entitled to rescind the contract, then if you have suffered loss you can keep the goods or retain the services and claim damages. Only if the seller or supplier can prove 'that he had reasonable ground to believe and did believe up to the time the contract was made that the facts represented were true' will he escape liability—and the odds are heavily against him.

In addition, Section 3 of the Act makes exclusion clauses void. 'If any agreement . . . contains a provision which would exclude or restrict—

(a) any liability to which a party to a contract may be subject by reason of any misrepresentation made by him before the contract was made; or

(b) any remedy available to another party to the contract by reason of such a misrepresentation; that provision shall be of no effect except to the extent (if any) that, in any proceedings arising out of the contract, the court or arbitrator may allow reliance on it as being fair and reasonable in the circumstances of the case.'

I know of no case in which the proviso has been put into effect. In general, any exclusion clause of this sort is void.

The Government (at the time we go to press) is proposing to bring in equivalent legislation to make void any exclusion clause in any contract of sale which would take away a consumer's rights, where goods turn out to be 'unmerchantable' (or defective) or, in general, 'not suitable for the purpose supplied'. There is a good precedent in Section 3 of the Misrepresentation Act.

But these are civil remedies. They give the public no rights against the seller. The Trade Descriptions Act does that—while at the same time giving the buyer no right against that seller.

'Any person who, in the course of a trade or business—

(a) supplies a false trade description to any goods; or

(b) supplies or offers to supply any goods to which a false trade description is applied' may (in theory at least) be subject to two years' imprisonment or to a fine of unlimited amount—or both. And similar rules apply to those who are suppliers of services.

In general, where a trade description is 'false to a material degree'—or 'is misleading'—the offender could be prosecuted.

Suppose, now, that you put out a catalogue or a circular—or exhibit goods in your shop window. The civil law says that you are not bound to sell them to any particular purchaser, at the price marked or at all. You are only issuing an 'invitation to treat', and the chances are that you may lawfully say to a prospective client or customer: "I am sorry; we made a mistake; if you wish to buy, you will have to pay more than the price stated. . . ."

Unfortunately, though, you have almost certainly 'applied a false trade description' to the goods or services concerned—and although the buyer would have no civil remedy against you, he may report you to the local Weights and Measures Authorities—in which case, you may be prosecuted for your trouble.

So as a seller, mind your words. And as a buyer, remember the Misrepresentation Act—and also that a mere threat to refer a false trade description to the authorities may bring the seller to heel. And remember, too, that you may legitimately 'puff' to your heart's content. But if you state facts, you must stick to the truth.

Chapter 47

When You Sell Privately

If my aunt had wheels, goes the old French saying, she would be a bicycle. If you cannot get a decent price for your old car—or for that of your wife—then you may have to revert to cycling. This may do a lot of good for your physical health but is unlikely to benefit your business.

Suppose, then, that you decide to sell your old and personally owned vehicle, so as to raise the money for a new one. In cutting out the dealer/middleman, what are the snags you are likely to meet— and how can you best protect yourself against them? How should you interview a prospective customer, particularly one from another town, both courteously and agreeably—but with due security for yourself?

*   *   *

There was once a businessman who sold his car to a man with magnificent, written credentials—including driving licence, membership card from a motoring organisation and a pile of letters, all bearing his name or signature or other identification. The seller even telephoned to the man's bank to check up that he had an account there. All seemed well.

Unfortunately, it turned out that the purchaser had stolen the cheque book and all the other documents from the same wallet. Buyer and money disappeared and were never traced.

So the only way to get absolute security when you sell is to insist upon getting the money, before the goods are handed over. There is no reason why you should be discourteous or disagreeable with a purchaser when you tell him this. Point out politely that you do not know each other . . . or even if you do, that you have no knowledge as to the state of his bank account. If he gets offended and nasty, then there is probably something amiss with him, so you are better off if he disappears.

After all, if you tell a prospective manager, assistant or secretary that you propose to take out a fidelity bond and he or she demurs and looks uncomfortable, you need not waste your time or money. The sooner he or she is removed from your office the better. The same applies to purchasers of your goods who are unwilling to submit to scrutiny or to give you time to pass their cheques through their accounts.

Subject to these precautions, the private seller is actually in a much stronger position than his purchaser. The *Sale of Goods Act, 1893*, for instance, only protects those who buy from those who sell in the usual course of their business. When you buy from a private individual, there is no implied term in the contract that the goods will be 'of merchantable quality' or 'reasonably suitable for the purpose supplied'.

Naturally, the private seller is not allowed to make any misrepresentations or to engage in fraud. But even the *Trade Descriptions Act, 1968*, does not apply to him. He will not get fined or imprisoned if he 'applies a false trade description' to the goods. At worst, he could be forced to accept the return of the goods and to hand back the money or to pay damages, to compensate the buyer for the cost of putting the goods into proper order.

Still, the greatest peril for the buyer arises if the goods are stolen. How do you know that the seller really owns the vehicle? The fact that he has the log book will not give him title. And how sorry you would be if it turns out that the car is on hire purchase—that it is still owned by a finance company.

Before you buy privately from a stranger, you should ask your solicitor or local Citizens' Advice Bureau to check with Hire Purchase Information Limited, to ensure that the vehicle is not, so far as they know, the subject of an undischarged HP agreement. If you have any doubt as to the origins of the vehicle, then by all means check with the local police. After all, if it turns out that the vehicle is 'hot', the fact that you did not actually 'know' that it was stolen will not prevent you from being guilty of 'handling' —or, to use the old term, 'receiving' stolen property. Under the *Theft Act, 1968*, it is quite enough if you 'believe' it to be stolen. And if the price is sufficiently low, a jury may reasonably impute belief to you.

Putting all these miseries on one side, though, either buying or selling privately may prove a worthwhile proposition. But unless you watch your legal step, your deal may land you in far worse trouble and expense than if you received less or paid more (as the case may be), through using the services of a dealer.

Chapter 48

Your Duties to Your Creditors

The law says that the debtor must seek out his creditor. Normally, it is no excuse whatsoever to say that the creditor did not come to you to beg for his money. If you owe a debt, then your duty is to get your money to the person who has earned it—and this applies not just to your own employees but to those who provide you with the stock, materials, supplies or services without which you would go out of business. You have to live? Certainly—but so does he.

There are exceptions. First, in some cases you do not know the amount of a debt until you receive the invoice or statement. Then clearly the creditor must let you know the size of the debt and its breakdown. But once he has delivered his bill, you must pay him his money.

Again, you may specifically agree that payment must be made (perhaps) by the end of the month following receipt of the invoice. In that case there is an express term in your contract with your supplier, which effectively gives you the right to delay payment until after the invoice has arrived. But generally, your duty to pay for goods and services arises immediately they are supplied.

In legal terms: "In consideration of your supplying me with —, I agree to pay £X00." The moment you receive the goods, your supplier has complied with his side of the bargain. That leaves you to perform your obligations.

At this stage, it is absolutely no excuse for you to say: "I didn't get the usual statement," or: "If you had sent someone around to collect the money, you could have had it." I repeat: Your duty is to find your creditor and to pay him.

Or suppose that you are the unhappy recipient of a writ of summons. Obviously, you will not want judgment entered against you. Your credit may be excellent until such time as someone obtains judgment—at which stage all your creditors may demand payment at once—and there is nothing more likely than that to add the name of your business to the depressing list of current liquidations.

So you pay—protesting furiously that you received no 'letter before action'. "If you had warned me that you were going to sue, you would have got your money," you say. Fair enough, perhaps. It may have been very unkind of your creditor not to have followed the usual courtesies. On the other hand, he may have preferred to get his claim in first—and not to give you the warning which would have enabled you to put that particular company (perhaps) into liquidation. That is a matter for him.

Most people give plenty of warning before they sue. Quite apart from their natural (and sensible) dislike of litigation, the issue of a writ is hardly likely to promote goodwill and mutually useful business in the future. Still, warnings and 'letters before action' may be common and courteous commercial conduct, but they are not required by law.

So if all the creditors pounce at the same time, it is up to you to fend them off as best you can. Robbing Peter to pay Paul . . . 'flying kites at the bank' . . . shuffling the accounts . . . putting off the evil day . . . call it what you like—unfortunately, this sort of activity is sometimes necessary in the business world. But make no mistake about it—the moment a debt falls due for payment, the creditor is entitled to sue for his money. If he gives you a time to pay . . . opportunity to juggle your accounts or to placate your bank manager, that is a matter for him. He is fully entitled to issue his writ in the High Court or a summons in the County Court (for £750 or less), the moment you fail in your obligation to make the payment in accordance with your contract.

Your creditor is not bound to give you time, to extend you any courtesy or to give you what amounts to additional credit—whatever the reason for your lack of liquidity. It is for you to keep yourself in business and 'if you fail to do so then why should he have to suffer' says the law.

Naturally, these rules apply equally in reverse. If you are owed money, then it is up to you to decide whether or not to exercise restraint. You are entitled to sue for it the moment it falls due but remains unpaid. You are not bound to seek out your debtor and to demand payment. His job is to get his money to you. That, at any rate, is the theory. It is just as well for many businesses that the practice is usually different.

Chapter 49

Handling Your Creditors—In Writing

Ill health . . . unexpected expense . . . redundancies . . . or just bad planning—these are only a few of the reasons why debtors must be held, from time to time, at arm's length. If you can do so orally, then well and good. But the day will come when you have to answer their letters—or write your own. Here's how.

*   *   *

In general, frankness pays. Your creditor does not want to take you to court, if he can avoid it. Indeed, the more insubstantial your assets, the less likely he will be to wish to spend his money, chasing yours. At the end of the day, he may end up with an instalment order from a County Court, requiring you to pay 5 new pence a month—and that will do his business no good.

On the other hand, if you are a man of even moderate substance, you will be worth chasing. After all, what is the 'equity' on your house—how much would be left over, if you were to sell your house and 'realise your asset'?

So try this sort of gambit:

1 As I expect you know, I have unfortunately suffered from a severe illness, which has resulted in my having to shepherd my resources. However, I am pleased to say that I shall shortly be working full-time and, in the circumstances, I would be grateful if you would extend the period for my repayment. . . .

2 Thank you for your reminder. I can assure you that I shall

honour my obligation. However, due to circumstances entirely beyond my control, I must ask you to exercise patience. These circumstances are . . .

3 I confidently expect to be able to resume payments in reduction of my overdraft, by the end of next month. Until then, it is essential that I obtain the supplies necessary for my business . . . (or: that I complete the work on my home). Your continued co-operation and understanding will be appreciated.

The vital rule in any event, is to give every appearance of calm. AVOID PANIC. DO NOT FLAP. Any indication of lost confidence could be fatal.

* * *

Sometimes, crawling becomes an essential operation. Thus:

1 I appreciate that you have been most understanding. But unfortunately my wife's illness has meant that she has had to give up work for the moment. And our family finances have suffered as a result. I would be immensely grateful if you would extend to me the courtesy of a further moratorium. . . .

2 Robert—we are old friends. This is my time of trial. Please do use your influence with the company, to prevent it from driving me into insolvency. Given time, I can certainly pay.

* * *

Even the debtor is left with one weapon—to be used as a last resort and only with restraint. It is an indication to the creditor that it would be fatal to press too hard. Thus:

1 My business is young and depends for its survival upon continued credit. If you were to carry out your threat and to issue proceedings, no doubt my other creditors would take due note— and the financial fabric of my business would then collapse. While, given time, I am sure that I can repay the money which I owe to you, if I were to be driven into insolvency I fear that neither you nor anyone else would rescue much from the

133

wreckage. I firmly believe that, given time, this business will pay. Meanwhile, I ask for your further indulgence. OR
2 I fully appreciate that you may make me bankrupt. This, of course, would be a personal disaster for me. But I really do not think that it would assist you in obtaining payment of the money which you are owed.

*   *   *

There are laws against obtaining credit by fraud—and if you operate a business through a company, then if you allow that company to obtain credit when you know that the debt will not be repaid, you may have to fish into your own pocket to meet the liabilities. If your personal business affairs have reached such a sorry pass, my advice is: Consult a solicitor.

*   *   *

Anyway, tactful letters bring useful delay. And if the creditor fails to start his legal proceedings within six years from the date when the debt was originally incurred—or the last date when the debtor acknowledged his indebtedness, in writing—then the claim becomes 'statute barred'.

The essence of a first-class letter of delay is simple. It consists of the following elements:

1 A courteous apology.
2 An explanation for the delay.
3 An assurance that further patience will lead to payment in due course, and
4 A conclusion of calm thanks.

*   *   *

Assuming that your reason for delay is genuine and that you are dealing with a decent, honourable creditor, a fair, frank approach to him generally pays off. Almost invariably, business concerns are prepared to call a halt to instalments . . . delay payments . . . reduce instalments . . . even write-off part of the debt, in return for payment of the balance. Explain your difficulties and you may be luckier than you think. But to sit back and do nothing is generally fatal. Only where the creditor is grossly inefficient, or, in the case of a private creditor, where he feels that he cannot put pressure on you— is silence likely to prove golden.

But do remember that if you sign a letter in which you acknowledge your debt (directly or indirectly) the six-year 'period of limitation' starts to run all over again. And if you may have a defence to the creditor's claim, you should frame your letter with special care. Thus:

1 I agree that the goods were delivered. But I would refer you to my letters of complaint, with which you have not dealt. I have had to have the goods repaired at a cost of £X. I enclose photocopies of the invoices herewith. Deducting the monies I have laid out from the monies that I owe you, the balance is —. I enclose my cheque in that sum herewith. Kindly acknowledge receipt in full settlement of your claim.
2 I was astonished to receive your bill for the extra work done on my house. I regard this as completely exorbitant. I enclose herewith my cheque for the agreed, basic, estimated sum. I am having the remainder looked over by a surveyor and will get in touch with you when I receive his report.
3 Unfortunately, it now transpires that the work done by your men on my home was shoddy and defective. Knowing the high standards to which your firm normally adheres, I would be very grateful if you would send in your team, to put things right. The moment the job is satisfactorily concluded, I shall be pleased to pay your bill.
4 I returned the — to your shop/works. In the circumstances, I presume that your account was sent to me in error and I return it herewith.

*　　*　　*

Finally, please remember always to keep copies of all letters of this sort.

Chapter 50

Collecting Debts

If you are owed money, you may need to write letters in order to collect it. These 'running letters' follow a fairly steady progression:

1 POLITE REMINDER "I am sorry to trouble you, but have you overlooked . . .?" Or: "May I please remind you that you promised me that you would repay to me the money which I lent you on the — (£—), by the end of last week. I do need it. . . ."

2 THE FIRM REMINDER Hence: "I am sure that your omission to pay me the money you owe me is entirely inadvertent. I would be very grateful if you could let me have your cheque by return." Or: "I find this embarrassing—but I do need the money. Please could you now let me have it?" Or, from a business: "We would refer you to our reminder of —. We would now be grateful if you would let us have your remittance without further delay."

3 NEXT, A MORE INSISTENT REMINDER "I am very sorry, but I cannot wait any longer for the repayment of the money you owe me." Or: "Please would you now let me have the £X which you owe us, without further delay."

4 THEN COMES THE TIME FOR THREATS But gentle ones. "It would be a very great shame if I had to put this matter in the hands of my solicitors." "The last thing in the world I would want to do would be to get lawyers involved." "It would be a very great pity if our happy relationship were to be destroyed. But soon you will leave me no option other than to inform my solicitors."

5 THEN THE THREAT BECOMES MORE POWERFUL Thus: "Unless I receive the money within seven days of today's date, I shall instruct my solicitors to take the appropriate steps." Or: "You leave me with no alternative. Unless I receive the money you owe me by —, I shall instruct my solicitors to issue proceedings." (Incidentally, if the sum involved is £750 or less, the odds are that the action will be commenced in the County

Court. A summons would be issued. If the amount involved is higher, then the lawyers would doubtless issue a High Court writ.)

6 FINALLY, THE CRUNCH "I have instructed my solicitors . . ." Or: "Tomorrow, a summons will be issued . . ."

After that, leave the collection to the lawyers—and the best of luck to you. The smaller the sum . . . the more insubstantial the debtor . . . the greater his prospect of proving some defence . . . the less worthwhile your proceedings are likely to be. But bolster yourself with this happy thought: The vast majority of cases never reach trial. At some stage along the trail—even if it is only on the issue of the summons or writ, the debtor usually concedes defeat. Usually . . .

Chapter 51

Unlawful 'Harassment'

Debt collecting is an unpleasant occupation—made more hazardous by the *Administration of Justice Act, 1970,* which recently came into force.

The first reported case under the Act involved a debt collecting firm which attempted to obtain money from a housewife, in payment for goods supplied. It sent a letter, threatening that a van marked 'Debt Collection Company' would arrive at her home. The proprietor was charged under Section 40 of the Act, which says this:

'A person commits an offence if, with the object of coercing another person to pay money claimed from the other as a debt due under a contract, he

(a) harasses the other with demands for payment which, in respect of their frequency or the manner or occasion of making any such demand, or of any threat or publicity by which any demand is accompanied, are calculated to subject him or members of his family or household to alarm, distress or humiliation. . . .'

The debt collector had harassed the housewife. He was duly convicted and fined.

The act makes it unlawful 'falsely to represent, in relation to the money claimed, that criminal proceedings lie for failure to pay it'. By all means threaten to put the matter in the hands of solicitors or of a debt collecting agency. But do not say that you will call in the police, when you know perfectly well that the debtor is guilty of no criminal offence.

If a person 'concerts with others' in the taking of such action, then he may 'notwithstanding that his own course of conduct does not by itself amount to harassment', be guilty of an offence. If you plan harassment with some debt collecting agency, you may find yourself in legal trouble, even though you have taken no specific action on your own behalf or that of your company or firm.

Penalties? Fine of up to £100 for the first offence; up to £400 thereafter.

One defence is provided: The rules do not apply 'to anything done by a person which is reasonable (and otherwise permissible in law) for the purpose—

(a) of securing the discharge of an obligation due, or believed by him to be due, to himself or to persons for whom he acts, or protecting himself or them from future loss; or

(b) of the enforcement of any liability by legal process.'

Businessmen who are owed money may take reasonable steps to induce the debtor to pay. Usual requests, demands and eventual threats of legal action remain entirely permissible. They may amount to 'harassment' in fact, but by law they are 'reasonable'—and even if the debt is only believed to be due and has actually been paid, the collector will avoid legal trouble.

On the other hand, those debt collectors who use humiliation as a weapon will be in trouble, along with the traders who put lists of debtors into their windows. If your firm or company employs an agency with way-out methods, you should watch your step. 'Concert' with them and you may join them in a legal difficulty. But you may still take such steps as are 'reasonable and otherwise permissible in law' to get payment—and the best of these is to threaten legal action and, where necessary, to let your lawyers get on with the job.

Meanwhile, if you suspect that your firm's 'dunning' letters or methods exceed the bounds of reasonableness and that they may amount to 'harassment', now is the time to change them. Otherwise the 'alarm, distress or humiliation' may be yours—even though you are only attempting to get in for your employers, your firm or yourself money that is genuinely and properly owed.

Chapter 52

The Noble Art of Borrowing from the Bank

You would never think that banks make a living from lending money, would you? You advance towards the manager's desk, rise from your knees and beg for 'facilities'. Graciously, he extends them —thereby keeping himself in business. Alas, he has the whip-hand— if only because you need the money and it would cost much more to borrow it elsewhere. And I cannot improve your credit rating. But if you know the basic laws which affect (or afflict) the borrower from the bank, your posture need perhaps be less prostrate than you think.

It is, of course, necessary to recognise that when the bank 'grants you overdraft facilities', it creates the normal relationship of lender to borrower. The fact that the money is lent by way of overdraft in no way alters the general rule—that money lent is repayable on demand, unless there is some special arrangement to the contrary. You have no legal right to an overdraft in the first place, and once facilities are granted, they may 'in the absence of agreement to the contrary' be withdrawn forthwith and without notice. You may be told to reduce your overdraft or to liquidate it completely, as and when the bank sees fit.

So make sure that there is some clear agreement, stating when the situation will be reviewed. If your facilities are granted (for instance) for three months or six, then until the dread day of review arrives you are entitled to keep the bank's money for your own purposes. Conversely, when that day does arrive, the bank may pounce—on you or on your securities.

The bank is not bound to insist upon your overdraft being secured. Equally, a manager is fully entitled to demand securities. And if you do not meet your obligations, the bank may realise those securities—in a word, sell them. From the proceeds of sale the bank will recoup the money you owe it. Any balance will be returnable to you.

Once you have failed to repay your loan, the bank may forthwith dispose of the securities. It is not bound to give you further time to pay, nor the opportunity to find the money somewhere else, so as to release your securities. Generally, the manager will oblige—banks generally use their powers with restraint. Even if the manager has decided that your future goodwill is scarcely worth having, he does not want trouble. If you will pay quietly, then his superiors will smile—and he will rejoice.

Remember, then, that the manager has a living to earn. The odds are that his Head Office will have relied upon him, in deciding to grant you the advance in the first place. If his confidence in you proves unjustified, then his position is unlikely to be reinforced. The bank manager is not expected to act as guarantor for the customers whom he obliges on the bank's behalf. But if his judgment goes astray too often, he is unlikely to attain the heights of his profession.

So understand your manager—and help him. Here are some suggestions:

1 Keep your account properly regulated. If you are going to exceed the limit agreed—in time or amount—then give advance warning. The more reliable a manager finds you, the more confidence he will repose in your word—and the more of the bank's money he will be prepared to place behind your business.

2 You must give the manager sufficient confidence in you to enable him to pass the feeling on to his superiors. So avoid any appearance of panic. A famous politician recently remarked that a week is a long time in politics. In general, it is also a short time in the life of a banker. So preserve your 'cool'. In speech and in writing, maintain an appearance of utter calm.

3 Make a clear arrangement with the manager concerning the period during which the advance may remain outstanding. This will undoubtedly be recorded in the manager's notes.

4 Make a clear agreement also as to the interest to be charged on your overdraft. This may be 2–4 per cent above the current bank rate, or whatever other rate is agreed between you. It is up to the banker and yourself to agree on terms.

5 Keep your own records straight—and if you are in any doubt as to the precise terms of your agreement with the manager concerning your overdraft, then write and confirm. And finally

6 Remember that the bank manager is (fortunately) human. Treat him with calm, confident courtesy. If he learns to rely upon you, you will be able to rely upon him—and that matters above all else.

Chapter 53

After an Accident—Make a Loan

There is more than one way to provide money for an injured employee. Simply hand over his wage or salary and even if he later shows that the accident was caused through the negligence of a third party, neither he nor you will get the money back. But lend him the cash—even if you would otherwise be bound in any event to pay it to him—and the chances are that you will save your company a good deal of money. The reason lies in the nature of damages.

Suppose that your employee is injured in a road accident, caused through the negligent driving of another man. He is off work, ill. Either because the man is entitled to be paid when away due to illness or accident or because you do not wish to see his family suffer due to the unhappy disaster, you pay the man his normal remuneration.

The day comes when a court is asked to award damages against the wrongdoer. Your employee will obtain his damages for personal injuries—and (if appropriate) the cost of repairing or replacing his car. But he will get no damages for loss of earnings because he will have suffered no such loss.

'Then we will join in the action, and claim the money we have had to pay to the employee, in return for no work. We have lost his services, for which we have paid.'

No good, says the law. First, you may have been under no legal obligation to pay the employee in the circumstances. In that case, you made a voluntary payment and you cannot claim that against a negligent third party.

Alternatively, the man was entitled to his sick pay. And—thanks to what many regard as a defect in English law—an employer cannot obtain damages for loss of services. This was decided in a case in which a police officer was knocked down, when on point duty. His employing authority obtained no damages.

It follows that when you pay a person injured through an accident, you wave farewell to your money—forever.

In some cases, an employer can shrug wearily—and pay up without any worry. The money comes from his insurers' pockets, and the worst that can happen to him will be an increase in premium on the next renewal date. But here it is most unlikely that any employer will have his remedy against his insurers. Usually, insurers only cover

141

legal liability of an employer to his employee, arising out of the employer's negligence—and not that of a third party. If you make this sort of payment, you must expect to bear its weight on your own financial shoulders.

So what should you do? Make the employee a loan. Write to him in this vein:

> Dear Mr Jones,
>   We were extremely sorry to hear of your accident. You will, I am sure, be pleased to know that the company intends to stand behind you and to pay you your full remuneration (less the amount of any National Insurance or other benefits which you will receive), for — months/at any rate for the moment/ until you are able to return to us/ during the subsistence of your contract of service. But such payment will be made by way of a loan. All monies will be repayable to the company if—and only if—you succeed in recovering them from the other driver or his insurers.
>   To set your mind at rest, may I emphasise that the loan will be repayable only in the event of—and to the extent that—monies are recovered by you from the other party to the accident.
>   We wish you a swift return to good health.

The effect of this arrangement will be to enable the employee to include a claim for his salary or wage, in any proceedings against the other party. He has received no remuneration—only a loan, repayable if his action succeeds. Your employee is no worse off—and you may have saved the old firm a great deal of money.

Now suppose that a female employee comes to you and says: "I am sorry, but I shall have to give up work in order to look after my husband, who was injured in an accident." What do you say to her?

If the lady loses her job—or even if you give her unpaid leave of absence—she cannot claim her lost wage or salary from the negligent driver. The 'damages' are too remote. It does not arise as a direct or foreseeable result of the negligence.

Nor can the husband obtain damages because his wife is bringing less into the household. But if he were to pay his wife a wage for looking after him, that would be a properly claimable 'head of damage', in any action against the other driver. After all, if you knock someone down and injure him, you must foresee the possibility that he will require nursing. You may have to pay reasonable cost of

142

nursing services. If those services are provided by a wife, she is just as entitled to proper payment as is any stranger.

"But what if the husband has no money with which to pay his wife for caring for him?"

Then let him owe it to her. She is not bound to demand immediate payment. Debts can mount up. Let your accountants do the lady a favour and work out how much tax should be deducted from her pay when it arrives. Put the whole transaction on the same footing as if the nurse were a stranger and the fact that she is the man's wife will not allow the Revenue to refuse the lady her tax allowances— nor the guilty party or his insurers to refuse to meet the expense of her services.

All this, of course, is simply one of the tricks of the legal trade. But that in no way makes them illegitimate. It pays to know your law on loans.

Chapter 54

Can You be made Personally Liable for the Company's Debts?

In general, businesses are carried out under the beneficent umbrella of limited liability. If the business has to be put into liquidation, then a shareholder can be forced to pay any money due on his shares—but nothing else. Even if he is a director, the company's creditors will not be able to get hold of his private assets. In return for this benefit, those interested in companies pay much more tax; they must (in general) make considerable disclosure of the company's assets, liabilities and business for all the world—including actual and potential creditors—to inspect; and tax deductible expenses are a good deal harder to come by than in the world of individual traders and those who operate in partnerships.

Still, if the balloon goes up, there is one way in which creditors may succeed in forcing directors to meet the debts personally.

If a company becomes insolvent and is wound up, Section 332 of the Companies Act says that if the liquidator can show that the business 'has been carried on with intent to defraud creditors of the company . . . or for any fraudulent purpose', then the officer or director whose fault this was may be held personally accountable. Luckily, one judge has ruled that you have to be guilty of 'actual dishonesty, involving—according to current notions of fair trading among commercial men—real moral blame', before you can be liable under Section 332. The person concerned must have been 'in some way a party to carrying on the business in any fraudulent manner . . .'.

In one recent case, a company secretary and financial adviser was faced with a claim in respect of the company's debts. It was alleged that he had 'failed to give certain advice to the directors', although he 'knew that the company was insolvent'. He had 'omitted to take steps which he should have taken to prevent the company from continuing to trade'.

Happily, his omission to give advice "did not render him a party to carrying on the business with intent to defraud", said the Judge. He was dismissed from the action.

Still, an officer or director of a company may be made liable 'without any limitation . . . for all or any of the debts or any other liabilities of the company as the court may direct', if he is guilty of misfeasance, under Section 332. He may also be imprisoned for up to two years or fined up to £500—or both. But at least we now know that board room directors, sleeping directors, professional advisers—and wives who are registered as company secretaries but are not 'concerned in the management or carrying on of the business' as such—will not find themselves burdened with the insolvent company's debts.

What, then, of the liabilities of a company official? If he is "merely performing his appropriate duties", said a judge, "he is not concerned in the management or carrying on of the business". Unless he is guilty of some 'positive act', he will not be 'party to the carrying on of the business' in such a way as to have to meet the company's debts out of his own pocket—unless, of course, he has been personally and fraudulently concerned in the milking of the shareholders or creditors. If a man engages in fraud, then—if caught—he can be forced to meet criminal penalties and civil liabilities. He cannot simply hide behind the cloak of the company. Conversely, if he simply does his job in a proper and non-fraudulent way, and disaster strikes, he will be in the clear.

So it is important for the insolvent firm to show that the fault lies in business circumstances, commercial misfortune—or some other cause than 'the carrying on of the business with intent to defraud creditors'. You must not allow your company to incur debts when there is no reasonable likelihood of the creditor ever being repaid. But otherwise, the end of the company may mean the death of your job, the end of your share capital or the loss of your prospects. But it will not involve your personal liability, civil or

COPING WITH CONTRACTS, CREDITORS AND COMPANIES

criminal. And in these hard times, that is a substantial mercy, for which the man who makes his business from commerce should be duly grateful.

Of course, if you operate as a private individual or as a firm, and without the benefit of limited liability, you (either individually or together with your partners) may be forced to pay the business debts out of your own private money.

If you have shares, your creditors may be able to get hold of them. And the sheriffs may 'distrain' on your private property.

Naturally, if the goods concerned do not belong to you, your creditors will have to hand them back. If you hire your television, for instance, it will belong to the owners and there will probably be a term in the agreement that if you go bankrupt the agreement will terminate and the owners will be entitled to collect their goods. And if you are married, some of your household property may belong to your wife.

But if you see insolvency looming up ahead, waste no time in putting goods or chattels—or, still less, houses or land or shares—into your wife's name. That will fool no one and will obviously be a 'disposition in defraud of creditors'. You should have thought of that step a very long time ago. Indeed, if you are looking forward to a wretched future, perhaps now would be a good time for you to consider transferring your assets to your wife, your mother or your sister. One day, you may be glad of it. But then again, the goods that belong to them are theirs and if you quarrel and cannot get anything back, that will be your own fault. You have been warned.

Chapter 55

Perils of Directors

The law expects every director to do his duty. Failure could lead to dismissal, personal liability—or prosecution. The prestige of the Boardroom brings perils in its wake. Here are the most important.

* * *

A director who carries out his duty in a proper manner is not personally liable for the defaults of the company. So what are his duties?

"It is impossible to describe the duty of directors in general terms," said Mr Justice Romer, in the famous case of *In re City Equitable Fire Insurance Company Limited*. "The position of a director of a company carrying on a small retail business is very different from that of a director of a railway company. . . . The duties of a director of one insurance company may differ from those of a director of another. . . .

"The larger the business carried on by the company, the more numerous and the more important the matters that must of necessity be left to the manager, the accountants and the rest of the staff. The manner in which the work of the company is to be distributed between the Board of the directors and the staff is, in truth, a business matter to be decided on business lines."

So to decide on the director's duties, you must consider not only the nature of the company's business, but also the manner in which the work of the company is, in fact, distributed between the directors and the officials of the company, provided always that this distribution is a reasonable one in the circumstances, and is not inconsistent with any express provisions of the Articles of Association.

"In discharging the duties of his position . . . a director must, of course, act honestly," said the Judge. "But he must also exercise some degree of both skill and diligence. . . . It has been laid down that so long as a director acts honestly, he cannot be made responsible in damages, unless guilty of gross or culpable negligence in a business sense."

Conversely, if a director acts dishonestly, he can be made personally liable to pay damages to compensate those who suffer as a result. He cannot shelter behind the fact that he was acting on behalf of the company.

Dishonesty is easy to define and to understand. But what of 'gross negligence'?

A director must take as much care of the company's interests as would an ordinary, reasonable person, acting for himself. A Court would ask: "Did this director exercise the ordinary degree of prudence which a person, acting on his own behalf, would have exercised, when entering into the transaction concerned?" Alternatively: "Did the director exhibit in the performance of his duties that degree of skill which may reasonably be expected of a person of his knowledge and experience?"

Again: "Did the director exceed the powers given to him under the Articles of the company?"

Many directors do nothing other than to attend Board meetings. This does not increase their liability. "A director is not bound to give continuous attention to the affairs of his company," said Mr

Justice Romer. "His duties are of an intermittent nature to be performed at periodical Board meetings and at meetings of any committee of the Board on which he happens to be placed. He is not, however, bound to attend all such meetings, though he ought to attend whenever, in the circumstances, he is reasonably able to do so."

A director cannot do the whole job. He is entitled to delegate. Unless he has grounds to suspect that the delegate is not capable of performing the job, then he will not personally be liable if he places the company's business into incapable hands.

In one famous case, the Court of Appeal asked: "Was it the director's duty to test the accuracy or completeness of what he was told by the General Manager and the Managing Director?... A business cannot be carried on on principles of distrust. . . ." In failing to check what he was told by others, he did not 'fail in his legal duties'.

"Men in responsible positions must be trusted by those above them, as well as by those below them, unless there is reason to distrust them. . . . For a director acting honestly himself to be held legally liable for negligence in trusting the officers under him, not to conceal from him what they ought to report to him, appears to us to be laying too heavy a burden on honest businessmen."

In the House of Lords, this decision was approved. "A director is bound to give his attention to and exercise his judgment as a man of business on the matters which are brought before the Board at the meetings which he attends. . . . He is entitled to rely upon the judgment, information and advice, of the Chairman and General Manager, as to whose integrity, skill and competence he had no reason for suspicion. . . .

"Directors are not bound to examine entries in the company's books . . . he is not guilty of negligence in not examining them for himself. . . ."

Not long ago, a company director was prosecuted and convicted of an offence under the *Customs and Excise Act, 1952*. Although she was a director of the company, she knew little about the conduct of the business, which she left to her co-directors and to the manager.

"It is not the duty of each director to exercise some degree of control over what is going on," said the Lord Chief Justice. "Nor is it right to say that there is a duty on a director to supervise the running of the company and, in particular, a co-director who is secretary." The lady was freed from liability—and responsibility.

So where a director acts honestly, prudently and sensibly—and without 'gross negligence'—he cannot be made personally liable for the company's debts or defaults.

If you are a director, you may concentrate on doing your job—

and leave your fellow directors and the other officials and servants of the company to do theirs.

Conversely, if you suffer as a result of the debt or default of some other company, it is extremely unlikely that you will be able to pin liability on to an individual director. Just as a company is entirely distinct from its shareholders, so even if a director owns 99 per cent of all the shares and is in effective charge of the day-to-day running of its business, his liability and that of the company are separate and apart.

How far can a director be made personally liable for the negligence of the company? In general, only where the negligence was really his own.

"Prima facie," said Lord Atkin many years ago, "a Managing Director is not liable for tortious acts done by servants of the company unless he himself is privy to the acts—that is to say, unless he ordered or procured the acts to be done. . . . If the directors themselves directed or procured the commission of the act, they would be liable in whatever sense they did so, whether expressly or impliedly."

So if you order, procure or are otherwise 'privy to' wrongful behaviour, you may have to pay for its results out of your own pocket. Otherwise, you have nothing to worry about.

One of the most real worries of the modern director rises from the *Trade Descriptions Act, 1968.*

Section 20: 'Where an offence under this Act which has been committed by a company is proved to have been committed with the consent or connivance of, or to be attributable to any neglect on the part of, any director, manager, secretary or other similar office in the body corporate, or any person who was purporting to act in any such capacity, he as well as the body corporate shall be guilty of that offence and shall be liable to be proceeded against and punished accordingly.'

So if you are a director (or manager or secretary or 'other similar officer') of a company, and the company causes a misleading description to be 'applied' to goods or services, you will not necessarily escape liability by saying: "It was the company, not I . . ." The company cannot (literally) be placed in the dock.

Other common problems, involving the criminal liability of a director? 'Causing' or 'permitting' the company to commit motoring offences.

In a recent case, a director was reported for failing to stop and give his name and address—he having shown a van driver how to drive a large, new, recently delivered vehicle. He scraped a parked car; stopped his own vehicle and went into his office, leaving his employee to give particulars to anyone who happened to require them.

He was convicted of an offence because he was under 'personal obligation' to stop and report—and it was not good enough for him merely to leave his driver to do so.

So the director must not 'cause' or 'permit' an offence to be committed—and if he commits one himself, then he will have to bear the brunt—personally.

Chapter 56

Beware of Brotherly Hate

Ever since the days of Cain and Abel, few human miseries have been more acute than those caused by brotherly dispute. And when members of families go into business together, the normal opportunities for wretched rows are multiplied. Hence the decision of Mr Justice Megarry in a winding-up action is worth some careful study by everyone who is actually or potentially in business with his brother—or, for that matter, with his father or son or any other relative.

Two brothers (whom I shall call X and Y) had an equal shareholding in two companies, one wholesale and the other retail. They were also the sole directors of the companies. X ran the wholesale company, Y the retail one. Each attended the Board meetings of the other. Unfortunately, the wholesale company 'fell upon hard times' and went into a creditors' voluntary liquidation.

The retail company was largely run by Y, who was its chairman with a casting vote on the Board and at meetings. X sought to wind up the company on the ground that it was 'just and equitable' to do so. His main complaints, said the Judge, fell under three heads. First, Y had opened a new bank account in his own name and was paying in and drawing out the company's money from it and had done so without consulting X. Next, X complained that Y would not employ him in the retail business and owing to the collapse of the wholesale company, he was now without employment. Third, X feared that Y would 'run the company for his own benefit, taking all the profits by way of director's remuneration'. There were other less important complaints, such as an alleged threat at one time made by Y to have X removed from the Board of Directors.

Counsel for X argued that this was "a case of a partnership carried on in the guise of a company" and on that footing there was now such a lack of confidence between X and Y as would justify the dissolution of a partnership, and that this was not exclusively attributable to X. "Accordingly," he said, "it was just and equitable that the company should be wound up and an order to this effect should be made."

It was accepted that each brother was a 'semi-sleeping partner in the business carried on by the other'. But was there any 'quasi-partnership', which should be wound up when the partners could not get on?

"The case is not one of the petitioning contributory complaining of the status quo being changed against his interests," said the Judge. "It is one where he complains that the status quo has not been changed in his favour. Even if this is a proper case for the application of the quasi-partnership concept (a matter upon which I feel some hesitation) I do not think that it is open to X to complain of Y continuing to do what was in accordance with the settled practice between them. The refusal of Y to employ X is thus in my judgment not merely not enough on its own . . . but it is also not a counter to be weighed in the scales with other matters. . . .

"Secondly, there is the question of lack of confidence, assuming (as for this purpose I do) that the quasi-partnership concept applies." In other words, if this is one of the cases in which there is deadlock in a quasi-partnership, was there such 'lack of confidence' which would justify the winding up of the company?

You have to look at "the facts which exist at the time of the hearing", said the Judge. Even if on the facts existing when the petition was presented it was then just and equitable to wind up the company, if it has ceased to be so thereafter, a winding up order should not be made. "No doubt if there were cogent grounds for complaint at the time when the petition was presented," the Judge continued, "but they afterwards melted away, there may be consequences in relation to costs: But a winding up order under this head must be based upon subsisting facts and not upon past history. . . ." And the petitioner "is confined to the heads of complaint set forth in his petition".

So the Judge then looked at the facts as they existed at the date of the hearing, and in the light of the evidence presented before him. "Whatever grounds Y may in the past have given X for the presentation of the petition," he said, "I have to decide in the case the light of the evidence now before me; and this includes the oral evidence of Y and X. . . ."

The Judge found Y "an impressive witness, frank, fair minded and businesslike. X, on the other hand, was at times confused and not very lucid. In so far as their evidence conflicts, I prefer the evidence of Y; and I think that he will try to act honourably and properly

in the management of this company. No doubt there will be differences of opinion about disputable matters; but taking the view of
Y that I did, I do not think that he will act unfairly, especially now
that he had acquired the knowledge of his duties towards his brother
which this case has brought him."

So there was an 'eleventh hour change of attitude' on the part of
Y. There was 'a delayed repentance, with last minute concessions'.
But that being so, there was no longer any deadlock or exclusion.
And the refusal of Y to employ X in the business, contrary to settled
practice, would not justify the winding up of a company.

"I do not accept," said the Judge, "that Y is proposing to run the
company for his own benefit. Even if one goes outside the four corners
of the petition, in the end X is left with complaints which in my
judgment are wholly insufficient to support the petition. The petition must therefore be dismissed." There was no order as to costs—
each brother presumably being left to pay his own.

This case, then, may have produced a happy ending. The company
lives on; the brother who runs it has had the views of the other
brother brought forcibly to his mind; and the dirty linen which has
been washed in public may now be dried in private.

In practice, few cases of this sort actually reach trial. Most of
them are settled on the way. But all of them produce far greater
heartbreak than those involving quarrels between directors who are
unrelated.

So how do you avoid this sort of situation arising? First, accept
the fact that it may arise. It may not be very clever to discuss divorce
as you march happily up to the altar, but whether you are entering a
partnership or a quasi-partnership, if you can decide upon the best
way to break up the union if need be, you reduce the prospects of
that break up occurring. And do not think that because your partner
happens to be a relative that the business marriage of convenience
will necessarily lead to life-long love. When poverty comes in the
door, says the sage, love flies out the window.

Next, if you can manage to compromise your difficulties without
having to call in the court, then so much the better. Otherwise you may find yourself in the same sad position as Messrs X and
Y, leaving the judge to sort out the mess—very likely with the same
result as you would have achieved, had you managed to resolve
your differences amicably.

Then, you may not be able to choose your relatives, but at least
you can decide whether or not to engage in business with them.
My advice? If in doubt, don't. Otherwise you may find yourself
applying to the court to wind up the business. And if the grounds
are insufficient . . . if your brother is operating his side of the business

along the lines previously agreed . . . if, despite your disagreements, the court takes the view that he is an honourable man . . . then you may find that the business goes on, whether you like it or not. Companies, like managers, are generally a good deal easier to create than to dissolve.

Chapter 57

At the End of a Business

Before the book concludes and you return the law to the dry-as-dust container in which it is usually found, let us consider the end of a business. How could you best put your business to rest?

You could be lucky and sell out for a small fortune and a large capital gain. You may prefer to stay on as a consultant or Board-room director, so as to continue to receive an earned income (with the appropriate tax allowances). It is up to you to make the best bargain you can—and do call in your own solicitor and accountant. There is no law which says that when you buy or sell a house, a business or anything else you may not use the other man's professional adviser. But don't. You want the guidance of someone who is concerned with your interests—and your interests alone.

Similar considerations apply if you decide to merge your business with another. You must plan carefully for the maximum capital gain, the minimum tax and the best benefits you can find. If you do not look after yourself, no one else will. As they said in the Bible: "If I am not for myself, who am I for? . . ."

The quotation continues: "But if I am only for myself, what am I?" Remember your staff and those who have served you well. To some extent, the law forces you to pay your debts—in cash. The idea that the closing down of a business means the end of a man's right to redundancy money is as common as it is fallacious. One of the most ordinary reasons for dismissing a man as redundant is if the business no longer requires his services because it is going into liquidation.

In the case of a merger or takeover, the rules get complicated. If the identity of the company remains the same and the man is offered similar work with the new Board, then he refuses it at his peril. But if the company itself closes its doors and its business is transferred elsewhere, the odds are that any dismissed employee is 'redundant'. If in doubt, consult your lawyer.

COPING WITH CONTRACTS, CREDITORS AND COMPANIES

If the business is itself wound up, then the law says how the debts are to be paid. Before any remaining proceeds are shared out, the creditors must be dealt with. Some of their claims are 'preferential'. If there is enough money to pay them all, then well and good. If not, then they share in the available assets, in the same proportion.

Rates and taxes (or, in any event, most of them) rank first. Then come the wages or salary of any clerk or servant earned during the four months preceding the death of the business. Whether you happen to be 'a clerk or servant' is a question of fact. Check up.

Third come wages of any labourer or workman, earned in the four months prior to the end—followed immediately by National Insurance contributions (or most of them).

Fifth comes purchase tax which is due and has become due within 12 months preceding the winding up. Finally, there is accrued holiday pay.

Once the preferential creditors are paid off, the rest of the world's lenders and creditors can queue up to share in the balance of the assets—once again, 'pari passu'—to each in due proportion to his debt.

If you recognise far enough in advance that the end is coming, you may decide to make sure that your own debts receive due preference. "I did the work to build up the company," you say, "and it was my money which laid the basis of the prosperity which has enabled us to pay off even the preferential creditors. So I am going to get my money back."

The chances are that you will find that you have made too few arrangements, too late. If you engage in 'fraudulent preferences', any payments may be called back into the corporate kitty. So consult your lawyer before you repay your friends and (above all) your family or yourself.

Even outside creditors need to be treated with some caution. If a creditor threatens to sue if you do not pay, while the others are prepared to lie low, it will probably not be a fraudulent preference if you deal with the one applying the pressure. There is then no voluntary preference. (A good rule to remember if you happen to suspect that your own debtor may 'go up the spout'. If there is to be a queue, get in first.)

Of course, it is when the first creditor issues his writ or advertises his winding-up petition that the balloon tends to rise into the sky. Creditors are sheep-like in their trusting natures. Provided that everyone else will give credit, they will. But if one creditor is unpaid and gets nasty, the hearts of the rest are struck with terror and they leap to the doors of the court, one after the other. The debtor can then sleep no more—as he counts the sheep leaping over the legal fences, he spends his nights deciding how best to wind up his affairs.

Once again, it is to the lawyer and the accountant that the unhappy debtor must turn. If the truth be told (which it seldom is) many of today's great industrial businesses have arisen Phoenix-like from the ashes of some none-too-savoury liquidation. "Out of the depths, I cried unto Thee. . . ." Well, prayer has its its place, no doubt—but it is definitely no substitute for the best professional advice that you can still afford. So before the creditors come marching in, you should rescue enough from the till to make the legal best of your bad situation.

As for us, may we meet again—in happy times.

Appendices

The Lawful Art of Tax Avoidance
by a Tax Expert

Summary of contents

Notes: libel disclaimer. Statutory references

Tax avoidance and tax evasion.

Changes in Government's attitude to tax avoidance – 1935 to 1960.

Historical background: capital and income, trade and investment.

A mythological figure – the composite tax avoidance tycoon.

A tax loss company.

Sugared sweets for share dealers.

A new dance – strip the assets!

Do not ask for whom the bell tolls – It tolls for thee.

Callaghan's Iceberg, or the *Finance Act, 1965*.

Current attractions – for the Exchequer.

Employees' stock options.

Sudden death of the tax-loss company.

Artificial transactions in land.

Shooting stars.

Forthcoming events: sale and leaseback; sales by instalments – deferred premiums; artificial tax losses.

Future ploys.

Was Napoleon right? Or are the English really a nation of tax avoiders? Hence their unique law of Trusts.

Of course they're after your money – or how to avoid millionaire's paranoia.

Random check list for tax avoider.

Libel disclaimer

The characters that flit through these pages are entirely imaginary.

Any resemblance to any individual alive or dead or to any organisation past or present is purely coincidental and due to the fact that even the most individualist and unique members of society or organisations must in some degree resemble the characters in any mythology—ancient or modern.

Statutory references

There are very few statutory references in the text. Readers seeking guidance should refer to the check list at the end of this appendix.

Tax avoidance and tax evasion

Taxmen love jargon. And no doubt the jargon helps to bring taxpayers gently down to earth. One of the favourite bits of jargon is the razor-edge distinction between tax *avoidance* and tax *evasion*. What is the difference? One Scottish judge put it like this:

"No man in this country is under the smallest obligation, moral or other, so to arrange his legal relations to his business or his property as to enable the Inland Revenue to put the largest possible shovel into his stores. The Inland Revenue is not slow—and quite rightly—to take every advantage which is open to it under the taxing statutes for the purpose of depleting the taxpayer's pocket. And the taxpayer is, in like manner, entitled to be astute to prevent, so far as he honestly can, the depletion of his means by the Inland Revenue." (Taken from the judgment of Lord Clyde, The Lord President of the Court of Session in *Ayrshire Pullman Motor Services and D. M. Ritchie* v. *CIR* 1929 14 TC 754.)

An English Judge put it thus:

"Every man is entitled if he can to order his affairs so that the tax attaching under the appropriate Acts is less than it otherwise would be. If he succeeds in ordering them so as to secure this result, then, however unappreciative the Commissioners of Inland Revenue or his fellow-taxpayers may be of his ingenuity he cannot be compelled to pay an increased tax." (Taken from the speech of Lord Tomlin in the *Duke of Westminster* v. *CIR* (1935) 19 TC 490.)

On these two statements of the law, succeeding generations of lawyers and accountants have built up the distinction between tax avoidance, which is legal, and tax evasion, which is not.

What does the distinction mean in practical terms? Take an example. If a man in business on his own account employs his wife to answer the telephone, or to keep the books, and pays her a small salary, that will be subject to the so-called 'wife's Earned Income Relief' and may altogether escape income tax (and surtax if applicable). That is tax avoidance and is legitimate. But if the husband merely pretends to employ the wife, and in fact pays her for doing nothing, or merely pockets the money himself, that is tax evasion, and if discovered may lead to penalties. This example shows that the distinction depends upon the element of deliberate dishonesty, and that element will be present in the vast majority of cases of tax evasion.

Changes in Government's attitude to tax avoidance—1935 to 1960

The two judgments mentioned were dated 1929 and 1935 respectively. Since then tax avoidance itself has been attacked in a variety of ways. Even the hardened tax avoider would, I think, admit that, in making such attacks, the Administration has done no more than curb the excesses of the professional tax avoiders. Notably, Government attacks have been concentrated on those activities which have resulted either in no tax being paid at all, or more particularly in taxpayers recovering from the Government more tax than they had actually paid. Many of these ploys are now useless, but their ingenuity is so appealing that they merit brief description.

Historical background: capital and income, trade and investment

To appreciate the ingenuity of these tax avoidance devices, one must recollect that our tax system is based on the taxation of *income*. *Income* is distinguished from *capital* and until 1962 capital appreciation was not taxed at all, except indirectly on death in the form of death duties. Further, in many cases only net income was taxed, so that losses on 'income' or 'revenue' account could be set off against income. Also relevant was the distinction between trade and investment. The whole of a trader's gains in respect of his stock in trade were and are still taxable. An investor's capital gains on his investments were not taxable at all until 1962.

A mythological figure—the composite tax avoidance tycoon

So take your mind back to the palmy days of 1935. Imagine yourself a successful entrepreneur flush with income, but resenting your surtax bill. Where do your random thoughts lead?

A tax loss company

Take first the possibilities of the tax loss company. Your old friend X confides in you that his seemingly prosperous company is in fact deep in the red. His accumulated losses amount in total to your company's profits for about five years. You've got a profitable new contract in the offing that will put you in the top surtax bracket.

Through your excitement, you hear X say that he'd be all right if only he could find somebody who would take the whole lot off his hands for a sum just big enough to enable him to retire. You hear yourself asking how much and when X mentions the derisory sum of £10,000 to your amazement you find you've clinched the deal. Out of sheer pity for poor old X of course. Next day your accountant confirms that if you channel the new contract through X's old company the entire profits for the next five years will be set against the accumulated losses and will thus be tax-free. You are staggered. Poor old X.

Ten years go by. It is 1945. You've had a good war, even with income tax at 10/- in the £, surtax at 9/6, and Excess Profits Tax. But the war is over and government contracts hard to come by. The beaches of commerce are littered with shells—shell companies that is—the used gourds of industrialised warfare. You don't even have to look for them. Their owners are weary of war and frightened of peace. So you buy. Not in your own name of course. By now you have a holding company and amongst its star-studded retinue of subsidiaries there is a share-dealing company.

Sugared sweets for share dealers

Your accountants, clever fellows, have explained to you that a share-dealing company treats the shares it owns as stock-in-trade. A bit technical of course but it means that if some shares go down you can chalk that loss up against any gains. What's more, the income you get from the shares is not included in your Case I Income Tax assessment as a share dealer. Is this a likely situation for a likely lad? It is! Quite heart-warming really.

A new dance—strip the assets!

So you buy the clapped-out companies whose directors are too sleepy to realise that you are steadily buying on the Stock Exchange or privately. Sometimes you pay cash and sometimes you pay with your own shares now riding agreeably high. Your people, who know a bit about property, sell off the old factories and warehouses, and of course the dreary old city centre head offices whose sites are now fetching a bomb. What trade is left you rationalise and put through your own factories where it takes up the slack. The old shell is now full of cash, which you pump out as dividends.

Some of these dividends, where they arise from capital disposals, will be capital dividends and as such not taxable at all. But lo and behold, the effect of these dividends is that the shares become worthless. That's a trading loss then, which can be set against gains on other shares. Your accountants, audacious fellows, even put in a claim for repayment of tax on War Loan held by the company. Unfortunately, some other fellow with a less meritorious case lost his appeal to the House of Lords on this very point and your claim was disallowed.

Do not ask for whom the bell tolls—it tolls for thee

So our imaginary tycoon, arch-exponent of the lawful art of tax avoidance, first hears the tolling of the bell, not unheard by others even at that time. Shall we put a date to it—say 1964? And that bell, pealing out its warning to tax avoiders, is going to go on ringing steadily into the seventies.

Look around, then, at the tax avoidance scene of that year. The anti-avoidance provisions of the *Finance Act, 1960*, particularly Section 28, are beginning to bite. So dividend stripping, whether of the 'forward-strip' or 'scissors' variety, is not what it was, even though Section 28 was far from being the first legislation against dividend-stripping. Redeemable debentures even if issued before 1960 are under attack. Capital sums derived from leases of assets are made taxable. The Labour Chancellor has issued his White Paper which, when it becomes the Finance Act of 1965, will abolish capital dividends, impose Corporation Tax, and add the so-called 'long term' Capital Gains Tax to the short term gains tax started in 1962.

Callaghan's Iceberg, or the *Finance Act, 1965*

If you were able to indulge in a Walter Mitty-like identification with the slap-happy tax avoiding tycoon on earlier pages, perhaps you will be able to follow him into the rather cooler climate of 1965. Note in particular the following changes.

1 Corporation Tax is now levied on companies, in addition to the Schedule F they must deduct from dividends. Corporation Tax is now at 40 per cent (compared with the 15 per cent of its predecessor Profits Tax). Schedule F is Income Tax at standard rate.

2 All dividends, whether derived from capital realisations, or profits, now bear Schedule F. The capital dividend no longer has any meaning for tax purposes.

3 The chargeable gains of companies are now subject to Corporation Tax. As the base date, in most cases April 1965,
recedes into the past, the majority of chargeable gains are taxable in a way that is indistinguishable from the taxation of
trading profits. The same applies to individuals, particularly if
they have substantial incomes, though the rate is 30 against 40
per cent for companies.
4 Obvious alternative ploys, like loans to directors and their
relations, have been dealt with.
5 Broadly speaking, a company will now pay Corporation Tax at
40 per cent on all its profits and post-1965 capital gains. Money
extracted from the company can only emerge in the form of
salary or dividend. Both will be subject to Income Tax and
Surtax, but the salary will qualify for earned income relief.

Current attractions—for the Exchequer

Now all that remains is to follow our chastened tycoon through the
six years since 1965. We are almost abreast with events, and must not
overlook the possibility of libel. However, taking the annual Finance
Acts as our guide we can draw the following conclusions.

Employees' stock options

Prior to 1966, an option to buy stock or shares granted to an
employee was an effective means of giving tax-free benefits. If
granted at market value or slightly above the option only bore a
modest amount of tax on grant, and if exercised in a later year bore
no tax on exercise and only capital gains tax (short term or long
term as appropriate) on disposal of the acquired stock. After 1966
such options were taxable on exercise. These rules will be altered
by the Finance Bill of 1972 which is before Parliament at the time
of writing—see Clauses 73–5 of the Bill.

Sudden death of the tax-loss company

In 1969 a final stop was put to the unwarranted manipulation of the
tax-loss company, though well-informed rumour-mongers claim it
was dead already. In the same year there were two wide-reaching
measures.

Artificial transactions in land

A new section dealt with artificial transactions in land. This narrowed
the gaps left for land developers practically to vanishing point, thus
completing the process begun in 1960. The only consolation was that

there was a provision for clearance of proposed transactions *before* they were undertaken.

Shooting stars

The second measure was a long section dealing with the 'sale by individual of income derived from his personal activities'. The measure was aimed at the entertainment world where various schemes had been devised to enable actors and others to take capital assets rather than income. In taxing arrangements of this kind inevitably some quite ordinary commercial or professional arrangements outside the entertainment world have been hit. The result is that any individual who now takes a reward for services in a capital form must consider whether or not he will be hit by the section and taxed as if the 'capital sum' he receives were income.

Forthcoming events

For the latest additions to the list of defeated tax avoidance ploys one must look not to the statute book but to two announcements made by the Inland Revenue.

Sale and leaseback

The first concerns persons who sell their trading premises on a lease-back arrangement, and thereafter pay a higher rent. Similar arrangements in respect of plant were dealt with in 1964. Now it appears that the Chancellor is limiting the new legislation to cases where the unexpired lease is for less than 50 years and the leaseback period is 15 years or less. For these cases the Chancellor is considering two alternatives for the future. Under the first the capital sum received by the vendor would be exempt from capital gains tax and income tax but only part of the new rent would be allowed as a deduction. The disallowed part would over the duration of the lease equal the capital sum received by the vendor.

The second alternative is to treat the lump sum as being taxable as income, with proportionate relief depending on the length of the base, and 'top slicing' relief. Leaseback arrangements entered into before 22 June 1971 will be dealt with on the basis that the whole rent will be allowable, but the capital sum derived from the sale will be subject to capital gains tax. Final details must probably await the *Finance Act, 1972* (see Clause 76 of the *Finance Bill, 1972*).

Sales by instalments—deferred premiums

The second concerns some extremely ingenious schemes to avoid capital gains tax and in some cases to create entirely artificial losses.

The postponement of capital gains tax was to be achieved by making use of the provisions relating to instalments. A sale by instalments for capital gains tax purposes is treated virtually as a series of separate sales, liability to capital gains tax only accruing on each instalment as it falls due (see Clause 109 of the *Finance Bill, 1972*).

So a sale by two hundred and fifty annual instalments, of which the first two hundred and forty-nine were of a nominal amount, and the two hundred and fiftieth instalment consisted of the balance plus interest, would effectively defer capital gains tax for two hundred and forty-nine years. Having completed that part of the bargain the vendor would then sell the right to receive the instalments and thus recover the full sale price without further delay, and it was claimed without paying any more capital gains tax (see Clause 109 of the *Finance Bill, 1972*).

Artificial tax losses

As an alternative, having postponed capital gains tax by the instalment method just described, the vendor then goes on to convert the lease granted into a short lease, by using a break clause exercisable early in the lease. This is in a form which protects sub-leases made before it is exercised. The effect of this is to initiate a claim for an artificial deduction. The Revenue have indicated that they reserve the right to attack existing schemes under the present law and that future schemes will be blocked by further legislation (see Clause 77 of the *Finance Bill, 1972*).

Future ploys

Having reached this point, how can I reward my readers for their patience? To point openly to remaining loopholes would almost certainly result in their closure. Indeed, so tightly has the net been drawn that any loopholes that remain are highly technical and must therefore be related to individual circumstances. In practice, combinations of the available reliefs and exemptions may often provide a satisfactory solution. The growing business is favoured by capital allowances, the repeal of salary restrictions, and small distributions. Full advantage should be taken of pension rights. If limited liability is unnecessary, a partnership will save the double charge to capital gains tax which a company suffers in liquidation. If avoidance schemes are contemplated, the two statutory procedures for clearance (Sections 464 and 488 of the *Income and Coporation Taxes Act, 1970*) should be used.

If, having made your pile, you wish to share it with your family, you may want to set up a trust. A short sermon on trust law follows—but do not let the title mislead you.

Was Napoleon Right? Or are the English really a nation of tax avoiders? Hence their unique law of Trusts

Lawyers are often called upon to create legal machinery governing relationships between individuals. This role is responsive rather than original, but occasionally in responding to popular need lawyers succeed in originating new forms of relationship. Thus mediaeval and Reformation lawyers, responding to their clients' need to avoid the taxes imposed by the Crown on inheritance at death, developed the 'use' which we now know as a trust. The gift 'to A for the use of B' has now become a gift 'to A to hold on trust for B'. The trust is a unique contribution made by English lawyers. It has virtually no exact counterpart in other systems of law, though it does of course appear in the legal systems of America and of some of the countries which were formerly part of the British Empire.

The English fondness for trusts has led to a considerable volume of anti-avoidance provisions relating to trusts or settlements. For example, a trust for the children of the settlor must be irrevocable. If not the trust income will be treated as the settlor's income. If the income is spent on minor children of the settlor, such expenditure will be treated as part of the settlor's income. If the trust owns shares in a family company, and there is accumulated, i.e. unspent, income in the trust, any capital sum paid to the settlor by the company will be treated as income of the settlor up to the amount of the accumulated income.

If the capital is vested in foreign trustees the beneficiaries resident here may find that the trust income is treated as their income even though they have not actually received it.

Recently there have been measures to aggregate the income of parents and their minor children so that the family would be taxed as one unit. These measures have now been repealed, as from April 1972.

Of course they're after your money—or how to avoid millionaire's paranoia

You can't take it with you, and you'll be lucky to keep it while you're still here.

So you've made a fortune, by luck, skill, industry and plain guts. This is no sermon. Just a casual suggestion that it may be salutary to think of your fortune in net terms—What you could keep after all your assets had been sold and taxes paid. Far less to worry about.

While you keep the business in your own hands you can in a sense play with the Revenue's money as well as your own. But if there is a spouse and children to consider this may not be a realistic approach. Death duties are outside the scope of this book, but they are relevant to the question of tax-avoidance because there is little point in saving income tax and capital gains tax merely in order to increase liability to estate duty. Marginal rates of estate duty now reach 45 per cent on an estate of £31,000 so that even at that comparatively modest figure estate duty may be more significant than capital gains tax and may well be as significant as income tax and surtax (allowing for earned income relief). Even by taking the net effective rate of estate duty the 45 per cent rate is reached on an estate of £90,000. These may be depressing figures. I mention them for the sake of realism only since they can make nonsense of desperate attempts to save income tax and surtax at all costs.

To assist in your planning, a random check list is given below. Its object is to indicate the closed loop-holes so that you will know what to avoid.

Random check list for the tax avoider

The statutory references are to the *Income and Corporation Taxes Act, 1970*, unless otherwise stated. Finance Acts are referred to thus— F.A. 1965. This list cannot of course be comprehensive.

Will there be an adventure in the nature of trade? That is, will profits be subject to income and surtax or to Corporation Tax and Schedule F?	Sections 108, 109, 526, 232, 238.
What expenses will be deductible?	Sections 130–135.
Will there be an acquisition and sale within twelve months?	Sections 160–167.
Will a capital sum be derived from assets, e.g. as compensation for loss?	Section 22 of F.A. 1965.
Will there be transactions between relatives or other 'connected persons' at artificial values?	Section 22 and Schedule 7 paras. 17 and 21 of F.A. 1965.
Will there be loans to directors and shareholders of family companies?	Sections 286 and 287.

Will there be transactions in securities followed by tax advantages, i.e. the receipt of money in untaxable form?	Sections 460–477.
Will assets or income be transferred abroad?	Sections 478–481 and 482.
Will any attempt be made to use up accumulated tax losses?	Section 483.
Will any individual sell his future income for a capital sum?	Sections 487, 489 and 490.
Will there be any 'artificial' transactions in land?	Sections 488–490.
Will land be sold and leased back?	Sections 491–496 and F.A. 1972.
Will there be dealings in leased assets other than land?	Sections 492–496.
Will there be sales by instalments over a long period?	Part III and Schedule 6 para. 14 of F.A. 1965 and F.A. 1972.
Will there be tax losses artificially created?	Sections 460–470 and F.A. 1972.
Will settlements be created and if so will the beneficiaries be children of the settlor?	Sections 437–459.
Will any of these settlements own shares in family (or 'close') companies. If so will these companies pay capital sums to the settlor?	Section 451.
Will short leases, i.e. for less than 50 years, be granted at a premium?	Sections 80, 83 and 85 and F.A. 1972.
Will land be sold with a right to reconveyance?	Section 82.
Will directors or employers exercise options to purchase shares?	Section 186 and F.A. 1972.
Will directors or employers receive benefits in kind or expense allowances?	Sections 195–203.
Will directors or employers receive benefits under a non-approved pension scheme?	Section 220.

Appendix 2

Industrial Relations Code of Practice

Like the Highway Code of the road, the Code of Industrial Relations has no legally binding effect. If you break it, you will not be prosecuted—or sued. But if you are hauled before a Court or an Industrial Tribunal and it can be shown that you have violated the Code, then your chances of emerging victorious are considerably reduced.

The Code sets out the conduct expected of industrial and commercial executives, when dealing with their employees. Clearly, it must be included in this book, in full.

The Code is not, in my view, a particularly shattering or useful document—a wise personnel manager told me that he regarded it as a revision primer for backward personnel directors—but potentially useful, as a means of convincing the Board that current practice is both sensible and necessary.

Anyway, the Code is unlikely to require comment or explanation. In case you need it, here it is.

Industrial Relations Code of Practice*

This Code has been issued with the authority of Parliament (Resolutions passed 2 February 1972 by the House of Commons and 10 February 1972 by the House of Lords). It came into effect, by order of the Secretary of State, on 28 February 1972. A full index will be found at the end of this appendix.

Introduction

The purpose of the Code is to give practical guidance for promoting good industrial relations. It does so in accordance with the four general principles set out in the Industrial Relations Act. These stress the importance of freely conducted collective bargaining, orderly procedures for settling disputes, free association of workers and employers and freedom and security for workers.

* Crown copyright. Reproduced with the permission of The Controller of Her Majesty's Stationery Office.

The Code interprets industrial relations in the widest sense. It does not confine itself to procedural matters such as collective agreements and negotiating machinery. It is also concerned with human relations, and therefore with policies which directly affect the individual employee[1] in the performance of his job.

Two main themes underlie the Code:

i the vital role of collective bargaining carried out in a reasonable and constructive manner between employers and strong representative trade unions;[2]

ii the importance of good human relations between employers and employees in every establishment,[3] based on trust and confidence.

In any undertaking,[4] management needs to use its resources efficiently, while employees look for continuity of employment, security of earnings and satisfaction in their work. Both have a common interest in the undertaking's success because without it their aims cannot be achieved. But some conflicts of interest are bound to arise. With good industrial relations they can be resolved in a responsible and constructive way.

Good industrial relations are a joint responsibility. They need the continuing co-operation of all concerned—managements, trade unions, employers' associations and individual employees—and the discussion of day-to-day problems as they occur. The Code is designed to encourage and assist that co-operation.

Application and Use

The Code applies wherever people are employed. Most of it will apply in most employment situations. But some of the detailed provisions may need to be adapted to suit particular circumstances, especially in small establishments, or particular types of employment. Any adaptations should be consistent with the Code's general intentions.

In many cases, changes will be needed to meet the standards set by the Code. Where they cannot be made at once, those concerned should ensure that there is reasonable and continuing progress towards achieving the Code's standards.

[1] Employee includes any worker covered by the Industrial Relations Act (see Section 167 of the Act).

[2] Trade union and employers' association include unregistered organisations, except where otherwise indicated.

[3] Establishment means an individual factory, plant, office, shop, etc. in which employees work.

[4] Undertaking means a business or organisation controlling one or more establishments.

171

The Code complements the provisions of the Industrial Relations Act. It provides guide-lines for all concerned with the day-to-day problems of industrial relations, as well as for the Commission on Industrial Relations and for Courts of Inquiry and similar bodies.

The Code imposes no legal obligations. Failure to observe it does not by itself render anyone liable to proceedings. But Section 4 of the Industrial Relations Act requires any relevant provisions to be taken into account in proceedings under the Act before the National Industrial Relations Court or an industrial tribunal.

Revision

The Code sets standards which reflect existing good industrial relations practice. It is not meant to restrict innovation and experiment or to inhibit improvements on those standards.

Industrial relations can never be static. Just as individual undertakings should review and improve their own practices, so the Code will need to be revised periodically. Under the Industrial Relations Act this must be done after consultation with the Trades Union Congress and the Confederation of British Industry, and after taking account of advice from the Commission on Industrial Relations.

Responsibilities

MANAGEMENT

1 The principal aim of management is to conduct the business of the undertaking successfully. Good industrial relations need to be developed within the framework of an efficient organisation and they will in turn help management to achieve this aim.

2 One of management's major objectives should therefore be to develop effective industrial relations policies which command the confidence of employees. Managers at the highest level should give, and show that they give, just as much attention to industrial relations as to such functions as finance, marketing, production or administration.

3 Good industrial relations are the joint responsibility of management and of employees and trade unions representing them. But the primary responsibility for their promotion rests with management. It should therefore take the initiative in creating and developing them.

4 Where trade unions are recognised for negotiating purposes management should:

    i maintain jointly with the trade unions effective arrangements for negotiation, consultation and communication, and for settling grievances and disputes;

    ii take all reasonable steps to ensure that managers observe agreements and use agreed procedures;

    iii make clear to employees that it welcomes their membership of an appropriate recognised union and their participation in the union's activities.

5 Where trade unions are not recognised for negotiating purposes management should:

    i maintain effective arrangements for consultation and communication and for settling grievances;

    ii take all reasonable steps to ensure that managers use those arrangements;

    iii make clear to employees that it respects their rights under the Industrial Relations Act to join a registered trade union and to take part in its activities, which include seeking recognition for negotiating purposes.

6 Effective organisation of work is an important factor in good industrial relations. Management should therefore ensure that:

    i responsibility for each group of employees is clearly defined in the organisational structure;

    ii each manager understands his responsibilities and has the authority and training necessary to do his job;

    iii individual employees or work groups know their objectives and priorities and are kept informed of progress towards achieving them.

7 All managers should receive training in the industrial relations implications of their jobs. This is as necessary for line managers, including supervisors, as for personnel managers.

8 The supervisor[5] is in a key position to influence industrial relations. Management should ensure that he:

    i is properly selected and trained;

    ii has charge of a work group of a size that he can supervise effectively;

    iii is fully briefed in advance about management's policies as they affect his work group;

    iv is an effective link in the exchange of information and views between management and members of his work group.

[5] In this Code supervisor means a member of the first line of management, who is responsible for his work group to a higher level of management.

9 Management should recognise that each employee has his individual needs and aspirations at work and should take this into account in its day-to-day conduct of business. In particular, management should recognise the employee's need to achieve a sense of satisfaction in his job and should provide for it so far as practicable.

TRADE UNIONS

10 The principal aim of trade unions is to promote their members' interests. They can do this only if the undertakings in which their members are employed prosper. They therefore have an interest in the success of those undertakings and an essential contribution to make to it by co-operating in measures to promote efficiency. They also share with management the responsibility for good industrial relations.

11 Trade unions should therefore:

i where appropriate, maintain jointly with employers' associations and others concerned, effective arrangements at industry or other levels for settling disputes and for negotiating terms and conditions of employment;

ii maintain, jointly with individual managements, effective arrangements for negotiation, consultation and communication and for settling grievances and disputes;

iii take all reasonable steps to ensure that their officials, including shop stewards (see paragraph 100), and members observe agreements and use agreed procedures;

iv maintain effective procedures for resolving particular issues with other unions and, where appropriate, make full use of the procedures established by the Trades Union Congress for settling inter-union disputes.

12 Trade unions should ensure that officials, including shop stewards:

i understand the organisation, policies and rules of the union;

ii understand their powers and duties;

iii are adequately trained to look after their members' interests in an efficient and responsible way.

13 To ensure their organisation is effective, trade unions should also:

i employ enough full-time officials to maintain adequate contact with management and with their members in every establishment

174

where the union is recognised, and with any employers' associations concerned;

ii maintain effective communication, including the exchange of information and views, between different levels in the union;

iii encourage their members to attend union meetings and to take part fully in union activities by holding branch meetings at times and places convenient to the majority; and where there is a large enough membership, consider basing the branch organisation on the establishment;

iv maintain effective procedures for settling disputes within the union.

14 Members of a trade union should be prepared to provide their union with the authority and resources needed to carry out its functions.

EMPLOYERS' ASSOCIATIONS

15 The principal aim of employers' associations is to promote those interests of their members which can best be served by co-operation at industry or other appropriate levels.

16 Employers' associations should therefore:

i where appropriate, maintain jointly with the trade unions concerned effective arrangements at industry or other levels for settling disputes and for negotiating terms and conditions of employment;

ii encourage their members to develop effective arrangements for settling grievances and disputes at the level of the establishment or undertaking;

iii take all reasonable steps to ensure that their members observe agreements and use agreed procedures;

iv identify trends in industrial relations to help their members to anticipate and keep abreast of change;

v collect and analyse information about industrial relations and distribute it to their members;

vi provide an advisory service to their members on all aspects of industrial relations.

17 Members of an employers' association should be prepared to provide their association with the authority, resources and information needed to carry out its functions.

THE INDIVIDUAL EMPLOYEE

18 The individual employee has obligations to his employer, to his trade union if he belongs to one, and to his fellow employees. He shares responsibility for the state of industrial relations in the establishment where he works and his attitudes and conduct can have a decisive influence on them.

19 The legal relationship between employer and employee derives from the individual contract of employment. Often many of its terms are fixed by collective bargaining and stated in collective agreements. With certain exceptions, employees are entitled to a written statement about their main terms and conditions of employment (see paragraphs 60–61).

20 Each employee should:
  i satisfy himself that he understands the terms of his contract and abide by them;
  ii make himself familiar with any arrangements for dealing with grievances and other questions which may arise on his contract, and make use of them when the need arises.

21 Some employees have special obligations arising from membership of a profession and are liable to incur penalties if they disregard them. These may include obligations, for example, in regard to health, safety and welfare, over and above those which are shared by the community as a whole.

22 A professional employee who belongs to a trade union should respect the obligations which he has voluntarily taken on by joining the union. But he should not, when acting in his professional capacity, be called upon by his trade union to take action which would conflict with the standards of work or conduct laid down for his profession if that action would endanger:

  i public health or safety;
  ii the health of an individual needing medical or other treatment;
  iii the well-being of an individual needing care through the personal social services.

23 Professional associations, employers and trade unions should co-operate in preventing and resolving any conflicts which may occur between obligations arising from membership of a profession and those which the professional employee owes to his employer and to his trade union if he belongs to one.

Employment Policies

24 Clear and comprehensive employment policies are essential to good relations between management and employees. They help management to make the most effective use of its manpower resources and give each employee opportunity to develop his potential.

25 Management should initiate and accept primary responsibility for these policies. But they should be developed in consultation or negotiation, as appropriate, with employee representatives.

26 The Race Relations Act 1968 makes it unlawful to discriminate on grounds of colour, race or ethnic or national origins about recruitment, terms and conditions of employment, training, promotion and dismissal. But management should not merely avoid such discrimination; it should develop positive policies to promote equal opportunity in employment.

27 Management should equally ensure that its employment policies are not influenced by conditions relating to age, sex or other personal factors except where they are relevant to the job.

PLANNING AND USE OF MANPOWER

28 Manpower planning in the undertaking consists of:

   i taking stock of existing manpower resources;
  ii working out future manpower needs;
 iii identifying what should be done to ensure that future manpower resources match those needs.

29 Manpower planning should be conducted in ways suited to the size and nature of the undertaking and should be:

   i backed by the authority of management at the highest level;
  ii integrated with other aspects of planning in the undertaking;
 iii based on adequate and up-to-date personnel records.

30 In operating its manpower policies management should:

   i avoid unnecessary fluctuations in manpower;
  ii where changes are necessary, make them with as little disruption as is practicable to the employees concerned;
 iii maintain arrangements for transferring employees from one job to another within the undertaking;
 iv record information which will help it to identify the causes of, and to control, absenteeism and labour turnover.

RECRUITMENT AND SELECTION

31 In recruiting and selecting employees management should:

   i decide the qualifications and experience needed by applicants;
  ii consider filling vacancies by transfer or promotion from within the undertaking;

177

iii obtain as much information about applicants as is relevant to selection for the job, but avoid enquiries which are unnecessary for that purpose;

iv base selection on suitability for the job;

v explain the main terms and conditions of employment and give any relevant information about trade union arrangements before an applicant is engaged.

32 Management should also:

i check recruitment and selection methods regularly to ensure that they are effective;

ii ensure that those who carry out recruitment and selection are competent to do so.

TRAINING

33 Management should ensure that new employees are given:

i induction training, include information about the matters referred to in paragraphs 60 and 62;

ii any training in the job needed to supplement previous education, training and experience.

34 Management should ensure that young people entering employment for the first time are also given broader initial instruction covering:

i a general introduction to their working life, including the importance of health and safety precautions;

ii basic training in related skills, where appropriate, as well as specific training in their particular job.

35 Management should:

i ensure that any necessary further education and training is provided when there is a significant change in the content or level of the job;

ii encourage employees to take advantage of relevant further education and training opportunities at all stages of their careers.

PAYMENT SYSTEMS

36 Payment systems vary according to the nature and organisation of the work, local conditions and other factors, but the following principles apply generally.

37 Payment systems should be:

i kept as simple as possible, consistent with their purpose, so that employees can understand them;

178

ii based on some form of work measurement where payment is linked to performance;

iii jointly negotiated where trade unions are recognised.

38 Differences in remuneration should be related to the requirements of the job, which should wherever possible be assessed in a rational and systematic way in consultation with employee representatives.

39 Payment systems should be kept under review to make sure that they suit current circumstances and take account of any substantial changes in the organisation of work or the requirements of the job.

STATUS AND SECURITY OF EMPLOYEES

40 As far as is consistent with operational efficiency and the success of the undertaking management should:

i provide stable employment, including reasonable job security for employees absent through sickness or other causes beyond their control;

ii avoid unnecessary fluctuations in the level of earnings of employees.

41 Where practicable, management should provide occupational pension and sick pay schemes.

42 Differences in the conditions of employment and status of different categories of employee and in the facilities available to them should be based on the requirements of the job. The aim should be progressively to reduce and ultimately to remove differences which are not so based. Management, employees and their representatives and trade unions should co-operate in working towards this objective.

43 In deciding how and when the changes mentioned in paragraphs 41 and 42 are to be introduced, their cost should be taken into account as part of total labour costs.

44 Responsibility for deciding the size of the work force rests with management. But before taking the final decision to make any substantial reduction, management should consult employees or their representatives, unless exceptional circumstances make this impossible.

45 A policy for dealing with reductions in the work force, if they become necessary, should be worked out in advance so far as practicable and should form part of the undertaking's employment policies. As far as is consistent with operational efficiency and the success of the undertaking, management should, in consultation with employee representatives, seek to avoid redundancies by such means as:

  i restrictions on recruitment;
  ii retirement of employees who are beyond the normal retiring age;
  iii reductions in overtime;
  iv short-time working to cover temporary fluctuations in man-power needs;
  v re-training or transfer to other work.

46 If redundancy becomes necessary, management in consultation, as appropriate, with employees or their representatives, should:

  i give as much warning as practicable to the employees concerned and to the Department of Employment;
  ii consider introducing schemes for voluntary redundancy, retirement, transfer to other establishments within the undertaking, and a phased rundown of employment;
  iii establish which employees are to be made redundant and the order of discharge;
  iv offer help to employees in finding other work in co-operation, where appropriate, with the Department of Employment, and allow them reasonable time off for the purpose;
  v decide how and when to make the facts public, ensuring that no announcement is made before the employees and their representatives and trade unions have been informed.

WORKING CONDITIONS

47 The Factories Act and other legislation lay down minimum standards about working conditions. Management should aim at improving on these standards in consultation and co-operation with employees and their representatives.

48 Management should therefore take all reasonable steps to:

  i improve standards of "housekeeping" including the cleanliness, tidiness, lighting, heating, ventilation and general appearance of the workplace;
  ii reduce noise, strain and monotony as far as practicable;
  iii ensure that hazards are reduced to a minimum and the work done as safely as possible.

49 Management and employee representatives should:

  i take all reasonable steps to ensure that employees use protective equipment (for example, guards, safety helmets, goggles and ear defenders), observe the standards laid down by law and co-operate in agreed safety measures;

ii make the best use of arrangements for consultation about safety and health.

50 Every employee should:

i ensure that he understands the health and safety precautions and observes them;

ii make use of protective equipment.

Communication and Consultation

51 Communication and consultation are essential in all establishments. They are necessary to promote operational efficiency and mutual understanding, as well as the individual employee's sense of satisfaction and involvement in his job. Management, employee representatives and trade unions should co-operate in ensuring that effective communication and consultation take place.

52 Communication and consultation are particularly important in times of change. The achievement of change is a joint concern of management and employees and should be carried out in a way which pays regard both to the efficiency of the undertaking and to the interests of employees. Major changes in working arrangements should not be made by management without prior discussion with employees or their representatives.

53 When changes in management take place, for example, following a merger to take-over, the new managers should make prompt contact with employee representatives and take steps to explain changes in policy affecting employees.

COMMUNICATION

54 In its day-to-day conduct of business, management needs both to give information to employees and to receive information from them. Effective arrangements should be made to facilitate this two-way flow.

55 The most important method of communication is by word of mouth, through personal contact between each manager and his immediate work group or individual employees, and between managers and employee representatives.

56 Personal contact should be supplemented as necessary by:

i written information provided through, for example, notice boards, house journals or handbooks;

181

ii training, particularly induction courses for new employees;

iii meetings arranged for special purposes.

57 Subject to the limitations on disclosure of information, referred to in paragraph 98, management should regularly provide employees with information about:

i the performance and plans both of the establishment and, so far as they affect it, of the undertaking;

ii organisational and management changes which affect employees.

58 Management should ensure that:

i managers, including supervisors, regard it as one of their principal duties to explain management's policies and intentions to those responsible to them and have the information needed to do so;

ii work instructions are conveyed clearly.

59 Management, in co-operation with employee representatives, should:

i provide opportunities for employees to discuss matters affecting their jobs with those to whom they are responsible;

ii ensure that managers are kept informed of the views of employees and of the problems which they may face in meeting management's objectives.

60 The Contracts of Employment Act, as amended in Schedule 2 of the Industrial Relations Act, entitles every employee, other than those in certain categories,[6] to be notified in writing within 13 weeks of starting a job, about:

i his main terms and conditions of employment;

ii his rights under Section 5 of the Industrial Relations Act in respect of trade union membership;

iii how he can seek redress for a grievance.

61 The written statement should be as comprehensive and easy to understand as possible. Where it refers the employee to another document, the Act requires that he must have reasonable opportunities of reading that document in the course of his employment or that it must be made reasonably accessible to him in some other way. He should be told clearly, in the written statement, where he can see the document.

[6] Contracts of Employment Act 1963, Section 4(8) and 6.

62 Apart from the statutory requirements, management should ensure that each employee is given information about:

   i the requirements of his job and to whom he is directly responsible;

  ii disciplinary rules and procedures and the type of circumstances which can lead to suspension or dismissal;

 iii trade union arrangements;

 iv opportunities for promotion and any training necessary to achieve it;

  v social or welfare facilities;

 vi fire prevention and safety and health rules;

vii any suggestion schemes.

63 Employee representatives and trade unions should:

  i ensure that they have the means to communicate effectively with those whom they represent;

 ii recognise that management has a responsibility for communicating directly with its employees.

64 Management, employee representatives and trade unions should co-operate in keeping employees informed of the conclusions reached through negotiation and consultation.

CONSULTATION

65 Consultation means jointly examining and discussing problems of concern to both management and employees. It involves seeking mutually acceptable solutions through a genuine exchange of views and information.

66 Consultation between management and employees or their representatives about operational and other day-to-day matters is necessary in all establishments, whatever their size. Establishments with more than 250 employees should have systematic arrangements for management and employee representatives to meet regularly.

67 Management should take the initiative in setting up and maintaining consultative arrangements best suited to the circumstances of the establishment, in co-operation with employee representatives and trade unions concerned. The arrangements should not be used to by-pass or discourage trade unions.

68 In setting up the consultative arrangements, management should ensure that:

  i the arrangements provide opportunities for employees to express their views on proposed changes which affect them and encourage discussion, at whatever level is most appropriate, of matters closely associated with the work situation;

ii employee representatives have all the information they require to enable them to participate effectively in discussions;

iii senior managers take an active part in consultation;

iv the arrangements include effective means of reporting back to employees.

69 Where committees are set up, management and employee representatives should agree on:

i the composition, objectives and functions of the committee and of any sectional or functional sub-committees;

ii the arrangements for the election or nomination of representatives;

iii the rules of procedure;

iv the range of subjects to be discussed.

70 Consultation and negotiation are closely related but distinct processes. Management and employee representatives should consider carefully how to link the two. It may often be advantageous for the same committee to cover both. Where there are separate bodies, systematic communication between those involved in the two processes is essential.

Collective Bargaining

71 Freely conducted collective bargaining is a joint activity which establishes a framework for relations between management and employees. It requires from both sides a reasonable and constructive approach in negotiation, with due regard to the general interests of the community, and a determination to abide by agreements which have been made.

72 Collective bargaining may take place at various levels, ranging from an industry or part of one to a group of employees within an establishment. Negotiations for the same group of employees may be conducted at different levels about different subjects.

73 Where negotiation takes place at more than one level, the matters to be bargained about at each level should be defined by agreement. The aim should be to assign to each level the matters which can be realistically settled at that level. Equally, whatever the level at which an agreement is reached, its terms should be capable of being applied effectively at the place of work.

74 Collective bargaining in an establishment or undertaking is conducted in relation to defined groups of employees which can appropriately be covered by one negotiating process. In the Industrial Relations Act and in the Code these are called "bargaining units".

75 Although bargaining unit is a new term, it describes what has long been established as part of the pattern of negotiation. Any negotiating arrangements need periodic review, but arrangements which are found to be working well should not be disturbed without good reason.

76 A bargaining unit should cover as wide a group of employees as practicable. Too many small units make it difficult to ensure that related groups of employees are treated consistently. The number of separate units can often be reduced by the formation of a joint negotiating panel representing a number of unions.

77 The interests of employees covered by a bargaining unit need not be identical, but there should be a substantial degree of common interest. In deciding the pattern of bargaining arrangements, the need to take into account the distinct interests of employees who form a minority group (including professional employees) should be balanced against the need to avoid unduly small bargaining units.

78 Factors which should be taken into account in defining a bargaining unit include:

   i the nature of the work;
  ii the training, experience and professional or other qualifications of the employees concerned;
 iii the extent to which they have interests in common;
 iv the general wishes of the employees concerned;
  v the organisation and location of the work;
 vi hours, working arrangements and payment systems;
 vii the matters to be bargained about;
viii the need to fit the bargaining unit into the pattern of union and management organisation;
 ix the need to avoid disruption of any existing bargaining arrangements which are working well;
  x whether separate bargaining arrangements are needed for particular categories of employees, such as supervisors or employees who represent management in negotiation.

79 When proposals are made for establishing or varying a bargaining unit, the first aim of management and unions should be to reach agreement on a voluntary basis. Where this proves impossible, either or both parties should consider:

  i referring the matter to the employers' association, where appropriate, and to a higher level within the trade union;
  ii seeking advice and conciliation from the Department of Employment;
  iii asking the Department of Employment to refer the matter to the Commission on Industrial Relations for examination and advice.

80 Failing a solution by any of these means, the employer, a registered trade union involved, or the Secretary of State may apply to the National Industrial Relations Court for a settlement under Sections 45–50 of the Industrial Relations Act.

81 In certain circumstances individual employees have a right under Sections 51–53 of the Industrial Relations Act to apply to the National Industrial Relations Court for their bargaining unit to be varied.

RECOGNITION OF TRADE UNIONS

82 A trade union may claim recognition for negotiating purposes either where management already has agreed bargaining arrangements with other unions or where no arrangements exist. In either case management should take into account:

  i the extent of support for the claim among the employees concerned, whether members of the union or not;
  ii the effect of granting recognition on any existing bargaining arrangements;
  iii whether or not recognition should be granted to the same union (or section of a union) in respect of supervisors and of the members of their work groups.

83 Management is entitled to know the number, but not the identities, of the employees covered by the proposed bargaining unit who are members of the union making the claim. Where the extent of support cannot be agreed, it should be determined by arrangements agreed between the parties, for example, a secret ballot.

84 Where a trade union has members in a category of employees for which no union has secured negotiating rights, management should consider receiving representations from an official of the union on behalf of any of those members about grievances or other matters which can be dealt with on an individual basis.

85 Responsibility for avoiding disputes between trade unions about recognition lies principally with the unions themselves and, in the case of affiliated unions, with the Trade Union Congress. Unions concerned should make full use of the available procedures.

86 Claims for recognition should, as far as possible, be settled voluntarily between the parties. If they cannot reach agreement the procedures set out in paragraphs 79–81 may be used.

AFTER RECOGNITION

87 Relations between management and trade unions which it recognises for negotiating purposes should be based on agreed procedures which provide a clear set of rules and a sound basis for resolving conflicts of interest.

88 Management should agree with recognised unions the provision of reasonable facilities to enable them to keep in touch with their members and to represent them effectively.

89 Management and recognised unions at the highest level should facilitate and encourage personal contact and discussion between managers and officials of the unions, including shop stewards. Contacts should not be left until trouble arises.

COLLECTIVE AGREEMENTS

90 Collective agreements deal with matters of procedure and matters of substance which are of joint concern to management and employees. A single agreement may contain provisions of both kinds or they may be dealt with in separate agreements. In either case, the agreement should be in writing and there should be agreed arrangements for checking that procedural provisions have not become out of date.

91 Procedural provisions should lay down the constitution of any joint negotiating body or specify the parties to the procedure. They should also cover:

 i the matters to be bargained about and the levels at which bargaining should take place;
 ii arrangements for negotiating terms and conditions of employment and the circumstances in which either party can give notice of their wish to re-negotiate them;
 iii facilities for trade union activities in the establishment and the appointment, status and functions of shop stewards;

   iv procedures for settling collective disputes and individual griev-
      ances and for dealing with disciplinary matters;
   v the constitution and scope of any consultative committees.

92   Substantive provisions settle terms and conditions of employment. They should indicate the period for which they are to apply,
and cover:

    i wages and salaries and, where appropriate, overtime rates,
      bonuses, piecework and other systems relating earnings to
      performance;
   ii hours of work, and, where appropriate, provisions for overtime,
      and shift working;
  iii holiday entitlement and pay.

93   Agreements may also cover such matters as:

    i techniques for determining levels of performance and job grad-
      ing, for example, work measurement and job evaluation;
   ii procedures for handling redundancy and temporary lay-offs;
  iii guaranteed pay, sick pay and pensions schemes;
   iv the deduction by management of trade union contributions from
      the pay of members.

94   There is advantage in agreeing at industry level as much as is
suitable for adoption over the industry as a whole, including:

    i terms and conditions of employment suitable for general
      application;
   ii general guide-lines for negotiating at a lower level matters which
      cannot be decided satisfactorily at industry level;
  iii a procedure for settling disputes, either for the industry as a
      whole or as a model for individual undertakings to adopt by
      agreement.

95   To maintain fair and stable pay structures, an agreement reached
at the level of the establishment or undertaking should define:

    i how and within what limits any negotiations at a lower level
      should be conducted;
   ii how it relates to any relevant industry-wide agreement.

DISCLOSURE OF INFORMATION

96   Collective bargaining can be conducted responsibly only if managements and unions have adequate information on the matters being negotiated.[7]

97 Management should aim to meet all reasonable requests from trade unions for information which is relevant to the negotiations in hand. In particular it should make available, in the most convenient form, the information which is supplied to shareholders or published in annual reports.

98 Management is not obliged to disclose certain kinds of information, including information which would be of advantage to a competitor. (See Industrial Relations Act, Section 158(1)).

Employee Representation at the Place of Work

99 Employees need representatives to put forward their collective views to management and to safeguard their interests in consultation and negotiation. It is also an advantage for management to deal with representatives who can speak for their fellow employees.

100 This function is widely carried out by employees who are accredited as union representatives to act on behalf of union members in the establishment where they themselves are employed. The title given to these representatives varies, but the most usual one is "shop steward". This is therefore used in the Code.

101 A shop steward has responsibilities both to trade union members in the establishment and to the union organisation outside it, in addition to his responsibilities as an employee. Most shop stewards spend only a part of their time in shop steward duties, but their role in the effective conduct of industrial relations at the place of work is always important.

102 Where there are shop stewards, trade unions should:

  i provide for their election or appointment;
  ii define the manner in which they can be removed from office;
  iii specify their powers and duties within the union.

[7] Section 56 of the Industrial Relations Act will require employers to disclose certain information about their undertakings to representatives of registered trade unions which they recognise for negotiating purposes. As we go to press, this section of the Act is not yet in operation. It will be brought into force, and this part of the Code amended to provide further guidance, when the results of the inquiry carried out by the Commission on Industrial Relations have been considered, and after consultation with interested organisations.

103 A shop steward's functions at the place of work cover:

  i trade union matters such as recruitment, maintaining membership and collecting contributions;

  ii industrial relations matters such as handling members' grievances, negotiation and consultation.

104 His role varies according to the industrial relations system in which he operates. Agreements at the level of the industry may lay down, or provide guidelines on, some of his functions. Others are best determined in the individual establishment. But all the functions of a shop steward should be clearly defined and those relating to industrial relations agreed between the parties.

105 A shop steward should observe all agreements to which his union is a party and should take all reasonable steps to ensure that those whom he represents also observe them.

APPOINTMENT AND QUALIFICATIONS

106 Trade unions and management should seek agreement on:

  i the number of shop stewards needed in the establishment, including senior stewards and deputies;

  ii the work groups for which each steward is responsible.

Both will depend on the size and organisation of the establishment and the number of union members employed.

107 Trade unions should decide on any conditions of eligibility for election and appointment such as a minimum age and length of service in the establishment. These matters may be the subject of consultation between management and unions.

108 To encourage union members to vote in elections of shop stewards, management should offer the trade unions facilities to conduct elections in the establishment and to publicise the dates and details.

109 Trade unions should notify management promptly in writing when shop stewards are appointed and when changes are made.

STATUS

110 Trade unions should:

  i give their shop stewards written credentials, setting out their powers and duties within the union, including any authority to call for industrial action;

ii seek agreement with management on the issue of joint written credentials setting out the relevant rights and obligations of the stewards and of management.

111 All credentials should state:

i the period of office of the shop steward;
ii the work group he represents.

CO-ORDINATION

112 In an establishment where there are a number of shop stewards of one trade union, they should consider electing a senior steward to co-ordinate their activities.

113 Where more than one union is recognised but each union has only a small number of members, the unions should seek to agree on the election of one steward to represent all their members in the establishment.

114 Where there are a number of senior shop stewards of different unions which negotiate jointly, the unions should seek to agree on the election of one of them to co-ordinate their activities in the establishment.

115 In each of these cases trade unions should seek agreement with management on the co-ordinating functions of the steward concerned.

FACILITIES

116 The facilities needed by shop stewards will depend on their functions. The nature and extent of these facilities should be agreed between trade unions and management. As a minimum, they should be given:

i time off from the job to the extent reasonably required for their industrial relations functions; permission should be sought from the appropriate manager and should not be unreasonably withheld;
ii maintenance of earnings while carrying out these functions.

117 Management should also make available other facilities appropriate to the circumstances. These may include:

i list of new employees;
ii accommodation for meetings with the employees whom they

191

represent, with other stewards and with full-time union officials;

iii access to a telephone and the provision of notice boards;

iv the use of office facilities where the volume of the steward's work justifies it.

TRAINING

118 Trade unions and management should:

i review the type of training most appropriate for the steward's needs and take all reasonable steps to ensure that stewards receive the training they require;

ii seek to agree on the arrangements for leave from the job to attend training courses, including compensation for loss of earnings;

iii accept joint responsibility for training in the use of arrangements for communication and consultation and for handling grievances.

119 Each union should ensure that its own shop stewards are adequately informed about its policies and organisation and about the agreements to which it is a party. Management should ensure that the stewards are adequately informed about its objectives and employment policies.

Grievance and Disputes Procedures

120 All employees have a right to seek redress for grievances relating to their employment. Each employee must be told how he can do so (see paragraph 60).

121 Management should establish, with employee representatives or trade unions concerned, arrangements under which individual employees can raise grievances and have them settled fairly and promptly. There should be a formal procedure, except in very small establishments where there is close personal contact between the employer and his employees.

122 Where trade unions are recognised, management should establish with them a procedure for settling collective disputes.

123 Individual grievances and collective disputes are often dealt with through the same procedure. Where there are separate procedures they should be linked so that an issue can, if necessary, pass from one to the other, since a grievance may develop into a dispute.

INDIVIDUAL GRIEVANCE PROCEDURES

124 The aim of the procedure should be to settle the grievance fairly and as near as possible to the point of origin. It should be simple and rapid in operation.

125 The procedure should be in writing and provide that:

i the grievance should normally be discussed first between the employee and his immediate superior;

ii the employee should be accompanied at the next stage of the discussion with management by his employee representative if he so wishes;

iii there should be a right of appeal.

COLLECTIVE DISPUTES PROCEDURES

126 Disputes are broadly of two kinds:

i dispute of right, which relate to the application or interpretation of existing agreements or contracts of employment;

ii disputes of interest, which relate to claims by employees or proposals by management about terms and conditions of employment.

127 A procedure for settling collective disputes should be in writing and should:

i state the level at which an issue should first be raised;

ii lay down time limits for each stage of the procedure, with provision for extension by agreement;

iii preclude a strike, lock-out, or other form of industrial action until all stages of the procedure have been completed and a failure to agree formally recorded.

128 The procedure should have the following stages:

i employee representatives should raise the issue in dispute with management at the level directly concerned;

ii failing settlement, it should be referred to a higher level within the establishment;

iii if still unsettled, it should be referred to further agreed stages, for example, to a stage of an industry-wide procedure, or to a higher level within the undertaking.

129 Independent conciliation and arbitration can be used to settle all types of dispute if the parties concerned agree that they should. Arbitration by the Industrial Arbitration Board or other independent arbitrators is particularly suitable for settling disputes of right, and its wider use for that purpose is desirable. Where it is used the parties should undertake to be bound by the award.

Disciplinary Procedures

130 Management should ensure that fair and effective arrangements exist for dealing with disciplinary matters. These should be agreed with employee representatives or trade unions concerned and should provide for full and speedy consideration by management of all the relevant facts. There should be a formal procedure except in very small establishments where there is close personal contact between the employer and his employees.

131 Management should make known to each employee:

   i its disciplinary rules and the agreed procedure;
  ii the type of circumstances which can lead to suspension or dismissal.

132 The procedure should be in writing and should:

    i specify who has the authority to take various forms of disciplinary action, and ensure that supervisors do not have the power to dismiss without reference to more senior management;
   ii give the employee the opportunity to state his case and the right to be accompanied by his employee representative;
  iii provide for a right of appeal, wherever practicable, to a level of management not previously involved;
  iv provide for independent arbitration if the parties to the procedure wish it.

133 Where there has been misconduct, the disciplinary action to be taken will depend on the circumstances, including the nature of the misconduct. But normally the procedure should operate as follows:

    i the first step should be an oral warning or, in the case of more serious misconduct, a written warning setting out the circumstances;
   ii no employee should be dismissed for a first breach of discipline except in the case of gross misconduct;
  iii action on any further misconduct, for example, final warning, suspension without pay or dismissal, should be recorded in writing;
  iv details of any disciplinary action should be given in writing to the employee and, if he so wishes, to his employee representative;
   v no disciplinary action should be taken against a shop steward until the circumstances of the case have been discussed with a full-time official of the union concerned.

Index to Appendix 2

The City Code on Take-overs and Mergers*

Introduction

The City Code on Take-overs and Mergers first appeared in its present form in March 1968. It was prepared and issued by the City Working Party, a body originally set up in 1959 and reconvened by the Governor of the Bank of England in 1967 for that purpose. On it are now represented the Issuing Houses Association, the Accepting Houses Committee, The Association of Investment Trust Companies, the British Insurance Association, The Committee of London Clearing Bankers, the Confederation of British Industry, the National Association of Pension Funds and The Stock Exchange, London. This new edition incorporates a limited number of revisions and additions made by the City Working Party in the light of experience gained in its operation since that date. Certain of these modifications are the result of suggestions made by the Panel on Take-overs and Mergers established in September 1967 on the proposal of the Governor to supervise the operation of the Code. The Code, nevertheless, both as to its principles and rules, remains substantially in the form in which it was originally issued.

It is generally accepted that the choice before the City in the conduct of Take-overs and Mergers is either a system of voluntary self-discipline based on the Code and administered by the City's own representatives or regulation by law enforced by officials appointed by Government. The City Working Party are firmly of the opinion that the voluntary system is more practicable and more effective.

The provisions of the Code fall into two categories. On the one hand, the Code enunciates general principles of conduct to be observed in bid situations. On the other, it lays down certain rules, some of which are precise, and others no more than examples of the application of principles. The general principles and these latter rules are of their very nature imprecise.

The City Working Party point out that some of these general principles of the Code, based upon a concept of equity between one shareholder and another, whilst readily understandable in the City may not easily lend themselves to legislation. The City Working

---

* Since going to press, the code has been revised in parts. Details available from The Issuing Houses Association, 20 Fenchurch Street, London EC3M 3DB.

Party believe that a code administered by the Panel would possess a degree of flexibility and speed in action which would be difficult to achieve in any more legalistic procedures imposed by statute. They consider also that the reconstituted Panel representative of the City and with its permanent secretariat would be capable of more useful functions before or during the course of a transaction than would be possible if a statutory body were charged with the responsibility of enforcing rigid regulations which would have in the end to be interpreted by the Courts.

Although the Code was drafted with quoted public companies particularly in view, the spirit of the Rules and, except where inappropriate, the letter, should be observed where unquoted public companies are concerned. The Rules and their spirit may also be relevant to transactions in the shares of private companies.

The Panel on Take-over and Mergers

The Panel referred to in the Introduction is now situated at The Stock Exchange, and communications intended for it should be addressed to The Secretary of the Panel on Take-overs and Mergers, P.O. Box No. 226, The Stock Exchange Building, London, E.C.2.

Attention is drawn to the fact that, in addition to its function as a supervising body in regard to all take-over and merger transactions, the Panel will be available for consultation at any stage before a formal offer is made to a company as well as during the course of a transaction. **Accordingly, in any case of doubt the Panel should be consulted.**

Since, however, it is a matter for a shareholder to decide for himself when and how to dispose of his shares, the Panel cannot be expected to pronounce on the merits or demerits of any individual offer.

Definitions

The Panel means the Panel on Take-overs and Mergers set up at the request of the Bank of England.

Associate. It is not thought practicable to define an 'associate' in precise terms which would cover all the different relationships which may exist in a take-over or merger transaction.

The term 'associate' is intended to cover all parties (whether or not acting in concert with the offeror or offeree company or with one another) who directly or indirectly own or deal in the shares of the offeror or offeree company in a bid situation and who have (in addition to their normal interest as shareholders) an interest or potential interest, whether commercial, financial or personal, in the outcome of the offer.

Without prejudice to the generality of the foregoing the term 'associate' may, in the circumstances of the case, include subsidiary, fellow-subsidiary and parent companies of either the offeror or offeree company; bankers or stockbrokers who normally act for any of the companies concerned and the financial advisers of any of such companies; the Directors (together with their close relatives and related trusts) of the offeror or offeree company or of an 'associate' company; the pension funds of such companies or any pension fund, investment company or unit trust which is accustomed to act on the instructions of any company or individual included in the foregoing description of 'associate'; and any company or individual directly or indirectly holding or acquiring during the course of the bid an interest which (together with any holding it had at the outset of the bid) represents 10 per cent. or more of the equity capital of the offeror or offered company.

Offer. Offer includes, wherever appropriate, take-over and merger transactions howsoever effected.

Offeror Company. Offeror company includes companies incorporated inside or outside the United Kingdom and individuals wherever resident.

Offer Period. Offer period means the period from the date when an offer is announced until the offer is declared or becomes unconditional or lapses.

Unconditional. References to an offer becoming or being declared unconditional include cases in which the offer has as a result of the receipt of sufficient acceptances been announced to have become or been declared unconditional subject only to one or more other previously stated conditions including for example the creation of additional capital, the grant of quotation etc. etc., being fulfilled.

General Principles

1.   It is considered to be impracticable to devise rules in such detail as to cover all the various circumstances which arise in take-over or merger transactions. **Accordingly, persons engaged in such transactions should be aware that the spirit as well as the precise wording of these general principles and of the ensuing rules must be observed.**

2.   While the Boards of an offeror company and of an offeree company and their respective advisers and associates have a primary duty to act in the best interests of their respective shareholders, they must accept that there are limitations in connection with take-over and merger transactions on the manner in which the pursuit of those interests can be carried out. Inevitably therefore these principles and the ensuing Rules will impinge on the freedom of action of Boards and persons involved in such transactions.

3. Shareholders shall have in their possession sufficient evidence, facts and opinions upon which an adequate judgement and decision can be reached, and shall have sufficient time to make an assessment and decision. No relevant information shall be withheld from them.

4. At no time after a *bona fide* offer has been communicated to the Board of an offeree company or after it has reasonably come within the contemplation of the Board of an offeree company that a *bona fide* offer is likely to be forthcoming, shall any action be taken by the Board of the offeree company in relation to the affairs of the company, without the approval in general meeting of the shareholders of the offeree company, which could effectively result in any *bona fide* offer being frustrated or in the shareholders of the offeree company being denied an opportunity to decide on its merits.

5. It must be the object of all parties to a take-over or merger transaction to use every endeavour to prevent the creation of a false market in the shares of an offeror or offeree company.

6. A Board which receives an offer or is approached with a view to an offer being made should normally in the interests of its shareholders seek competent outside advice.

7. Rights of control must be exercised in good faith and the oppression of a minority is wholly unacceptable.

8. All shareholders of the same class of an offeree company shall be treated similarly by an offeror company.

9. If, after a bid is reasonably in contemplation, an offer has been made to one or more shareholders of an offeree company, any subsequent general offer made by or on behalf of the same offeror or his associate to the shareholders of the same class shall not be on less favourable terms.

10. During the course of a take-over or merger transaction, or when such is in contemplation, neither the offeror company, the offeree company nor any of their respective advisers shall furnish information to some shareholders which is not made available to all shareholders. This principle shall not apply to the furnishing of information in confidence by an offeree company to a *bona fide* potential offeror company or *vice versa*, nor to the issue of circulars by members of a Stock Exchange to their own investment clients provided such issue shall previously have been approved by the Panel.

11. Directors of an offeror or an offeree company shall always, in advising their shareholders, act only in their capacity as Directors

and not have regard to their personal or family shareholdings or their personal relationship with the companies. It is the shareholders' interests taken as a whole which should be considered, together with those of employees and creditors.

12.   Any document or advertisement addressed to shareholders containing information, opinions or recommendations from the Board of an offeror or offeree company or its respective advisers shall be treated with the same standards of care as if it were a prospectus within the meaning of the Companies Act 1948. Especial care shall be taken over profit forecasts.

Rules

THE APPROACH

1.   The offer should be put forward in the first instance to the Board of the offeree company or to its advisers.

2.   If the offer or an approach with a view to an offer being made is not made by a principal, the identity of the principal must be disclosed at the outset.

3.   A Board so approached is entitled to be satisfied that the offeror company is or will be in a position to implement the offer in full.

4.   Where an offer is being made by a parent company for minority shareholdings of a subsidiary, or in any other case where the offer is not completely at arm's length, it is essential that competent outside advice be obtained in order to ensure, and to satisfy the offerees, that their interests are fully protected.

EARLY STAGES

5.   When any firm intention to make an offer is notified to a Board from a serious source (irrespective of whether the Board views the offer favourably or otherwise), shareholders must be informed without delay by Press notice. The Press notice should normally be followed as soon as possible by a circular.

Where there have been approaches which may or may not lead to an offer, the duty of a Board in relation to shareholders is less clearly defined. There are obvious dangers in announcing prematurely an approach which may not lead to an offer. By way of guidance it can be said that an announcement of the facts should be made forthwith as soon as two companies are agreed on the basic terms of an offer and are reasonably confident of a successful outcome of the negotiations.

In any situation which might lead to an offer being made, whether welcome or not, a close watch should be kept on the share market; in the event of any untoward movement in share prices an immediate announcement, accompanied by such comment as may be appropriate, should be made.

6. Joint statements are desirable whenever possible, provided that agreement thereon does not lead to undue delay. The obligation to make announcements lies no less with the potential offeror company than with the offeree company.

7. The vital importance of absolute secrecy before an announcement must be emphasised.

8. When an offer is announced, the identity of the offeror company must be disclosed and that company must disclose any existing holding in the offeree company which it owns or over which it has control *or which is owned or controlled by any person or company acting in concert with the offeror company in relation to the offer.*

BOARD CONSIDERATION OF AN OFFER

9. Directors must always have in mind that they should act in the interests of the shareholders taken as a whole. Shareholders in companies which are effectively controlled by their Directors have to accept that in respect of any offer the attitude of their Board is decisive. Exceptionally, there may be good reasons for such a Board preferring a lower offer or rejecting an offer. Nevertheless, where a Board recommends acceptance of the lower of two offers, or, being a controlling Board, accepts such lower offer or rejects an offer, thus in effect frequently forcing the minority shareholders to act similarly, it must very carefully examine its motive for so doing and be prepared to justify its good faith in the interests of the shareholders as a whole.

10. Directors whose shareholdings, together with those of their families and trusts, effectively control a company, or shareholders in that position who are represented on the Board of a company, and who contemplate transferring control, should not, other than in special circumstances, do so unless the buyer undertakes to extend within a reasonable period of time a comparable offer to the holders of the remaining equity share capital, whether such capital carries voting rights or not. In such special circumstances the Panel must be consulted in advance and its consent obtained.

11. Any information including particulars of shareholders given to a preferred suitor should on request be furnished equally and as

promptly to a less welcome but *bona fide* potential offeror. In case of difficulty the Panel must be consulted and its consent obtained.

12.   It is essential that after an offer has been announced the offer document and a letter setting out the views of the Board of the offeree company should be circulated as soon as practicable.

If any offeror who has announced his intention to make an offer does not proceed with the formal offer within a reasonable time, he must be prepared to justify the circumstances of the case to the Panel.

FORMAL OFFERS, DOCUMENTS SUPPORTING AN OFFER OR RECOMMENDING THE ACCEPTANCE OR REJECTION OF AN OFFER

13.   Any document or advertisement addressed to shareholders under these headings must be treated with the same standards of care with regard to the statements made therein as if it were a prospectus within the meaning of the Companies Act 1948. This applies whether the document or advertisement is issued by the company direct or by an adviser on its behalf. Each document sent to shareholders of the offeree company must state that the Board of the offeror company and/or, where appropriate, of the offeree company (or a Committee of the Board duly authorised by the Board so to act) have considered all statements of fact and opinion contained therein and accept, individually and collectively, responsibility therefor and consider that no material factors or considerations have been omitted.

A copy of the authority from the Board of the company (or the Committee, as the case may be) for the issue of such document must be lodged with the Panel Secretariat.

14.   Shareholders must be put into possession of all the facts necessary for the formation of an informed judgement as to the merits or demerits of an offer. Such facts must be accurately and fairly presented and be available to the shareholder early enough to enable him to make a decision in good time. The obligation of the offeror company in these respects towards the shareholders of the offeree company is no less than its obligation towards its own shareholders.

15.   Without in any way detracting from the imperative necessity of maintaining the highest standards of accuracy and fair presentation in all communications to shareholders in a take-over or merger transaction, attention is particularly drawn in this connection to profit forecasts and asset valuations.

Notwithstanding the obvious hazard attached to the forecasting of profits, profit forecasts must be compiled with the greatest possible care by the Directors whose sole responsibility they are.

When profit forecasts appear in any document addressed to shareholders in connection with an offer, the assumptions, including the commercial assumptions, upon which the Directors have based their profit forecasts, must be stated in the document.

The accounting bases and calculations for the forecasts must be examined and reported on by the auditors or consultant accountants. Any Merchant Bank or other adviser mentioned in the document must also report on the forecasts. The accountants' report and, if there is an adviser, his report, must be contained in such document and be accompanied by a statement that the accountants and, where relevant, the adviser, have given and not withdrawn their consent to publication.

Wherever profit forecasts appear in relation to a period in which trading has already commenced, the latest unaudited profit figures which are available in respect of the expired portion of that trading period together with comparable figures for the preceding year must be stated. Alternatively, if no figures are available, that fact must be stated.

When revaluations of assets are given in connection with an offer the Board should be supported by the opinion of independent professional experts and the basis of valuation clearly stated.

16. The offer document must state the shareholdings of the offeror company in the offeree company together with the total of the shareholdings in the offeree company in which Directors of the offeror company are interested and the shareholdings in the offeree company which any person or company acting in concert with the offeror company in relation to the offer owns or controls (with names of such persons acting in concert). The document of the offeree company advising its shareholders on an offer (whether recommending acceptance or rejection of the offer) must (a) detail the shareholdings of (i) the Directors of the offeree company in the offeree company and the offeror company and (ii) the offeree company in the offeror company and (b) inform shareholders whether the Directors of the offeree company intend, in respect of their own beneficial shareholdings, to accept or reject the offer. If any such shareholdings referred to in this Rule have been purchased during the period commencing one year prior to the announcement of the offer and ending with the latest practicable date prior to the posting of the offer document, the details, including dates and costs, must be stated. If no such purchases have been made, this fact must be stated.

17. Where the offer is for cash or includes an element of cash, the offer document must include confirmation by the adviser or by another appropriate independent party that resources are available to the offeror company sufficient to satisfy full acceptance of the offer.

18. Documents sent to shareholders of the offeree company recommending or rejecting offers must contain particulars of all service contracts in force for Directors with the offeree company or any of its subsidiaries which have more than twelve months to run and, if entered into within six months of the date of the document, the dates of the contracts and particulars of any immediately preceding contracts. Offer documents on behalf of the offeror company should state whether its Directors' emoluments will be affected by the acquisition of the offeree company.

19. In order to facilitate the work of the Panel, copies of all public announcements made and all documents bearing on a take-over or merger transaction must be lodged with the Panel Secretariat at the same time as they are made or despatched.

MECHANICS OF THE FORMAL OFFER

20. No offer for the whole of the equity share capital of a company (or for a proportion of such equity capital which, if accepted in full, would result in the offeror company having voting control of the equity share capital of the offeree company) shall be made unless it is a condition of such offer that the offer will not become or be declared unconditional unless the offeror company has acquired or agreed to acquire (either pursuant to the offer or by shares acquired or agreed to be acquired before or during the offer) by the close of the offer shares carrying over 50 per cent of the voting rights attributable to the equity share capital. Accordingly no such offer shall become or be declared unconditional unless the offeror company has acquired or agreed to acquire more than the said 50 per cent.

21. An offer must initially be open for at least twenty-one days after the posting of the offer and, if revised, it must be kept open for at least eight days from the date of posting written notification of the revision to shareholders: an acceptor shall be entitled to withdraw his acceptance in any case after the expiry of twenty-one days from the first closing date of the initial offer, if the offer has not by such expiry become or been declared unconditional; such entitlement to withdraw shall be exercisable until such time as the offer becomes or is declared unconditional.

No offer (whether revised or not) shall be capable of becoming or being declared unconditional after the expiration of 60 days from the date the offer is initially posted, nor of being kept open after the expiry of such period unless it has previously become or been declared unconditional.

Other than in the circumstances that a competing offer has been declared or has become unconditional, a formal offer may not be withdrawn during its currency except with the permission of the Panel. An offer which is allowed to lapse because of the non-fulfilment of a condition is not to be treated as withdrawn for the purpose of this Rule.

22. After an offer has become or is declared unconditional, the offer must remain open for acceptance for not less than fourteen days, except in the event that the offer becomes or is declared unconditional on an expiry date and the offeror company has given at least ten days' notice in writing to the shareholders of the offeree company that the offer will not be open for acceptance beyond that date.

If in accordance with the provisions of Rule 24 an unconditional declaration becomes void and is subsequently reinstated, the period of fourteen days above referred to will run from the date of the second declaration.

23. An offeror company which has extended an offer must announce the fact not later than 9.30 a.m. on the working day next following the day on which the offer would otherwise have expired.

24. By 9.30 a.m. at the latest on the working day next following the expiry of the first offer, or of any extended or revised offer, whichever may be the later (the relevant day), the offeror company shall announce and simultaneously inform the Stock Exchange:

(a) either that the offer has become or is declared unconditional or that the offer has been allowed to lapse, and in the first event,
(b) the total number of shares (as nearly as practicable) (i) for which acceptances of the offer have been received (ii) held before the offer period and (iii) acquired or agreed to be acquired during the offer period.

If the offeror company is unable within the above time limit to comply with any of these requirements, the Stock Exchange will consider the suspension of dealings in the offeree company's shares and, where appropriate, in the offeror company's shares until the relevant information is given. If the offeror company, having declared an offer unconditional, fails by 3.30 p.m. on the relevant day to comply with any of the requirements of sub-para (b) of this Rule, its unconditional declaration shall be void. Immediately thereafter and until the offer is again declared unconditional any acceptor shall be entitled to withdraw his acceptance. Subject to the provisions of the second paragraph of Rule 21, the offeror company may again declare the offer unconditional after it has satisfied the requirements of sub-para (*b*) of this Rule but not before the expiry of eight days after the relevant day.

25. The obligations of the offeror company and the rights of the offeree company shareholders under Rules 20–24 must be specifically incorporated in the offer document.

26. Generally speaking bids for less than 100 per cent of the equity capital of an offeree company not already owned by the offeror company or any of its subsidiaries are undesirable. If there are circumstances in which a general offer for less than 100 per cent is in the opinion of the offeror company justified, it must be made to all shareholders of the class and arrangements must be made for those shareholders who wish to do so to accept in full for the relevant percentage of their holdings. Other than in special circumstances (in which case the consent of the Panel must be obtained) no partial bid may be made to which Rule 20 would not apply. A partial bid to which Rule 20 is not applicable may not be declared unconditional unless acceptances are received for the number of shares bid for.

It is recognised that there may be very exceptional circumstances where in the interests of all the shareholders a deal might be made with a significant minority without a similar offer being made to the other shareholders. In such circumstances the Panel must be consulted in advance and its consent obtained.

27. Where an offer is made for more than one class of share, separate offers must be made for each class and the offeror company should state that it will resort to compulsory acquisition powers under Section 209 of the Companies Act 1948, only in respect of each class separately.

28. Where an offer is made for equity capital and there are convertible securities outstanding, arrangements must be made to offer to the holders of such securities such amendment of the conversion terms or other appropriate arrangements as to ensure that their interests are not prejudiced. Where options or subscription rights are outstanding this Rule also applies *mutatis mutandis*.

DEALINGS

29. Save in so far as appears from this Code, it is considered

undesirable to fetter the market. Accordingly, all parties to a take-over or merger transaction (other than to a partial bid) and their associates are free to deal at arm's length subject to daily disclosure to The Stock Exchange, the Panel and the Press (not later than 12 noon on the dealing day following the date of the relative trans-action) of the total of all shares of any offeror company or the offeree company acquired or sold by them or their respective associates for their own account on any day during the offer period in the market or otherwise and at what average price.

In addition all purchases and sales of shares of any offeror or the offeree company made by associates for account of investment clients who are not themselves associates must be similarly reported to The Stock Exchange and to the Panel, but need not be disclosed to the Press.

In the case of a partial bid the offeror company and its associates may not deal in shares of the offeree company during the offer period for their own account, nor in the case of a partial bid to which Rule 20 does not apply may the offeror company or its associates, unless the Panel specifically so agrees, purchase shares of the offeree company for their own account during a period of twelve months beginning on the last day of the offer period.

29A.   If (a) the total of the shares of any class under offer in the offeree company purchased for cash either through the market or otherwise by the offeror and any person or company acting in concert with the offeror during the offer period and within one year prior to its commence-ment exceeds 15 per cent of that class:
or
(b) in the view of the Panel there are exceptional circum-stances which render such a course necessary in order to give effect to General Principle 8;

then, except with the specific approval of the Panel in cases falling under (a) above, the offer for that class shall be in cash or accom-panied by a cash alternative at not less than the highest cash price (excluding stamp duty and commission) paid for shares of that class acquired during the offer period and within one year prior to its commencement.

If the offeror considers that the 'highest cash price' (as defined above) should not apply to a particular case (if, for instance, it considers that there has been a general change in market prices since the relevant purchase or facts have been published causing a change in the market value of the securities of the offeree company) the offeror should consult the Panel which will have discretion to agree an adjusted price.

In any situation where the provisions of this Rule apply no provisions of Rule 31 shall be applicable.

30. No dealings of any kind (including option business) in the shares of the offeror and offeree companies by any person who is privy to the preliminary take-over or merger discussions or to an intention to make an offer may take place between the time (a) when the initial approach is made or intimated or (b) when there is reason to suppose that an approach or an offer will be made and the announcement of the approach or offer or of the termination of the discussions as the case may be.

31. If the offeror company alone or in association with others purchases shares in the market or otherwise during the offer period at above the offer price (being, in the event of the terms of an original offer being revised, the final bid price under the revised terms of an offer) then it shall offer an increased price to all acceptors, such price being not less than the weighted average price (excluding stamp duty and commission) of the shares so acquired during the offer period. If the offer involves a further issue of already quoted securities, the value of such securities shall normally be calculated for the purpose of ascertaining what increased price shall be paid (but not for the purpose of establishing whether any purchase was made at a price above the offer price) by reference to the average of the mean of the daily quotation (as stated in the Stock Exchange official list) of the securities during the offer period. If the offeror company considers that the terms of the previous sentence should not apply to an offer (if, for instance, it considers there has been a general change in market prices during the offer period or facts have been published causing a change in the market value of the securities of the offeror company) the offeror company should consult the Panel. If the offer involves the issue of securities which are not already quoted the value shall be based on a reasonable estimate of what the opening price might be.

32. Since arrangements to deal, purchases and sales with special conditions attached are not capable in every circumstance of being extended to all shareholders, such arrangements to deal, purchases and sales whether during, or in anticipation of, a bid must not be made.

33. Since dealings in the market or otherwise by an associate of an offeror or offeree company may result in a *bona fide* offer being frustrated or may affect the outcome of a bid, such associate is

advised to consult the Panel in advance and where he has not done so must be prepared to satisfy the Panel that his action was not prejudicial to the interests of shareholders generally of the offeror or the offeree company as the case may be.

CHANGES IN THE SITUATION OF A COMPANY DURING A BID

34. During the course of an offer, or even before the date of the offer if the Board of the offeree company has reason to believe that a *bona fide* offer is imminent, the Board must not, except in pursuance of a contract entered into earlier, without the approval of the shareholders in general meeting, issue any authorised but unissued shares, or issue or grant options in respect of any unissued shares, create or issue or permit the creation or issue of any securities carrying rights of conversion into or subscription for shares of the company, or sell, dispose of or acquire or agree to sell, dispose of or acquire assets of material amount or enter into contracts otherwise than in the ordinary course of business. Where it is felt that an obligation or other special circumstance exists, although a formal contract has not been entered into, the Panel must be consulted and its consent obtained.

REGISTRATION OF TRANSFERS

35. The Board and officials of an offeree company should take action to ensure during a take-over or merger transaction the prompt registration of transfers so that shareholders can freely exercise their voting and other rights. Provisions in Articles of Association which lay down a qualifying period after registration during which the registered holder cannot exercise his vote are highly undesirable.

Panel on Take-overs and Mergers

28th April, 1969.

POLICY STATEMENT

The Panel on Take-overs and Mergers has reached understandings with various City bodies, with the Bank of England and with the Board of Trade, as a consequence of which it is now able to give an indication of its future policy with regard to the administration of the City Code on Take-overs and Mergers.

It remains the belief of the City bodies who have framed the Code (and who are represented on the Panel) that the conduct of the City in take-over matters can best be governed by voluntary principles rather than regulated by statute. They have nevertheless recognised the need to place beyond doubt their determination that the voluntary system should both function effectively and command the respect of all those concerned with it. They have, therefore, authorised the Panel to draw attention to the means which are available to it to enforce this respect.

The Director-General or his Deputy are available at all times to give rulings on points of interpretation of the Code. They will endeavour to give these rulings as promptly as is necessary to the free functioning of the take-over and merger business. Companies and advisers are invited to make full use of this service.

In the event of disagreement, applicants may appeal to the Panel, whose decision will be final. If there is a breach of the Code, the Panel will have recourse to private or to public censure or, in a more flagrant case, to further action designed to deprive the offender temporarily or permanently of his ability to practise in the field of take-overs and mergers. No finding of a breach of the Code nor any censure or further action will take place without the alleged offender having had the opportunity of a hearing and the right of an appeal to a special Appeal Committee of the Panel.

In order the better to implement the Code the Council of The Stock Exchange will propose such amendments of their Rules and Regulations as are necessary to provide that the findings of the Panel or the Appeal Committee, as the case may be, will be accepted by the Council of The Stock Exchange as proof that the Code has been broken. It will be for the Council then to consider the appropriate measures to be taken in accordance with its disciplinary Rules which include the power to censure, suspend or expel a member. Similar arrangements have been agreed with the Federated Stock Exchanges. An expelled member of a Federated Stock Exchange is, as such, precluded from carrying on his business.

Similarly the Executive Committee of the Issuing Houses Association will propose amendments to the Association's Rules agreeing on behalf of their members to accept the jurisdiction of the Panel and empowering them to suspend or expel a member. Whilst the suspension and still more the expulsion of a member of the Issuing Houses Association would involve public reprobation of a grave kind it would not, however, in law prevent the Issuing House involved from continuing in business.

In any case where it appeared that a breach involving an Exempted or a Licensed Dealer was of such a nature that public reprobation might not be an adequate sanction, the Panel would report the matter to the Board of Trade inviting them to take the report into consideration with a view to the possibility of action under the

Prevention of Fraud (Investments) Act 1958. Under this Act, the Board may revoke the exemption of an Exempted Dealer or the licence of a Licensed Dealer, in the latter case subject to an appeal procedure. Such revocation would have the effect that the person concerned would no longer be permitted (subject to the exceptions stated in the Act) to carry on the business of a dealer in securities or to circulate any offer to buy or sell securities. The Panel has been assured by the Board of Trade that they will take into prompt consideration the facts relevant to the exercise of their powers and disclosed in any such report by the Panel.

During the currency of a take-over bid the Panel may request the Council of The Stock Exchange to suspend quotation of any security. It is the Panel's policy to make such a request primarily where it is in the Panel's view necessary to prevent dealings in securities during a bid situation in the absence of adequate information or clarification of some position or state of affairs. The Panel may, however, also request the Council to refuse quotation for new securities to be issued in connection with an acquisition, where a breach of the Code has been committed or where other circumstances exist which make it necessary, in the Panel's opinion, that an offer should not become unconditional.

In the event of a take-over involving Exchange Control consent the Panel will keep in close consultation with the Bank of England during the currency of such offer in order that the Bank of England may satisfy itself that the conditions under which such consent is granted are properly observed.

The Panel has had discussions with the chairmen of the Association of Stock and Share Dealers, the Association of Canadian Investment Dealers and Members of the Toronto and Montreal Stock Exchanges in Great Britain and the Association of New York Stock Exchange Member Firms having Representation in the United Kingdom, all Recognised Associations of Dealers in Securities in the terms of the Prevention of Fraud (Investments) Act 1958. The chairmen have agreed to propose amendments to their statutes corresponding to those being proposed by the Council of The Stock Exchange.

As regards persons who propose to carry out take-over transactions under S.14 of Prevention of Fraud (Investments) Act 1958 (sub-section (2) of which empowers the Board of Trade to permit the distribution of offer documents to shareholders) the Board of Trade have agreed to consult the Panel in future about the exercise of their powers under the sub-section in any case where it appears that the interests of the Panel might be involved.

The Board of Trade have informed the Panel that they are considering amendment of the Licensed Dealers (Conduct of Business)

Rules in the light of the new arrangements established by the Panel and the revised Code.

The Panel has further had discussions with the Accepting Houses Committee, the Association of Investment Trust Companies, the British Insurance Association, the Committee of London Clearing Bankers and the National Association of Pension Funds, all of which bodies are sponsors of the Code and are represented on the Panel, and also with the Chairman of the Association of Unit Trust Managers. The chairmen or other representatives of these bodies with whom discussions took place all expressed their support for the Code and the Panel and agreed to take appropriate steps to engage the support of their membership.

In the event of the Panel taking or requesting disciplinary action as outlined above, the firm or person concerned will have the alternative of accepting the finding of the Panel or of appealing to a new Appeal Committee. This Appeal Committee will be presided over by Lord Pearce, who has agreed to accept the appointment, and will have three further members of the Panel (but not persons who will have sat at the first hearing) one of them representing the City body (if any) to which the alleged offender belongs. In the event of an appeal being made, publication of the Panel's findings will be delayed until after appeal proceedings have been concluded.

Panel memoranda of interpretation and practice

PRACTICE NOTE NO. 1

PRIVATE COMPANIES AND UNQUOTED PUBLIC COMPANIES

The Introduction to the City Code states (Paragraph 5):

> 'Although the Code was drafted with quoted public companies particularly in view, the spirit of the Rules and, except where inappropriate, the letter, should be observed where unquoted public companies are concerned. The Rules and their spirit may also be relevant to transactions in the shares of private companies.'

This Note sets out the Panel's current views on the application of this paragraph in take-over and merger transactions.

1.   A company is considered for the purpose of this Note as being a private company if it complies with S.28 Companies Act, 1948, that is to say, it restricts the right to transfer its shares, limits the number of its members to 50 (excluding employees) and prohibits any invitation to the public to subscribe for any of its shares or debentures. But in the rare cases of private companies which have

a quotation for any of their issued securities the Code applies to them as if they were public companies, and for the purpose of this Note they are treated as if they were public companies.

2. For the purposes of the Code, public companies having no quotation are treated in the same way as those having a quotation. References in Rule 24 of the Code to information to be given to and action to be taken by the Stock Exchange should be disregarded where these are inappropriate.

3. The Panel would not normally expect to be informed, or to have documents submitted, in the case of a merger or take-over transaction between two private companies. In such cases the parties are enjoined to have regard to such provisions of the Code as may be applicable to the transaction. The Panel's advice is available on request.

4. Where the offeror is a public company (quoted or unquoted) and the offeree a private company, the offeror is expected to conduct the operation in accordance with the General Principles of the Code. The Panel, however, would not normally require to be informed of such transactions or to have documents submitted; an exception would be where, for instance, the relative sizes of the two companies and other circumstances are such that the transaction effectively constitutes a reverse take-over and where a change in effective control of the offeror would result. Dealings in the shares of the public company during the offer period should, however, be disclosed in all cases in accordance with Rule 29.

5. Where the offeror is a private company and the offeree is a public company the Code applies to the offeror in the same way as if it were a public company and also applies to the offeree.

6. The foregoing provisions apply whether the transaction involves all or part only of the capital of the company concerned.

This Note should be read in conjunction with the particular section of the Code to which it refers. It is intended to serve as a guide only and is subject to amendment in the light of experience. If this Note in itself or in conjunction with the Code gives rises to difficulties, the Panel should be consulted. The Panel welcomes comment from interested parties and representations for clarifications or changes to this Note to take account of particular situations not envisaged when it was drafted.

PRACTICE NOTE NO. 2

DIRECTORS' EMOLUMENTS AND PARTICULARS OF SERVICE
CONTRACTS

Rule 18 of the Code states:

'Documents sent to shareholders of the offeree company recommending or rejecting offers must contain particulars of all service
contracts in force for Directors with the offeree company or any
of its subsidiaries which have more than twelve months to run and,
if entered into within six months of the date of the document, the
dates of the contracts and particulars of any immediately preceding
contracts. Offer documents on behalf of the offeror company
should state whether its Directors' emoluments will be affected by
the acquisition of the offeree company.'

This Rule is one where there is frequently recourse to the Panel for
interpretation.

The following sets out the Panel's current views on how this Rule
should be complied with in offer documents:

1. *Directors of an offeree company—particulars of service contracts*
   The relevant document should contain either:

   (i) a statement that there are no service contracts in force for
   any Director of the offeree company with the company or
   any of its subsidiaries with more than 12 months to run,
   which cannot, within the next 12 months, be terminated by
   the company, without payment of compensation, or
   (ii) particulars of any such service contract, that is to say:
      (*a*) the name of the Director under contract;
      (*b*) the expiry date of the contract;
      (*c*) the amount of fixed remuneration payable under the
      contract (irrespective of whether received as a Director or
      for management, but excluding arrangements for company
      payments in respect of a pension or similar scheme); and
      (*d*) the amount of any variable remuneration payable under
      the contract (e.g. commission on profits) with details of the
      formula for calculating such remuneration.
   Where there is more than one contract, a statement of the
   aggregate remuneration payable thereunder is normally
   regarded as fulfilling the requirements under (*c*) and (*d*)
   above, except to the extent that this method would conceal
   material anomalies which ought to be disclosed (e.g.
   because one Director is remunerated at a very much higher
   rate than the others). It is not regarded as sufficient to

refer to the latest annual accounts, indicating that information regarding service contracts may be found there, or to state that the contracts are open for inspection at a specified place.

(iii) A statement as to whether or not there have been any changes in service contracts, or any new contracts granted, during the preceding six months; if so, the same particulars as described above must be given in respect of the earlier contracts (if any) which have been amended or replaced as well as the current contracts, and particulars of remuneration payable under both the earlier and the current contracts must relate to each individual separately.

2. *Directors of an offeror company—Directors' emoluments*
Irrespective of whether the offer is for cash or for paper, the relevant document should contain a statement (if appropriate, a negative statement) indicating whether and in what manner the emoluments of the Directors of the offeror company will be affected by the acquisition of the offeree company, or any other associated relevant transaction. Such information should include any alterations to fixed amounts receivable or the effect of any factor governing commissions or other variable amounts receivable. Grouping or aggregating the effect of the transaction on the emoluments of several or all the Directors will normally be acceptable.

3. *Subsidiary documents*
The particulars described in paragraph 2 above should be contained in the offer document. Those described in paragraph 1 should be contained in the first major circular issued by the offeree company in connection with the offer (which may be the offer document when it contains a letter of recommendation). Documents subsequently sent to shareholders of the offeree company by either party should contain details of any changes in the relevant particulars since they were first published. Where there have been no changes that fact should be stated.

This Note should be read in conjunction with the particular section of the Code to which it refers. It is intended to serve as a guide only and is subject to amendment in the light of experience. If this Note in itself or in conjunction with the Code gives rise to difficulties, the Panel should be consulted. The Panel welcomes comment from interested parties and representations for clarifications or changes to this Note to take account of particular situations not envisaged when it was drafted.

Furthermore, it should not be overlooked that, as a guide to certain provisions of the Code, this Note does not attempt to deal with Stock Exchange requirements which may be applicable in any given case, particularly where the offer document is to be sent to the shareholders of the offeror company for information about the effect of the proposed acquisition, and to which requirements separate reference should therefore be made.

PRACTICE NOTE NO. 3

PUBLICATION OF INFORMATION

General Principle 10 of the Code states:

'During the course of a take-over or merger transaction, or when such is in contemplation, neither the offeror company, the offeree company nor any of their respective advisers shall furnish information to some shareholders which is not made available to all shareholders. This principle shall not apply to the furnishing of information in confidence by an offeree company to a *bona fide* potential offeror company or *vice versa*, nor to the issue of circulars by members of a Stock Exchange to their own investment clients provided such issue shall previously have been approved by the Panel.'

This Principle seeks to ensure that information about companies involved in a bid situation is made equally available to all shareholders as nearly as possible at the same time and in the same manner. A number of matters have arisen:

1. *Shareholders' meetings*
   Several companies and advisers have asked Panel permission to hold 'briefings' for selected shareholder groups to discuss offers and indeed such meetings, as for instance with institutional investors, have not been uncommon in the past. It is considered, however, that the implications of such meetings need consideration in the light of the Code. The Panel's view is that, whatever the intention at the outset, there is a strong possibility that fresh information will be forthcoming at meetings of shareholders at which directors of companies or their advisers express their views during a bid. Such information is not covered by a Board responsibility statement within the provisions of Rule 13. Nevertheless such meetings are not precluded provided that the following safeguards (which apply irrespective of whether the meeting is convened by the offeree or an offeror) are observed:

(*a*) A meeting should not be held until the offer document has been issued and the offeree board has published its views.

(*b*) All shareholders should be sent invitations to attend the meeting at least three days (Sundays and public holidays excluded) beforehand. In special circumstances the Panel may accept that paid press advertisement of a meeting is sufficient notice.

(*c*) The press and news agencies should be invited.

(*d*) If at the meeting any material new information is forthcoming or significant new opinions are expressed, a circular giving details should be sent to shareholders immediately thereafter: in the later stages of a bid it may be necessary to make use of paid newspaper space as well as a circular. The circular or advertisement should include the Board responsibility statement. If such new information is not capable of being substantiated as required by the Code—e.g. a profit forecast—this should be made clear and it should be formally withdrawn in the circular or advertisement.

2. *Television, etc.*

Parties involved in bids should take particular care not to release fresh material orally by way of television or other news media. If any fresh information is made public in this way, shareholders should be circularised and (where appropriate) newspaper space taken as described in 1 (*d*) above.

3. *Circulars issued by associate brokers*

The Panel does not wish to prevent brokers who are associates in a bid from circularising their own clients with material on the company with which they are associated, but associate brokers should bear in mind the essential point that fresh information about a bid must not be restricted to a small group. Accordingly such circulars should not contain any statements of fact or opinion derived from information not generally available; in particular, profit forecasting (unless, and then only to the extent that, the offer documents contain forecasts) should normally be avoided. The broker's associate status should be clearly disclosed. Clearance before issue may in many cases be effected by telephone but where there is doubt a draft of the circular should be sent to the Panel.

This Note should be read in conjunction with the particular section of the Code to which it refers. It is intended to serve as a guide only and is subject to amendment in the light of experience. If this Note in itself or in conjunction with the Code gives rise to difficulties, the

Panel should be consulted. The Panel welcomes comment from interested parties and representations for clarifications or changes to this Note to take account of particular situations not envisaged when it was drafted.

PRACTICE NOTE NO. 4

PROFIT FORECASTS AND ASSET VALUATIONS

Rule 15 of the Code states:

'Without in any way detracting from the imperative necessity of maintaining the highest standards of accuracy and fair presentation in all communications to shareholders in a take-over or merger transaction, attention is particularly drawn in this connection to profit forecasts and asset valuations.

Notwithstanding the obvious hazard attached to the forecasting of profits, profit forecasts must be compiled with the greatest possible care by the Directors whose sole responsibility they are.

When profit forecasts appear in any document addressed to shareholders in connection with an offer, the assumptions, including the commercial assumptions, upon which the Directors have based their profit forecasts, must be stated in the document.

The accounting bases and calculations for the forecasts must be examined and reported on by the auditors or consultant accountants.

Any Merchant Bank or other adviser mentioned in the document must also report on the forecasts. The accountants' report and, if there is an adviser, his report must be contained in such document and be accompanied by a statement that the accountants and, where relevant, the adviser, have given and not withdrawn their consent to publication.

Wherever profit forecasts appear in relation to a period in which trading has already commenced, the last unaudited profit figures which are available in respect of the expired portion of that trading period together with comparable figures for the preceding year must be stated. Alternatively, if no figures are available, that fact must be stated.

When revaluations of assets are given in connection with an offer the Board should be supported by the opinion of independent professional experts and the basis of valuation clearly stated.'

This Rule is one of the most difficult in the whole of the Code. Many aspects of it are not capable of amplification except on an *ad hoc* basis, but this Note attempts to clarify such aspects as can usefully be the subject of general comment.

1. Dividend forecasts are not, normally, of themselves considered to be profit forecasts for the purposes of this Rule, unless, for example, they are accompanied by an estimate as to dividend cover.

2. (a) The fact that a forecast has already been made outside a bid situation (e.g. in an interim statement or annual report) does not in any way reduce the requirement for it to be reported on if it is repeated in a document issued in a bid context. If such a forecast is in existence the parties may consider it of material importance to repeat it in the document (having it examined and reported on in accordance with this Rule), since, even if it is not referred to in the document, it is likely to be mentioned by financial commentators and thus made an important factor in shareholders' decisions.

(b) A similar principle might in some cases apply to directors' estimates of asset values which are published with a company's accounts in accordance with the Companies Act 1967, and which are consequently reproduced with a statement of assets in an offer document or defence circular. However, the Panel would not regard such estimates as 'given in connection with an offer' unless asset values are a particularly significant factor in assessing the relevant bid and the estimates are accordingly given considerably more prominence in the appropriate circulars than merely being referred to in a note to a statement of assets in an Appendix. In these circumstances, of course, such estimates must be supported (subject to paragraph 7 below) by independent experts in accordance with this Rule.

3. An estimate of profits for a period which has already expired should be treated as a profit forecast within this Rule unless the figures for the whole of the relevant period are up to publication standard, i.e. they have received the same degree of examination and carry the same degree of authority as normally apply to published but unaudited interim or preliminary final results of the company in question. Any profit figures which have not been prepared to such a standard must be examined and reported on in the manner described in this Rule. Where figures of publication standard are incorporated in a forecast for a longer period the reports should, of course, cover the whole period.

4. The reference in the penultimate paragraph of this Rule to 'the latest unaudited profit figures which are available' should be read as a reference to figures which have been prepared to such a standard as not to require reporting on under paragraph 3 above. It is considered that the dangers of reproducing figures of a lesser

standard in a document circulated in a bid context outweigh any advantages likely to be gained from so doing. Where, however, a profit forecast is to be reported on, there is no objection to accountants or other financial advisers referring to their reports to the fact that they have taken available management figures into account in reviewing it.

5. Once a forecast has been reported on in accordance with this Rule, reference may be made to that profit forecast in any document published within 60 days thereafter. However, where a forecast is repeated in the context of a different transaction from that for which the forecast was initially reported on the original reporting letters should be reproduced and the directors should confirm that they know of no reason why the original forecast should not stand.

6. It should be appreciated that even when no particular figure is mentioned certain forms of words may constitute a profit forecast. Examples are 'profits will be somewhat higher than last year' or 'the profits of the second half-year are expected to be similar to those earned in the first half-year' (when interim figures have already been published). It is impossible to generalise but broadly whenever a form of words puts a floor under (or, in certain circumstances, a ceiling on) the likely profits of a particular period or whenever a form of words contains the data necessary to ascertain an approximate figure for future profits by an arithmetical process, the Panel takes the view that there is a profit forecast which, except to the extent that in exceptional circumstances specific dispensation has first been obtained, must be reported on in accordance with this Rule. In cases of doubt professional advisers are strongly urged to consult the Panel executive in advance.

7. In exceptional cases companies, in particular property companies, which are the subject of an unexpected bid may find difficulty in obtaining the opinion of independent professional experts to support an assets revaluation, as required by the last paragraph of this Rule, before their recommending or rejecting circular has to be sent out. In such cases the Panel may be prepared exceptionally to waive strict compliance with this paragraph. The Panel will only do this where the interests of shareholders seem on balance to be best served by permitting informal valuation to appear coupled with such substantiation as is available. Advisers to offeree companies who wish to make use of this procedure should consult the Panel at the earliest opportunity.

8. Where revaluations of assets are given the name of the independent professional expert or experts should be stated in the offer document and the valuation made available for inspection.

9. It is not necessary for copies of accountants' and other financial advisers' letters reporting on forecasts to be lodged with the Panel.

This Note should be read in conjunction with the particular section of the Code to which it refers. It is intended to serve as a guide only and is subject to amendment in the light of experience. If this Note in itself or in conjunction with the Code gives rise to difficulties, the Panel should be consulted. The Panel welcomes comment from interested parties and representations for clarifications or changes to this Note to take account of particular situations not envisaged when it was drafted.

PRACTICE NOTE NO. 5

DISCLOSURE OF DEALINGS

Rule 29 of the Code states:

'Save in so far as appears from this Code, it is considered undesirable to fetter the market. Accordingly, all parties to a take-over or merger transaction (other than to a partial bid) and their associates are free to deal at arm's length subject to daily disclosure to The Stock Exchange, the Panel and the Press (not later than 12 noon on the dealing day following the date of the relative transaction) of the total of all shares of any offeror company or the offeree company acquired or sold by them or their respective associates for their own account on any day during the offer period in the market or otherwise and at what average price.

In addition all purchases and sales of shares of any offeror or the offeree company made by associates for account of investment clients who are not themselves associates must be similarly reported to The Stock Exchange and to the Panel, but need not be disclosed to the Press.

In the case of a partial bid the offeror company and its associates may not deal in shares of the offeree company during the offer period for their own account, nor in the case of a partial bid to which Rule 20 does not apply may the offeror company or its associates, unless the Panel specifically so agrees, purchase shares of the offeree company for their own account during a period of twelve months beginning on the last day of the offer period.'

There are set out below a number of rulings and interpretations which have been given by the Panel following enquiries from stockbrokers, merchant banks and other advisers and which have a general application. Attention is drawn particularly, in the interpretation of this Rule, to the denfinition of 'Associate' in the section of the Code headed 'Definitions'. This Note applies to all dealings whether undertaken through a recognised stock exchange or outside the market.

1. *Method of disclosure*

   (*a*) Announcements of dealings by or on behalf of an associate which are disclosed in writing (or by Telex) to The Stock Exchange, London, are published on the floor of The Stock Exchange and arrangements have been made for copies of such announcements to be sent by The Stock Exchange to the Panel and the Press. Separate disclosure to the Press and to the Panel is therefore unnecessary.

   (*b*) Announcements of dealings by an associate on behalf of investment clients which are disclosed in writing (or by Telex) to The Stock Exchange, London, are not published on the floor of The Stock Exchange nor sent to the Press. Copies of such announcements are sent by The Stock Exchange to the Panel to whom separate disclosure is therefore unnecessary.

   (*c*) Dealings by a principal (i.e. an offeror or the offeree) in a bid situation or by an associate may be disclosed by the party concerned or by an agent (merchant bank, stockbroker, etc.) who acts on their behalf. In cases where there is more than one agent (i.e. a merchant bank and a stockbroker, or a London broker and a country broker) particular care should be taken to ensure that the responsibility for disclosure is agreed between the parties and that publication is neither overlooked nor duplicated.

2. *Details of disclosure*

   (*a*) When dealings by or on behalf of a principal are disclosed, the principal must be named. (Included in the foregoing are any dealings where the investment risk is directly or indirectly borne by one of the principals, e.g. where a financial adviser has the right to sell any shares purchased on to one of the principals at an agreed price.)

   (*b*) When dealings by or on behalf of an associate are disclosed, the associate need not normally be named, but it should be indicated with which principal he is associated. An associate should, however, be named if he is an associate by reason of the size of his holding in one of the principals.

   (*c*) The references in this Rule to 'shares' should be taken to means securities which could have a bearing on the offer, i.e.:

       (i) securities of the offeree which are being bid for or which carry voting rights;

(ii) equity share capital of offeree and offeror(s);

(iii) securities of the offeror(s) which carry substantially the same rights as any to be issued as consideration for the offer;

(iv) securities of offeree and offeror(s) carrying conversion or subscription rights into any of the foregoing, where variations in the price of such securities are likely to affect the price of the securities into which they are convertible or over which they carry subscription rights;

(v) options in respect of any of the foregoing.

(d) The requirement to disclose dealings applies also to dealings in the shares of unquoted public companies.

3. *Exceptions from disclosure requirements*
   The following need not be reported:

   (a) Dealings in securities of an offeror where the consideration for the offer is cash or fixed-income securities not carrying conversion or subscription rights.

   (b) Dealings for investment clients where a merger is being effected by a Scheme of Arrangement under the Companies Act.

   (c) Dealings in offeror or offeree company securities after a merger or takeover has been referred to the Monopolies Commission. In such cases the bid is regarded as suspended for the time being. In the event of the bid being subsequently revived the Rules of the Code will apply as in the case of a fresh merger or takeover.

4. *Contested bids*
   The reference in this Rule to 'any offeror company' means that in a contested bid situation dealings by one offeror (or his associates) in the shares of the other offeror company (or companies) should be disclosed. This applies whether the deals are for associates or for investment clients.

5. *The offer period*
   The obligation to disclose under this Rule commences with the announcement of the offer (whether or not details of the terms are announced) but not with an announcement only that talks are being held which may or may not lead to an offer. (In the latter event Rule 30 would effectively prevent dealings prior to the announcement of the terms of the offer by persons privy to the negotiations.) The obligation ceases when the offer either lapses or is reported unconditional.

6. *Clearing Banks*
   It is not necessary for dealings for investment clients to be disclosed by a clearing or other banker whose sole relationship

with a party to a take-over is the provision of normal commercial banking services or such activities in connection with the offer as confirming that cash is available, handling acceptances and other registration work, and handling an alternative cash offer, since such a relationship is not considered by itself to constitute that of associate.

7. *Associates' discretionary clients*
Dealings by associates on behalf of discretionary investment clients must be disclosed as dealings for associates (and so become available to the Press). Discretionary investment clients include individuals and funds for whom the associate is accustomed to make investment decisions without prior reference. Such disclosures may contain a reference to the nature of the clients.

This Note should be read in conjunction with the particular section of the Code to which it refers. It is intended to serve as a guide only and is subject to amendment in the light of experience. If this Note in itself or in conjunction with the Code gives rise to difficulties, the Panel should be consulted. The Panel welcomes comment from interested parties and representations for clarifications or changes to this Note to take account of particular situations not envisaged when it was drafted.

PRACTICE NOTE NO. 6

THE ASSUMPTIONS ON WHICH A PROFIT FORECAST IS BASED

Requirement to state the assumptions
1.   The City Code on Take-overs and Mergers was issued in its present form in April 1969. Revisions made at that time to the original Code included the requirements for an accountants' report on a profit forecast and for a statement of the assumptions on which the forecast is based to be included in an offer document. After two years' experience it is appropriate to see how the practice of meeting these requirements has developed. This Practice Note, which has been written after consultation with the Institute of Chartered Accountants in England and Wales, reviews the types of assumptions often listed in practice as the basis for a forecast and indicates how such assumptions can be framed so as to be of maximum assistance to the reader. These indications can by their very nature only be suggestions and accordingly it is not proposed that this Practice Note should be enforced as literally as its predecessors.

2. The following extracts from Rules 13, 14 and 15 of the Code are relevant to a consideration of the assumptions on which a profit forecast is based:

'13. Any document or advertisement addressed to shareholders . . . . must be treated with the same standards of care with regard to the statements made therein as if it were a prospectus within the meaning of the Companies Act 1948.

14. Shareholders must be put into possession of all the facts necessary for the formation of an informed judgment as to the merits or demerits of an offer. Such facts must be accurately and fairly presented. . . .

15. Without in any way detracting from the imperative necessity of maintaining the highest standards of accuracy and fair presentation in all communications to shareholders in a take-over or merger transaction, attention is particularly drawn in this connection to profit forecasts and asset valuations.

Notwithstanding the obvious hazard attached to the forecasting of profits, profit forecasts must be compiled with the greatest possible care by the Directors whose sole responsibility they are.

When profit forecasts appear in any document addressed to shareholders in connection with an offer, the assumptions, including the commercial assumptions, upon which the Directors have based their profit forecasts, must be stated in the document.

The accounting bases and calculations for the forecasts must be examined and reported on by the auditors or consultant accountants. Any Merchant Bank or other adviser mentioned in the document must also report on the forecasts.'

3. The main object of such circulars is often to persuade shareholders either to accept or to reject an offer. However objective a board of directors tries to be, their forecast may be coloured by the case being advocated by them or by their advisers. In addition, whereas in a prospectus it is properly the practice to make a conservative estimate of profits, in this type of circular it may be doing a disservice to shareholders to err on the conservative side. Profit forecasts in any event are always the results of personal judgment and are liable to be affected by a number of substantial uncertainties.

4. It is important therefore that by listing the assumptions on which the forecast is based some information should be given to help

shareholders in forming a view as to the reasonableness and reliability of the forecast. This should include a summary of the conclusions reached by the directors on matters which required judgment as to the likely outcome of events, and should draw the shareholders' attention to, and where possible quantify, those uncertain factors which could materially disturb the ultimate achievement of the forecast.

5. From the standpoint of the directors making the forecast and of their advisers it is also right that they should be able to explain the uncertainties and so protect themselves from subsequent unjustified criticism if the forecast is not achieved.

6. The forecast and the assumptions on which it is based are the sole responsibility of the directors. However, a duty is placed on the financial advisers to discuss the assumptions with their client and to satisfy themselves that the forecast has been made with due care and consideration. One of the duties placed on the auditors or consultant accountants is to satisfy themselves that the forecasts, so far as the accounting bases and calculations are concerned, have been properly compiled on the footing of the assumptions made. Although the accountants have no responsibility for the assumptions, they will as a result of their review be in a position to advise the company on what assumptions should be listed in the circular and the way in which they should be described. The financial advisers and accountants obviously have substantial influence on the information given in a circular about assumptions. Neither should allow an assumption to be published which appears to them to be unrealistic (or one to be omitted which appears to them to be important) without commenting on it in their reports.

Detailed Considerations
7. The Code gives no guidance as to what is meant by the phrase 'assumptions, including the commercial assumptions, upon which the Directors have based their profit forecasts', and as would be expected this has been interpreted in a variety of ways.

8. Some assumptions have done no more than say that in making the forecast it has been assumed that the estimates used will prove to be right; for example:

'Sales and profits for the year will not differ materially from those budgeted for.'
'There will be no increases in costs other than those anticipated and provided for.'

Every forecast involves estimates of income and of costs and must obviously be dependent on these estimates. Assumptions of the type illustrated above do not help the shareholder and are better omitted, unless they are amplified so as to make them informative, e.g. by going on to say that sales x per cent up on last year's sales have been budgeted for.

9. There are inevitable limitations in the accuracy of some forecasts and shareholders will be assisted if these can be indicated. It will normally be helpful to include a description of the general nature of the business or businesses with an indication of any major hazards in forecasting in these particular businesses. So as to show the significance of any such hazards it may also be helpful if a breakdown of forecast sales and profits before tax by diverse activities can be given with a comparison with the similar figures for recent years which may have already been published under Section 17, Companies Act 1967.

10. The assumptions stated should not relate to the accuracy of the accounting systems. Examples have been:

'The book record of stocks and work in progress will be confirmed at the end of the financial year.'
'The estimate of stocks on hand at 30th September, 1970 will prove substantially accurate.'

If the systems of accounting and forecasting are such that full reliance cannot be placed on them, this should be the subject of some qualification in the forecast itself (perhaps also requiring a qualification in the reports of the financial advisers and accountants). It is not satisfactory for this type of deficiency to be covered by the assumptions, although any area in the estimates that is subject to special doubt should be indicated.

11. Reference has frequently been made in assumptions to unforeseen circumstances, such as:

'The profits anticipated will not be unduly affected by any unforeseen factors.'
'There will be no significant unforeseen circumstances.'

It must be expected that a forecast will take account of all *foreseen* circumstances and it does not seem necessary or helpful to have a general assumption about the unforeseen. However, it is a general practice in referring to profit forecasts in a prospectus to use such a phrase and this could be incorporated in the statement about the forecast in a circular, rather than as an assumption, e.g.:

'The directors forecast that, in the absence of unforeseen circumstances, the profits before tax for the year . . .'

12. Even the more specific type of assumption may still leave the shareholder in doubt as to its implications, for instance:

'No abnormal liabilities will arise under guarantees.'

'Provisions for outstanding legal claims will prove adequate.'

One might dismiss these on the grounds that the first relates to the unforeseen and the second to the adequacy of the estimating system. However, the reason for the inclusion of each of these assumptions was presumably because there was an unusual element of doubt about the liabilities under guarantees and claims. In both these examples it would have been more helpful if information could have been given about the extent or basis of the provision already made and/or about the circumstances in which unprovided liabilities might arise.

13. It may be helpful to indicate what the effect on the profit forecast would be if certain of the major assumptions were to prove to be wholly or partly invalid. For example, the effect might be shown if sales volume, selling prices, raw material costs, etc. were y per cent above/below estimate or if full production from a new factory were delayed by z months. It may be appropriate for maximum and minimum forecast profits to be given rather than a single figure.

General Rules

14. It is suggested that the following general rules should apply to the selection and drafting of assumptions:

(a) the reader should be able to understand their implications and so be helped in forming a judgment as to the reasonableness of the forecast and to the main uncertainties attaching to it;

(b) the assumptions should be, wherever possible, specific rather than general, definite rather than vague;

(c) all-embracing assumptions and those relating to the general accuracy of the estimates should be avoided;

(d) the assumptions should relate only to matters which may have a material bearing on the forecast.

There is, however, a need for brevity and simplicity which may restrict adherence to the foregoing in every detail. There may be occasions, particularly when the forecast relates to a period already ended, when no assumptions are required.

15. The larger and more complex the group, the more difficult it becomes to make the assumptions specific and definite, with reasonable brevity. In such instances it may be appropriate to give a division of profits and to relate the assumptions specifically to the various divisions.

Examples

16. Examples of assumptions which follow these rules are given below:

(*a*) 'The company's present management and accounting policies will not be changed.' (For a company being acquired.)

(*b*) 'Interest rates and the bases and rates of taxation, both direct and indirect, will not change materially.'

(*c*) 'There will be no material change in international exchange rates or import duties and regulations.'

(*d*) 'Percentage of time lost on building sites, due to adverse weather conditions, will be average for the time of the year.'

(*e*) 'Turnover for the year will be £1m. on the basis that sales will continue in line with levels and trends experienced to date, adjusted for normal seasonal factors; a reduction of £100,000 in turnover would result in a reduction of approximately £10,000 in the profit forecast.'

(*f*) 'Beer sales will increase in line with the trend established in the previous year, which corresponds to the national average rate of increase.'

(*g*) 'An increase of about 10 per cent. in subscriptions will be achieved as a result of increases in the prices of certain journals and an increase in the number of subscribers.'

(*h*) 'Trading results will not be affected by industrial disputes in the company's factories or in those of its principal suppliers.'

(*i*) 'The current national dock strike will not last longer than six weeks.'

(*j*) 'The new factory at Inverness will be in full production by the end of the first quarter. A delay of one month would cause the profit forecast to be reduced by £5,000.'

(*k*) 'Increases in labour costs will be restricted to those recently agreed with the trades unions.'

(*l*) 'Increases in the level of manufacturing costs for the remainder of the year will be kept within the margin of 2 per cent, allowed for in the estimates.'

(*m*)'The conversion rights attaching to all the convertible loan stock will be exercised on the next conversion date.'

This Note should be read in conjunction with the particular sections of the Code to which it refers. It is intended to serve as a guide only and is subject to amendment in the light of experience. If this Note in itself or in conjunction with the Code gives rise to difficulties, the Panel should be consulted. The Panel welcomes comment from interested parties and representations for clarifications or changes to this Note to take account of particular situations not envisaged when it was drafted.

Appendix 4

The Businessman's Guide to Good Health

By Dr Michael Cranley

What is good health?

Health means enjoying life and getting the full benefit from it. Health for leisure and sport as well as for work. Too many of us just throw it away. In spite of the great advances in medicine and surgery *your* expectation of life at 50 is not much better than it was at the turn of the century. WHY? Largely because of two groups of diseases. The first includes Coronary Thrombosis which increases in numbers, all the time attacking younger men.

The second includes the cancers—particularly cancer of the lung, which alone each year claims almost 20,000 victims in the United Kingdom. In addition, there are other disabling diseases of varying severity which are on the increase—such as Bronchitis and other chest troubles; gastric and duodenal ulcer!

Severe mental illness and less crippling forms of anxiety and depression; arthritis, rheumatism, sciatica and lumbago.

It is significant that General Practitioners and Company Directors have the greatest chance of getting coronary thrombosis while Church of England clergymen and farm workers have the least.

Work stress and strain

We obviously cannot alter the structure of our competitive society, improve the flow of traffic or stop its noise. Nor can we help breathing in diesel fumes or hearing the roar of traffic and jet planes. You cannot stop the 'phone ringing at all hours—but you can take it off the hook from time to time.

You and your car

Apart from the motor cycle the car is easily the most dangerous way of travelling between two places. Considerably more dangerous than going to the moon and back. Quite apart from the danger of being killed in an accident, if you drive you are subjecting yourself to all sorts of nervous tensions. Why are car drivers more prone to coronary thrombosis than other people? Recent research has shown that

232

adrenalin which is produced normally during any stressful pursuit gets used up by muscular activity but not when sitting driving. This has a harmful effect upon the heart. *Criminal injuries*

Certainly if you drive more than 10,000 miles a year—take care. Try and develop a new attitude to driving. If the other chap overtakes you, let him. As the psychiatrists say: "That is his problem not yours." Use the car as little as possible. For long journeys, go by train or boat. (Jet travel is another invention of the devil.)

If you can walk or cycle, you will be doing yourself a favour, and (incidentally) you won't be polluting the atmosphere.

Don't kill yourself in the dining room

It really is a sad commentary on the human race that while two-thirds of it goes hungry, Western Man ruins his health by eating too much of the wrong sorts of food. *Contributory negligence*

Obesity

This is a real killer and there is no doubt that excess weight predisposes to heart and lung disease and to almost any illness you can think of, including of course all forms of rheumatism and arthritis.

Imagine what a fourteen pounds sack of potatoes would do to your bad back. About half of the men in this country are over weight and 3 stones excess weight at the age of forty will probably cut your life short by at least ten years. Food—like life—is to be enjoyed, but sensible eating can be as much fun as over-eating and the rewards are indeed golden. *Grievous bodily harm*

Your ideal weight

I'm afraid the 'weight for height' tables that one often sees are not of much help. They are mostly based on the *average* weight of men of a given age and height. As we've seen, this is not the same as the ideal weight. Also some of us have heavier bony structures than others. Common sense is a good guide. If you can pick up a bulge of fat under the arms or around the waist you are certainly overweight.

What to eat

HOW TO LOSE WEIGHT

Most of us eat too much carbohydrate. Any diet that cuts down the amount of bread, starch, potatoes and sugar should help us to lose weight fairly easily. *Standing orders*

233

CHOLESTEROL AND ALL THAT

There has been a lot of conflicting evidence as to whether a diet rich in animal fats, which contain cholesterol, causes heart disease and arteriosclerosis. There is no definite answer but probably excess fat *does* do you harm.

General damages

It is therefore a good idea to go easy on fatty meats, butter, cream and eggs. Pork and lamb are rich in cholesterol. If you like fish, chicken, veal, fruit and vegetables and the new vegetable margarines and cooking oils these are no problems in a low cholesterol diet. Ask your doctor what he thinks.

Expert witness

NATURAL EATING

With the increase of convenience foods such as white bread and refined sugar, a whole host of man-made illnesses have come along. Two of these are diverticulitis, which one never heard of thirty years ago, and cancer of the colon. Both of these are certainly due to the fact that we eat too much in the way of soft sloppy foods that do not give our bowels enough work to do. Try eating wholemeal bread, lightly cooked vegetables and plenty of fresh fruit including the skin.

If more people ate like this, you would want to start selling your laxative shares.

No smoking

What are the advantages of smoking? Well, the taxes certainly help pay for other people's education, roads and jet fighters. Also it does keep your weight down, but apart from this and its doubtful pleasure, it is difficult to find any advantages.

Scandalous behaviour?

The disadvantages, they really are extensive. Smoking certainly causes cancer of the lung. If you are a man and a heavy smoker you have a 1 in 8 chance of dying of it and if you are a non-smoker a 1 in 300 chance. Repeated reports from Medical Centres throughout the world have confirmed that these figures are correct.

Suicide?

In addition, smokers stand a 50 per cent greater chance of getting coronary thrombosis and probably get it about 4 or 5 years earlier than they would have otherwise. Peptic ulcer, sinusitis, bronchitis and all sorts of chest diseases are made worse by smoking.

Approximately 70,000 deaths a year in Great Britain are due to smoking cigarettes. Pipes and cigars are less dangerous but still cause trouble.

How to give it up

There is no guaranteed easy way of giving up smoking and if you are

234

not determined there are no tricks that will make you do so. However, if you do *want* to give up smoking, here are some useful tips:

1 On the day before you are determined to give it up smoke three Extraordinary resolution times your normal ration. The next morning you should have such an unpleasant head and taste that you will find it easier to start.
2 If you do not succeed straight away in giving up completely, write down each day's total of cigarettes.
3 If you feel you must have a cigarette first thing in the morning drink a 'bitter lemon' or tonic water instead.
4 Try and get your wife or a friend to join with you in giving up.
5 If the strain is too much ask your doctor for a tranquilliser. He will almost certainly agree to help.
6 Imagine how your wife would look in black—this year.

Alcohol

Too much in the way of beer will certainly add to your waist line and Liquid assets excess spirits cause a host of conditions, particularly liver trouble. In moderation and particularly with meals, alcohol makes life more pleasant.

Exercise

We were designed to keep moving and not to sit still and grow fat. No loitering Don't actually shoot the lift-man, but do make sure that you walk or run up and down stairs. The Managing Director of Volvo insists that the lifts in his factory are only for the use of the old, the sick and men below executive level. Cycle or walk to work or at least to the nearest Underground or bus station.

Sports

Golf is fine, but you really do want something that puts a little bit of pressure on you. Try squash, tennis or swimming or whatever you fancy. Don't overdo things, however, and if you haven't played any games for twenty years do go easy.

If you have little time get yourself an excellent book brought out Discretion by Penguin: *Physical Fitness*. This takes about 11 minutes a day and starting gradually gets you up to the maximum desired exercise for your age.

Preventive medicine

> *Physicians of the utmost fame*
> *Were called at once; but when they came*
> *They answered as they took their fees*
> *There is no cure for this disease.*

BELLOC

But of course nowadays there *is* so often a cure, providing that your doctors can spot it early enough.

ANNUAL CHECK-UP

Highway robbery?

'My Father never had one and he lived to be twenty-eight.'

A check-up may seem expensive, but surely your health is worth the price of a new exhaust system for your limousine?

No one wants to make people into hypochondriacs but it really is sensible, once you are past the age of thirty-five, to have a thorough check-up every year. If your doctor is able and willing to do one, he will want to carry out a full medical examination with chest X-ray, blood tests (which will show whether you are anaemic or suffering from any severe illness), urine tests and an electrocardiograph. Examination may show that other tests are necessary. In the past two years, I have picked up at least three cases of serious illnesses which have been treated *before* they caused any trouble.

If your Doctor is not able to do this for you, excellent ones can be arranged through private Agencies including BUPA and the Institute of Directors.

ANTI-FLU INJECTIONS

Flu is a disabling condition. The new anti-flu injections give you and your employees considerable protection.

AFTERNOON NAPS

Like any other machine the body shouldn't be allowed to work flat out for too long. If you can possibly take a brief rest after lunch, do so. It helps take much of the stress and tension off the day and even 10 minutes can work wonders. Distinguished people famous for their devotion to the cat nap have included Winston Churchill, Napoleon —and Ewan Mitchell.

EVERYONE NEEDS TRANQUILLISERS

Due relief

Last year 300 million tranquillisers and sedative tablets were prescribed in Great Britain. Although tranquilliser tablets are better than nothing, they certainly ought not to be a first resort. There are, however, plenty of tranquillisers that everyone should have—reading,

236

painting, fishing, gardening, photography. Perhaps even more important the good fortune to have a worth-while and interesting job, and (best of all) the peace and the support of a happy home. Above all take things easy.

Keep a sense of proportion and fun. As Shaw said: "Never run after a bus or a woman. There's always another following closely behind."

Index

Business premises—*cont.*
  reference to court, 93
  rent, basis of assessment, 93
  schedule of comparables, 94
  solicitor, advantage of employ-
    ing, 92
  terms of, 93, 95
  termination of, 91
Businessman's health guide. *See*
  Health guide

Capital gains tax, 161
City Code. *See* Take-overs and mergers
Civil Evidence Act, 1968, 62
Code of industrial relations
  application and use, 171
  collective
    agreements, 187–8
    bargaining units, 185
    communication, 181–3
  consultation, 183–4
  contents of, 5, 170–95
  disciplinary procedure, 194
  disputes procedure
    arbitration, 193–4
    collective disputes, 193
    establishment, 192
    individual grievances, 193
  employment policies, 176–81
  evidence, use in, 5, 170
  information, disclosure, 188–9
  manpower, planning and use of, 177
  payment systems, 178
  purpose of, 170–1
  racial discrimination, avoidance, 177
  recruitment and selection, 177–8
  redundancy, 180
  responsibilities
    employers' associations, 174
    individual employees, 175–6
    management, 172–4
    trade unions, 174–5
  revision, 172
  shop stewards. *See* shop stewards
  status and security, 179
  supervisor, functions, 173
  trade unions
    recognition, claim for, 186
    relations between management
      and, 187
    responsibilities, 174–5
  training, 178
  working conditions, 180–1
  forms of, 11

legal enforceability
  contracting out of, 9–11
  Industrial Court, jurisdiction, 9
  presumption of, 9, 11
  meaning, 9
Commission on Industrial Relations,
  20, 21
Committee of London Clearing
  Bankers, 198
Common fund costs, 67
Companies Act, 1948, 208
Company
  chargeable gains, 164
  corporation tax, 163
  director. *See* Director
  fraudulent purpose, carrying on for,
    143
  limited liability, advantages of, 143
  officers
    misfeasance by, 144
    ostensible authority, 125
    personal liability, 144
    Trade Descriptions Act, liability
      under, 148
  partnership in guise of, 149
  share-dealing, 162
  tax loss, 161–2, 164
  taxation, 163–4
  winding up. *See* winding up
Conciliation officer, 7, 8
Confederation of British Industry, 198
Contract
  acceptance, counter-offer, when
    amounting to, 119
  agent, ostensible authority, 124–6
  binding nature of, 119–20
  employment, of. *See* Contract of
    employment
  guarantee, of, 100
  hire, of, 121
  insurance, of. *See* Insurance
  offer
    conditional, 119
    final terms, advantage of, 120
    invitation to treat distinguished,
      119
    withdrawal, 119
  oral, validity, 100
  penalty clauses, 99
  sale of goods. *See* Sale of goods
  sale of land. *See* Conveyancing
  signature
    document different to that
      intended, 123

Health guide—*cont.*
obesity and slimming, 233–4
preventive medicine, 236
smoking, disadvantages, 234–5
tranquillisers, 236
Hearsay. *See* Evidence
Hedley Byrne & Company v. *Heller and Partners, Ltd.*, 114
High Court, audience in, 49
Hire, contract of, 121
Holiday pay entitlement, 15

In re City Equitable Fire Insurance Company Limited, 146
Income and Corporation Taxes Act, 1970, 167, 168
Industrial Court
collective agreements, enforcement by, 9
contempt of, 10
fine, jurisdiction to impose, 10
proceedings in, right to bring, 8
Industrial Relations Act
arrangement of sections, 5
Code. *See* Code of industrial relations
compulsory strike ballot, 21
contracting out
agency shop agreements, 8
apprentices, 8, 12–14
approved closed shops, 8
employees on fixed-term contracts, 8, 12–14
general prohibition, 8
non-legally enforceable agreements, 9
cooling-off period, 21
holiday entitlement, 15
Industrial Court. *See* Industrial Court
Industrial Tribunals, functions, 7
interpretation, 4
National Industrial Relations Court, 20–21
objects of, 5
territorial application, 4
unfair dismissal
compensation for, 5–7, 12
employees protected against, 5
Industrial Tribunal, jurisdiction, 12
presumption at law, 6, 12
what constitutes, 6
unfair industrial practices, 21

appeals from, 20
compensation, assessment by, 7, 12
Industrial Relations Act, functions under, 7, 12
jurisdiction, 20
redundancy, functions as to, 20
unfair dismissal, jurisdiction, 12, 33
Injunction
to restrain
leaving without notice, 36
poaching of staff, 40
Insurance
broker, payment by insurers, 104
claim
exaggeration, 105
fraudulent, *Theft Act* provisions, 105
notice, time for, 105
fire. *See* Fire insurance
Lloyd's underwriters, 106
policy. *See* Policy
problems of, 103–6
proposal form
concealment or misrepresentation in, 104
mistake without fraudulent intention, 104
shopping around for, 103
under-insurance, effect of, 105
Issuing Houses Association, 198

Joint negotiating panel, 18
Judge
error in law by, 64
flattering, 60
notes of evidence, 60

Land
taxation
artificial transactions, 164
sale and leaseback, 165
Land Compensation Act, 1961, 52
Landlord and Tenant Act, 1954, 91, 96, 100
Law of Property Act, 1969, 91, 96, 100
Leading questions, 61
Leasehold, nature of, 100
Legal aid
contributions, basis of, 77–78
costs, effect on, 78
excluded matters, 78
qualifications for, 77
Letters before action, 66–70, 81
Lien of solicitor, 66